D1267500

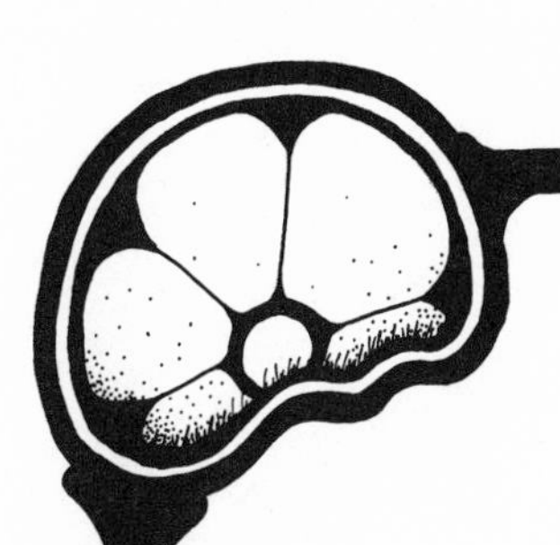
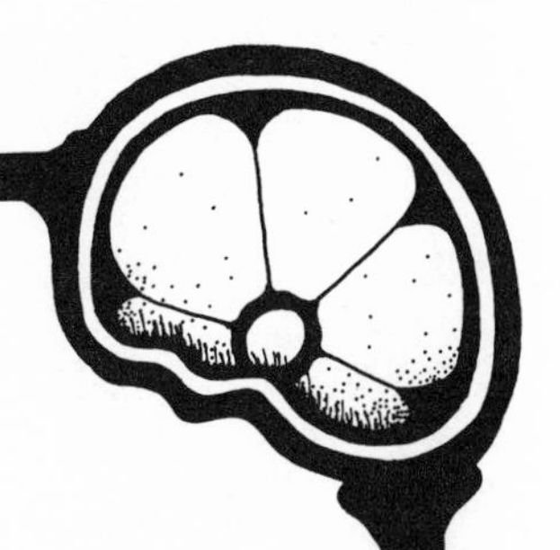

FARM WOMEN
ON THE PRAIRIE FRONTIER:

A Sourcebook for Canada and the United States

by

Carol Fairbanks
and
Sara Brooks Sundberg

Illustrations by Ted F. Myers

The Scarecrow Press, Inc. Metuchen, N.J., and London
1983

Library of Congress Cataloging in Publication Data

Fairbanks, Carol, 1935-
Farm women on the prairie frontier.

Bibliography: p.
Includes index.
1. Rural women--West (U.S.)--History--Addresses, essays, lectures. 2. Rural women--Northwest, Canadian--History--Addresses, essays, lectures. 3. Frontier and pioneer life--West (U.S.)--History--Addresses, essays, lectures. 4. Frontier and pioneer life--Northwest, Canadian--History--Addresses, essays, lectures.
5. American literature--Women authors--Bibliography.
6. Canadian literature--Women authors--Bibliography.

I. Sundberg, Sara Brooks. II. Title.
HQ1438.A17F34 1983 305.4'0971 83-4498
ISBN 0-8108-1625-3

Manufactured in the United States of America

In memory of

Ryan Fairbanks Myers

C. F.

For
Marshall

S. B. S.

CONTENTS

IN THE SUMMER AFTER "ISSUE YEAR" WINTER (1873)

Roberta Hill Whiteman

I scratch earth around timpsila
on this hill, while below me,
hanging in still air, a hawk
searches the creekbed for my brothers.
Squat leaves, I'll braid your roots
into such long ropes, they'll cover
the rump of my stallion.
Withered flower, feed us now
buffalo rot in the waist high grass.

Hear my sisters laugh?
They dream of feasts, of warriors
to owl dance with them
when this war is over. They don't see
our children eating treebark, cornstalks,
these roots. Their eyes gleam
in shallow cheeks. The wagon people
do not think relationship is wealth.

Sisters, last night the wind
returned my prayer, allowing me to hear
Dog Soldiers singing at Ash Hollow.

I threw away my blanket
stained with lies.
Above the wings of my tipi,
I heard the old woman in Maka Siċa
sigh for us. Then I knew
the distance of High Back Bone's death--
fire from another world away. Even they
may never stop its motion.

Yesterday at noon, I heard
my Cheyenne sister moan as she waded
through deep snow before soldiers
cut up her corpse to sell
as souvenirs. Are my brothers
here? Ghosts bring all my joy.
I walk this good road between rock
and sky. They dare not threaten with death
one already dead.

Notes on poem

I based the incidents in the poem on Batiste Good's Winter Count, which marks the years for the Brule Lakota between 1700-1880. One of the incidents mentioned was the 1856 capture of Little Thunder and Batiste Good and one hundred and thirty Lakota at Ash Hollow. In this instance Indian people were imprisoned, their horses and weapons stolen, the chiefs arrested or killed in order to force them into signing agreements which allowed for railroad construction, the improvement of the Bozeman Trail, and the establishment of military posts. The Dog Soldiers are one of the Warrior Societies which vowed to stake themselves to the ground and fight to the death defending their people. Reference is also made to Chivington's bloody spree at Sand Creek in 1864.

Another incident mentioned is the death of High Back Bone, a chief who was shot at long range by Crows and Shoshones in 1870-1871. Shooting from a great distance was contrary to plains warfare because a brave warrior touched his enemy with a coupe stick instead of firing from a safe distance. During the years mentioned in the poem, the Lakota, and their allies, the Arapahoe and the Cheyenne, confronted white diseases, decreasing buffalo herds, starvation, the further reduction of their lands by treaty agreements, which were then broken and resulted in battles with white soldiers. "Issue Year" refers to blankets and goods given to the Lakotas in 1873-1874. Incidentally, after the first "Issue Year" of 1858-1859, a small pox epidemic is listed two years after and in the year following 1873, another epidemic marks the year--"Measles and Sickness Used Up The People Winter."

Timpsila are prairie turnips.
Maka Sića is the badlands.

--R. H. W.

This poem serves as a reminder that prairie women's history and literature should be read with a continuing sense of another perspective--that of the Indian; the land once belonged to the Osage, the Kansa, the Lakota, the Pawnee, the Plains Ojibwa, and the Cree.

--C. F. and S. B. S.

ACKNOWLEDGMENTS

We would like to express our gratitude for the assistance we received in preparing this book:

For botanical illustrations: Marshall Sundberg, Department of Biology, University of Wisconsin-Eau Claire.

For critical reviews: T. A. Browne, Department of English, University of Wisconsin-Eau Claire; Arthur Geffen, Department of English, University of Minnesota; Robert Gough, Department of History, University of Wisconsin-Eau Claire; Gary Pennanen, Department of History, University of Wisconsin-Eau Claire; Leslie Polk, Department of Journalism, University of Wisconsin-Eau Claire; James Richtik, Department of Geography, University of Winnipeg; Nadine St. Louis, Department of English, University of Wisconsin-Eau Claire; Ingolf Vogeler, Department of Geography, University of Wisconsin-Eau Claire.

For library assistance at the University of Wisconsin-Eau Claire: Richard Bell; Bebeanna Buck; Eugene Engeldinger; Kay Henning.

For manuscript preparation: Caryl Laubach and Kari Tubbs.

For research funding by the University of Wisconsin-Eau Claire: Douglas Pearson, Chairman, Department of English; Lee Grugel, Dean, College of Arts and Sciences; Elmer Sundby, Assistant to the Vice Chancellor.

We would also like to thank Charley Ivey, Eau Claire, Wisconsin, and George Fairbanks, Fairport, New York, for loaning family manuscripts; Helen Sampson and Michael Hilger furnished photographs on which some of the drawings were based.

Portions of "Women and Their Visions: Perspectives

from Fiction" originally appeared in *The International Journal of Women's Studies* (September-October 1979); Editor Sherri Clarkson kindly gave permission to reprint. Leslie Polk, Editor of *Wisconsin Dialogue: A Faculty Journal of the University of Wisconsin-Eau Claire*, gave permission to reprint "A Usable Past: Women on the American Prairies" which originally appeared in the Winter 1983 issue.

NOTE TO READERS

This sourcebook is intended for students, teachers, and general readers who wish to explore the historical and literary materials of the grasslands of Canada and the United States. Those with minimal background on the subject will find the four essays in Part I useful introductions to the land and the people, the history and the fiction. In Part II the annotations direct readers and researchers to relevant materials in history and literature.

LIST OF ILLUSTRATIONS

PART I: ESSAYS

EARLY AGRICULTURAL SETTLEMENT ON THE INTERIOR GRASSLANDS OF NORTH AMERICA

The expansion of North American agriculture into the grasslands of central Canada and the United States was a remarkable drama. Within less than a century most of roughly 860, 300, 000 acres of virgin grassland succumbed to the plow. This change came largely through the efforts of nineteenth- and early twentieth-century agricultural pioneers, men and women who struggled to subdue the land, and to make it fulfill their visions. The content of their visions and the dynamics of their relationships with the grassland environments comprise a unique chapter in the history of the land and the people of North America. Pioneer farm women's experiences are an often neglected part of this chapter. To establish the setting for farm women's experiences it is necessary to describe the grassland environments and to survey their effects on agricultural settlement.

Grasslands are not unique to the United States and Canada. Similar regions are found in the steppes of Eurasia, the African veldt, and the Argentine pampas. In North America the grasslands stretch northward in an irregular line from western Indiana to the vicinity of Edmonton, Alberta. The western boundary of the grassland is the Rocky Mountains. The southern boundary follows a diagonal line from central Illinois to north central Texas. In addition to these boundaries isolated patches of grassland, outliers of the larger grassland formation, are found as far east as Ohio, and as far north as the Peace River drainage basin in Alberta. [See map page 4].

Even though the term grassland is applied to this vast region, the vegetation is far from uniform. Variation within the grassland is illustrated by the classification system used

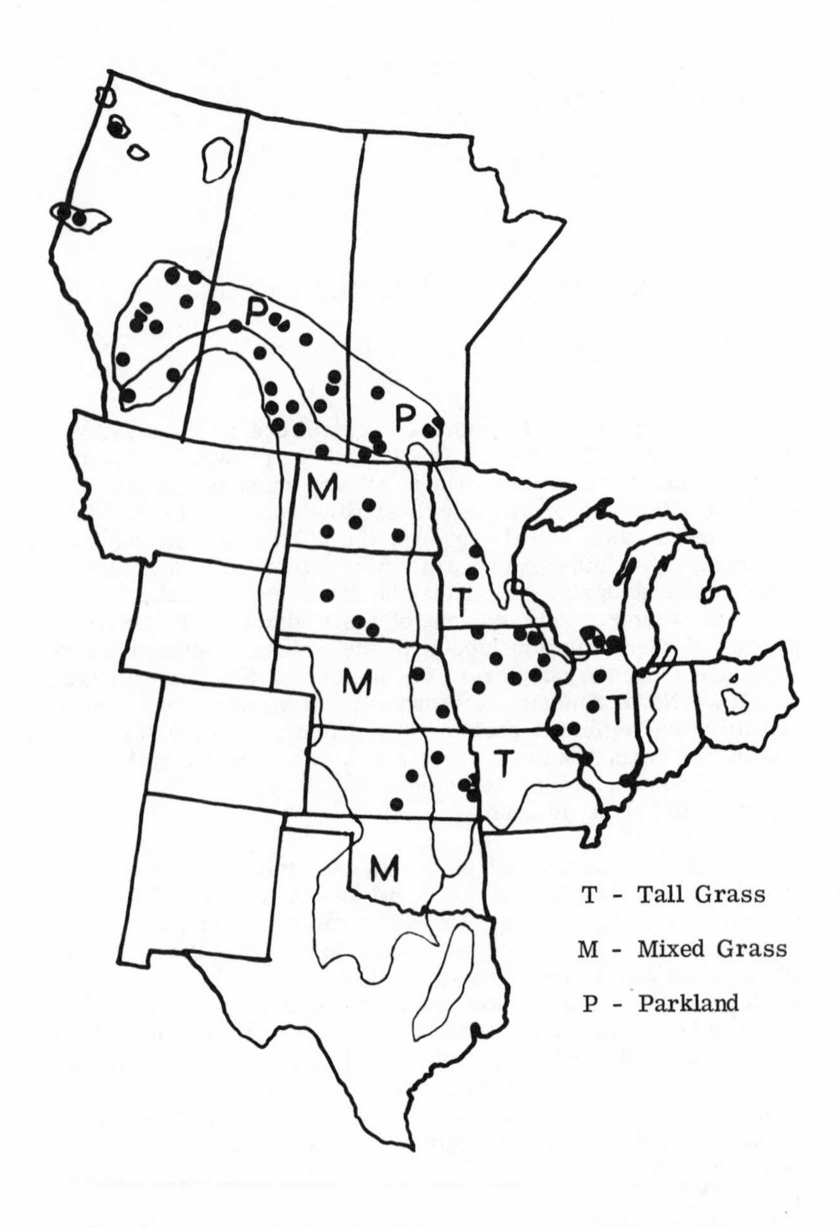

Map of Grasslands: Grassland Communities and Locations for Women's Writings (non-fictional works)

to identify the grasses. John L. Vankat divides the central North American grasslands into three communities, extending from east to west. They are tall grass, mixed grass, and short grass, which roughly correspond to variations in climate, soils, and vegetation. [1] The tall grass community is characterized by a humid climate, fertile soil, and grasses reaching heights of up to eight feet. [2] In contrast, grasses in the mixed grass community reach only two to four feet, and are composed of mid and short grass species. The climate of the mixed grass region ranges from subhumid to semi-arid and the soil is fertile. The short grass community is an extension of the mixed grass. Plant ecologists now believe that the appearance of areas dominated by short grasses is the result of overgrazing and does not represent true climax conditions. [3] Generally speaking short grasses, which reach heights of only three to seven inches are dominant in areas with a semi-arid climate. In this essay the mixed and short grass communities will be considered together. Because of the lack of precipitation, this region is the least conducive to cultivation. The northern portion of the grasslands form a fourth community, parkland. This community reaches its fullest extent in Canada, comprising approximately forty percent of the Canadian portion of the grasslands. Parkland has a subhumid climate, fertile soil, and combines tall grasses with some trees, mostly aspen and bur oak. [4]

The lack of uniformity between grassland environments played a principal part in the uneven development of agricultural settlement in central North America. Agricultural pioneers paused as they approached the grasslands, and paused again as they encountered new conditions within the grasslands. Consequently there was no single grasslands experience. At each new juncture individual pioneers were forced to reconcile the conflict between their conceptual image of the land and the reality of the land. Despite this fact, general patterns in the way farmers responded to new conditions within the grasslands can be identified. Because the heights of grasses are useful indicators of changes in environmental conditions, the category of tall grass and the general category of mixed grass are convenient units to examine both grassland environments and general patterns in the experiences of agricultural pioneers.

Explorers and travelers entering the grasslands from the east emerged from the forest edge into a sea of tall grasses. French explorers unaccustomed to the open landscape called this region prairie, meaning meadow. Even today the tall grass region is considered the "true prairie" of

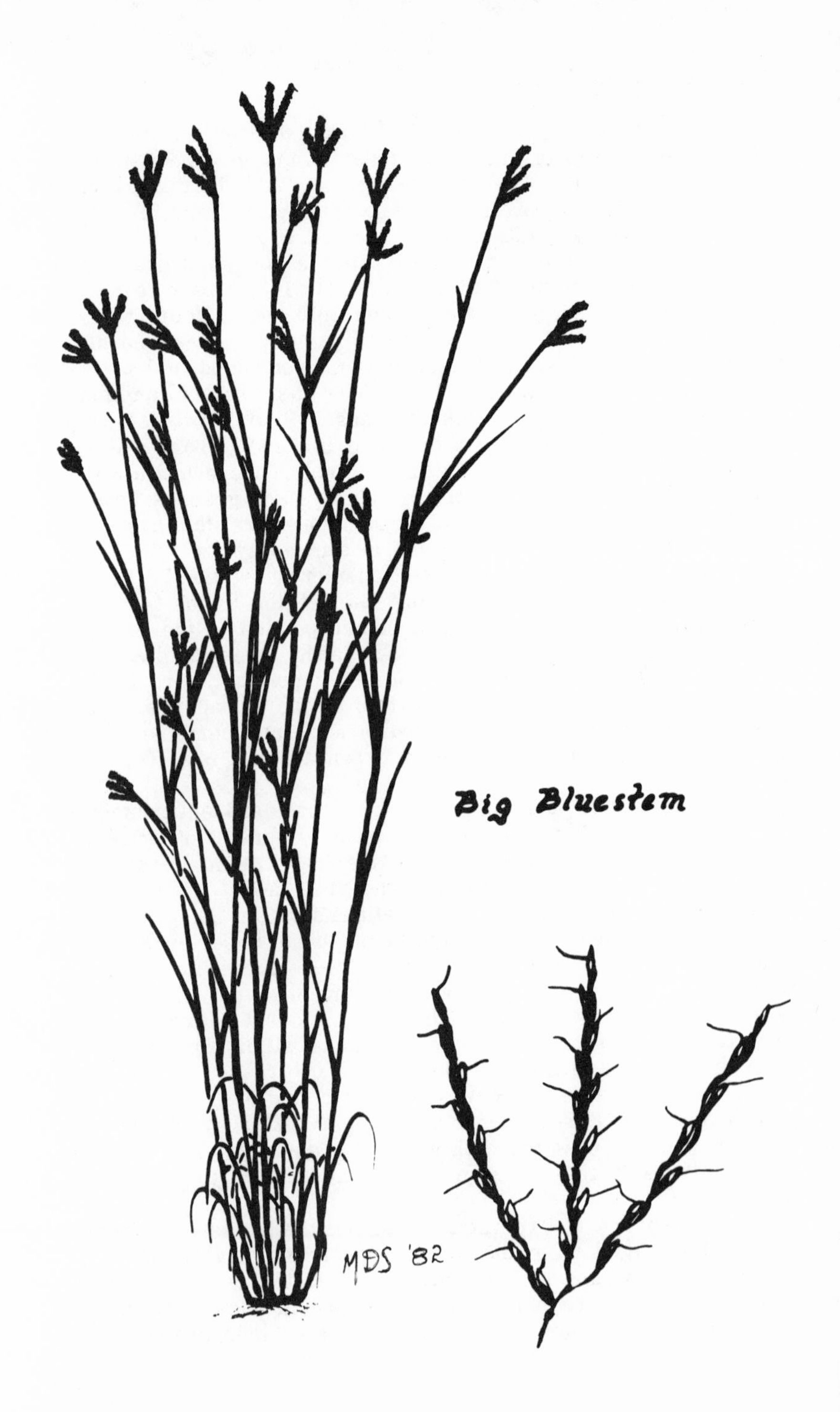
Big Bluestem
MDS '82

the North American grassland.[5] The "true prairie" or tall grass prairie named by the explorers was primarily located in the United States, although there is evidence to suggest that the tall grass region did extend into southern Manitoba along an area located between Winnipeg and Brandon, south of the Assiniboine River.[6] The original 400,000 acres of tall grass prairie below the 49th parallel occupied the central lowland states, with the greatest portion of tall grass being found east of the 98th meridian, in the states of Indiana, Illinois, Minnesota, Iowa, Missouri, Texas, Oklahoma, Kansas, Nebraska, and North and South Dakota.[7] Recording his journey through the tall grass country of Illinois during the years of 1679 and 1680, French explorer Father Louis Hennepin wrote, "The region we entered was a great open plain on which nothing grows except high grass...."[8] Hennepin was describing that part of the tall grass prairie known as the prairie peninsula, which protrudes into the deciduous forest as far east as Indiana and as far north as southwestern Ontario. He described the peninsula further: "Those limitless prairies are dotted with forests of full grown trees where every sort of building timber is to be found."[9] Hennepin's comments confirm the view that the original prairie vegetation of Indiana and Illinois combined grassland with some trees, with the trees usually located along rivers or streams or in isolated groves. Westward from Illinois trees became scarce and the prairie became dominant.[10]

John E. Weaver describes the tall grass prairie landscape as composed of "level land, knolls, steep bluffs, rolling to hilly land, valleys, and extensive alluvial plains."[11] Grasses thriving on the wetter lowland sites of this landscape were big bluestem, Indian grass, Canada wild-rye and cordgrass.[12] As he rode through a tall grass outlier in southern Ontario, Patrick Shirreff, an early voyageur among the grasses observed "two species of grass which occasionally reached the horses' ears."[13] Shirreff might have been referring to big bluestem and prairie cordgrass; both species reach heights of six to eight feet. Ecologist David Costello suggests that, "there were no more luxuriant stands of vegetation than those dominated by prairie cordgrass.... This coarse woody-stemmed grass ... produced shade so dense that other plants were virtually excluded from its presence."[14]

On the drier upland sites of the prairie, the taller grasses gave way to needlegrass, prairie dropseed, side oats grama, June grass, and little bluestem.[15] Although smaller in stature these grassland species were no less showy than their lowland neighbors. Costello illustrates this point:

> When the tall, flexible stems of needlegrass were mature, they reached a height of three to five feet and presented a magnificent sight as they bent in waves that ran with the wind. When the seeds with long awns were disseminated, the bleached stalks and leaves remained to give the prairie a snow-covered appearance when viewed from afar.[16]

The dramatic appearance of the grasses is matched only by the seasonal changes of the forbs, or broad leaved herbs. These forbs produce the colorful flowers characteristic of the prairie. Forced to adapt to the seasonal changes of the dense grasses, the heights of the different species of forbs, flowering successively throughout the growing season, correspond to the heights of the lofty grasses. In the early spring the lavender pasque flower signals the end of dormant winter. It is soon followed by Canada anemone, prairie phlox, and violets. Summer brings purple prairie clovers and blackeyed Susans. In the autumn sawtooth sunflower and goldenrod are conspicuous among the grasses.[17] Early descriptions of prairie vegetation frequently mentioned the engaging effects of these colorful forbs. Illinois pioneer Rebecca Burlend described the Grande Prairie:

> Let the reader imagine himself by the side of a rich meadow, ... decked with myriads of flowers of a most gorgeous and varied description.... Nothing can surpass in richness of colour, or beauty of formation many of the flowers which are found in the most liberal profusion....[18]

But not all prairie travelers recorded a favorable opinion of the prairie landscape, Caleb Atwater recorded this assessment of an Ohio prairie in 1818:

> To the traveler, who for several days traverses these prairies and barrens, their appearance is quite uninviting, and even disagreeable. He may travel from morning until night, and make good speed, but on looking around him, he fancies himself at the very spot whence he started ... a dull uniformity of prospect "spread out immense." Excepting here and there a tree, or a slight eleva-

> tion of ground, it is otherwise a dead level, covered with tall weeds and coarse grass.[19]

Despite this claim Atwater was quick to add, "but in order to make ample amends for any deficiency, nature has made them exuberantly fertile."[20]

Unlike Atwater, Burlend did not appreciate the fertility of the open prairies. Although she noted that prairie soils were "quite black," she concluded that prairie "land, though the soonest cultivated, is not the most productive being as the farmers term it, of a stronger quality than [woodland soil]."[21] Perhaps Burlend was referring to the toughness of prairie sod, resulting from the deep, dense root systems anchoring the prairie grasses. The root system of little bluestem can reach depths of seven feet or more. According to Costello, "a square yard of soil four inches deep may contain roots that would stretch for twenty miles if all were placed end to end."[22]

The deep root systems of the tall grass region are fastened in soil rich from the humus of abundant prairie vegetation. Most of the soil within the tall grass region is part of the Great Soils classification of prairie soil, a rich deep top soil, though Chernozem, a shallower soil, is found in the Dakotas and Minnesota. John Weaver notes the soils of the tall grass region offer nearly every feature generally considered favorable to plant production."[23]

Another characteristic of the prairie, adding to its productivity, is its climate. Although precipitation varies in the tall grass region, ranging from 40 inches in the east to 20 inches in the west, it usually falls during the growing season and drought is not a problem.[24] Temperatures vary widely in the grassland region ranging from extreme highs of 100° F or more to lows as extreme as -50° F. Because of the lack of physical barriers on the prairie, warm and cool air masses move rapidly across the grassland, causing swift changes in temperature. The early occurrence of frost is a constant concern for farmers.[25] Using the central Iowa city of Indianola as a point of reference, statistics show that over a forty-year period Indianola averaged 166 frost-free days with the latest spring frost on April 27 and the earliest fall frost on October 10.[26] The number of frost-free days, or length of growing season, tends to decrease in the north and increase slightly in the south. In addition to the danger of early frost the changeable prairie climate threatens crops with extreme heat, hail storms, dust storms, and drought.[27]

Another factor related to climate, which is noticeable on the prairie, but characteristic of the entire grassland, is wind. The almost constant presence of the wind was a source of fascination for some observers. Watching the wind form waves among the tall grasses, Illinois traveller Catherine Stewart observed, "oceans of blossoming fragrance, when the wind waves over the long luxuriant grass ... that expansion of feeling is produced as when at sea...."[28] For others, the incessant hum of the wind was a source of irritation. Costello notes that the wind and sky are effective barometers of the weather. Here he vividly describes the effect of strong winds on the prairie:

> Our windmills turned their faces from the wind and shut off when the wind blew at twenty to twenty-five miles per hour. In autumn the Russian thistles ran freely before the wind at thirty miles per hour and pushed down fences.... At forth to fifty miles per hour dust clouds streamed off the fields.... At wind speeds above that the whole landscape turned yellow with soil-laden air.... At seventy to one hundred miles per hour, when the Chinook blew, tin roofs from cow sheds sailed into the sky....[29]

The vegetation, climate, and soils of the tall grass prairie environment are the principal factors determining the success of agriculture on the prairie. Despite vagaries of the climate, prairie is some of the most valuable agricultural land in North America. This evaluation was not generally accepted by agricultural pioneers until well into the nineteenth century. As late as 1882 John Macoun, a Canadian expansionist, wrote: "the settler in Ontario feels that to be out of sight of woods is a calamity. He also believes that land covered with a forest is NEW and therefore richer than the prairie, and rejects the latter and takes to brush and forest."[30]

Attempts to establish agricultural settlements in the tall grass regions of North America began as early as 1812. In that year a small group of Scots and Irish settlers initiated settlement along the river banks at the junction of the Red and Assiniboine Rivers in present-day Manitoba. By the early 1820s U.S. farmers were approaching the open prairies of Indiana and Illinois, the prairie peninsula. The preferred areas of settlement, however, were not the fertile prairies but rather "oak openings," isolated patches of fertile grassland surrounded by oak groves. Only when these areas became crowded did U.S. settlers press onto the open prairie.[31]

Part of the explanation for the pioneers' hesitation derives from the discrepancy between their conceptual image of the tall grass region and the reality of the prairie environment. J. Wreford Watson argues that "it is the mental picture a man has about a region that will qualify his use of it."[32] In the case of some pioneers, their ability to assess the agricultural potential of the prairie accurately was biased by a conceptual image derived from their previous experience in the woodlands. Frontier historian Ray Billington summarizes this dilemma when he describes the U.S. experience:

> They had, for generations, judged the richness of land by the density of its forest growth, used wood for everything from homes to fences, and obtained fuel, game, and water from the wilderness. Now they must settle on a barren waste apparently incapable of supporting forests, unprotected from winter blasts or summer heat, without logs for their cabins, rails for their fences, or fuel for their fires. They must dig wells rather than depend on rippling forest streams, and provide drainage to carry spring rains from level lands. Worst of all they must devise some means of breaking the tough prairie sod which shattered the fragile wooden plows to which they were accustomed.
>
> Little wonder that settlers hesitated at the edge of the prairies....[33]

A second negative image, associated with the image of a barren land, affected evaluations of grasslands in the British Northwest. Because much of the early information concerning these grasslands came from fur traders and explorers using northern routes, the climate of the grasslands was popularly believed to be subarctic. The combination of treeless plains and frigid temperatures produced an image of a subarctic wasteland in the grasslands.[34] This image continued through the first part of the nineteenth century despite the contrary example of the Red River Settlement. Douglas Owram suggests that this was possible because the Red River Settlement was viewed as separate from the rest of the grasslands. It was an "oasis in the wilderness."[35]

Compounding these images was the inaccessibility of the prairies. Prairie roads were rough, waterways were scarce, and railways were distant. In the British Northwest the prairie was even more inaccessible because roads and trails had not penetrated the Precambrian Shield.

Exceptions to the negative assessments of the prairie as a place for agricultural settlement usually referred to prairie lands within easy reach of timber. As early as the seventeenth century Father Louis Hennepin praised the fertility of Illinois prairie soil saying, "the soil is capable of producing all sorts of fruit, herbs, and grain in greater abundance than the best European soils produce them."[36] Doug McManis, in his study of Illinois prairies, argues that during the first half of the nineteenth century, when serious settlement efforts were being considered in the United States, optimistic evaluations of prairie emerged as early as 1816.[37] Caleb Atwater's recommendation of prairie soil, mentioned earlier, was written in 1818.

Despite early positive assessments of the prairie, the complex set of mental and physical barriers obstructing agricultural advance onto the prairie did not significantly erode until the middle of the 1850s. Migration onto the open prairie was facilitated by a gradual process of adaptation which challenged the barren image of the prairie. Between 1812, when settlement reached the prairie edge in the British Northwest, and 1865, when it reached the western fringe of the tall grass region in the United States, settlers found new ways to make prairie accommodate the needs of agricultural settlement. The efforts of these settlers combined with the promotional activities of railroads, colonization companies, and state and territorial governments caused pioneers to re-evaluate the agricultural potential of prairie.

Pioneers establishing farms on prairie confronted two initial tasks: construction of some type of shelter and breaking the prairie sod. Most farmers settling on the prairie of Indiana, Illinois, Iowa, and Manitoba during the first four decades of the nineteenth century were fortunate to be located near rivers and streams where timber was available. Patrick Shirreff described the attitude of these early farmers: "Proximity to forest is chosen for the facility of obtaining building, fencing, and fuel timber, and a settler regards the distance of half a mile from forest an intolerable burden."[38] Areas distant from timber, such as the Grande Prairie in central Illinois, remained unsettled until the Illinois and Michigan canal and railroads brought timber to points within easy hauling distance.[39] As a result the initial shelters built by pioneers in western Indiana, Illinois, Iowa, and Manitoba were constructed of logs. Construction of these shelters, for the most part, did not depend upon acquiring new skills.[40]

Prairie Print No. 2 Dakota House

Farmers settling on the western fringe of the tall grass region during the second half of the nineteenth century were not as fortunate as their eastern counterparts. In these areas settlement preceded the railroads and timber was less abundant.

Beginning in the 1850s settlers gradually migrated into western Minnesota, northwestern Iowa, the eastern Dakotas, eastern Nebraska, and eastern Kansas. These settlers, like their neighbors in the east, relied upon timber supplies located near rivers and streams. As the demand for timber increased and as settlement moved further away from waterways, farmers developed a type of shelter built with prairie sod that would be the forerunner of sod houses found in the mixed grass plains. These shelters consisted of sod walls but various other materials were used for the rest of the house. Everett Dick describes a popular style of sod home found in eastern Kansas:

> It was built by setting up two rows of poles and then bringing them together at the top and thatching the sides with prairie hay. The house was all roof and gable; the windows and doors were in the end. The gables were built up with sod walls.[41]

It is not possible to draw precise lines separating areas where the modified sod shelter replaced the log cabin or where the true soddie replaced its modified version. Individual settlers varied both in their preference for housing and in the resources available to them for construction of housing. Some settlers could afford the cost of shipping timber long distances. Others preferred sod style homes even though timber might be available.[42] Nevertheless it is clear that new patterns of housing construction emerged on the open prairie. These patterns were unique adaptations to existing conditions within the grassland.

Another initial task encountered by settlers farming the prairie frontier was the breaking of prairie sod. Breaking the tough prairie sod was a challenge for farmers using tools inherited from their woodland experiences. The first plows adapted for use on the prairie were mammoth wooden structures, some with beams measuring six to twelve feet.[43] These plows, requiring as many as six yoke of oxen to pull them, cut a furrow up to three feet deep and thirty inches wide.[44] Because the sticky sod clung to the plow, farmers stopped frequently to scour the moldboard. Eventually these cumbersome plows were replaced by steel plows with finely ground moldboards. These plows scoured the sod faster and cleaner.[45] Even after the sod had been turned, axes were used to chop the turf so that the first seed could be planted. Cultivation was easier after the first breaking, but it took several years for all the dead roots and stems from the prairie vegetation to decompose and become part of the soil.[46] If farmers could not afford to purchase the team and plows needed to break the sod, they might exchange their labor for the use of their neighbor's equipment. Some farmers chose to hire a professional sod breaker at $2.00 to $4.00 an acre.[47] The work was hard and sometimes expensive but for some settlers it was preferable to farming in the woodlands. An optimistic English immigrant farming on the Illinois prairie in 1821 explained that it was "far preferable to clearing of woodland, which is attended with much trouble and expence."[48]

With the tasks of constructing a shelter and sod breaking accomplished, pioneers demonstrated their commitments to farming and their abilities to adapt to the prairie environment. But other obstacles remained to be overcome. As settlement advanced across the prairie frontier the problems of obtaining fuel and water increased. Settlers near the eastern edge of the prairie had access to water from nearby rivers and streams. These waterways were also a source of timber. Settlers who located beyond convenient reach of water supplies dug their own wells. If this was not possible, holding ponds were dredged to catch rain water, though this was usually less than desirable. In other cases farmers simply took the time to haul water in barrels from the nearest available source.[49]

The problem of obtaining fuel was no less difficult. Initially, settlers used buffalo and cow dung. When these resources were depleted they turned to the use of local grasses and hay. Sloughgrass, also called cordgrass, was a common fuel:

> Large wisps of this are twisted, doubled, and tied by hand, being thus brought into compact and convenient form for putting into the stove. One or two of these twisted bunches are supplied every five or ten minutes, and they maintain a hot fire as serviceable as that of wood or coal. The amount of hay thus used in a year for heating in an ordinary room is from eight to twelve tons. An hour's time is sufficient for twisting up a winter day's supply of this fuel.[50]

In the 1870s Mennonites in Manitoba used large brick ovens to burn combinations of manure, hay, and straw.[51]

Like the problem of obtaining fuel, the problem of obtaining materials for fencing was related to the absence of easily available timber. Farmers needed to protect their crops from wandering livestock. Wood fences were found throughout the prairie, but as settlement migrated westward, and as the population of farmers increased, timber became costly and scarce. As a result fencing in prairie areas took various forms, including the use of ditches, sod or stone walls, and hedges. In some cases farmers relied on the practice of herding, rather than the use of fences. These methods of corralling livestock and protecting crops remained in use even after the advent of barbed wire in the 1870s.[52]

With the act of breaking the prairie sod settlers demonstrated their desire to farm, and with the act of fencing they staked out their claims to the land. And as they overcame the obstacles of providing fuel, water, and shelter, farmers were gradually eroding the barren image of the treeless prairie. The expansion of agriculture on the western edge of the tall grass region in the United States during the second half of the nineteenth century illustrates this point. Gilbert Fite notes that in the 1860s the number of farms in Minnesota increased from 18,181 to 92,386. Between 1860 and 1880 in one county of northwestern Iowa the number of farms grew from only five to 697. Eastern Kansas and eastern Nebraska also experienced substantial growth.[53] This rapid filling-in of prairie meant that by the 1870s U.S. farmers would begin to look farther west for farmlands, this time to the mixed grassland of the Great Plains.

During the 1870s in Canada a different settlement pattern was taking place. As U.S. settlers moved onto the western edge of the tall grass prairie and beyond, settlers in Canada were just beginning to venture away from the prairie fringe along the banks of the Red and Assiniboine Rivers in Manitoba. Movement away from these rivers was delayed, at least in part, because the settlers preferred well-watered and partially-timbered areas. Other factors contributing to the delay were the lack of railroads, the poorly drained character of the Manitoba lowlands, and the fact that large portions of the lowlands were owned by land speculators.[54]

When settlers in Canada did venture away from the banks of the Red and Assiniboine Rivers, their choices were often another partially-timbered region, parkland. Parkland provided a settlement option similar to the oak openings preferred by farmers in the United States and Ontario during the early 1800s. Wood, water, and hay were easily accessible as well as open spaces of grassland ready for immediate plowing.

The agricultural potential of the parkland had been a subject of formal investigation as early as 1857. In that year the first of several expeditions began explorations of the land between the Red River and the Rocky Mountains. Although reports from these expeditions differed, they did agree on the suitability of parkland for agriculture. In fact the term Fertile Belt was often used to describe this region.[55]

Parkland forms a crescent-shaped belt within the interior of Canada. It is a long narrow transition zone separating the boreal forests and mixed grasslands within Manitoba, Saskatchewan, and Alberta. Parkland vegetation consists of tall grasses interspersed with clumps of trees. Captain John Palliser included this description of parkland in his report of explorations made in the late 1850s:

> It is ... a partially wooded country abounding in lakes and rich natural pasturage, in some parts rivaling the finest park scenery of our country. Throughout this region of country the climate seems to preserve the same character, although it passes through very different latitudes....[56]

The uniformity in vegetation observed by Palliser is evidence of the warm temperatures accompanying the northward loop of isotherms in western Canada. As a result of these isotherms spring appears in the parkland region of the Peace River in Alberta at nearly the same time as it appears along the Red River in Manitoba.[57] Throughout the region the growing season ranges from 130 to 160 days. The climate is classified as subhumid. Annual precipitation may reach twenty inches. Much of this precipitation falls during the growing season, allowing adequate moisture for crops. The soils of the region are rich and black, similar to those found in the tall grass region. The topography is also conducive to agriculture, varying from level plain to gently rolling hills.[58] In 1858 Henry Youle Hind made this recommendation:

> It is a physical reality of the highest importance to the interests of British North America that this

> continuous belt can be settled and cultivated from a few miles west of the Lake of the Woods to the passes of the Rocky Mountains, and any line of communication, whether by waggon road or railroad, passing through it, will eventually enjoy the great advantage of being fed by an agricultural population from one extremity to the other.[59]

This recommendation combined with similar recommendations from other expeditions greatly diminished the notion of a subarctic wasteland in British North America.[60]

The Canadian government acquired the interior grasslands of Canada in 1870 and almost immediately began the task of encouraging agricultural settlement. Plans were made in the early 1870s for construction of a transcontinental railroad line from Winnipeg to Edmonton using a parkland route. The lure of a potential railroad combined with the availability of wood, water, and hay stimulated settlement in the parkland during the early 1870s. These settlements suffered major setbacks in the 1880s after final plans were announced for a transcontinental railroad using a southern route through the plains. Without railroad connections, agricultural settlement on parkland, especially the more northerly sections in Saskatchewan and Alberta, could develop only very slowly. The occurrence of frost in these sections also affected the rate of settlement. Even with early ripening varieties of wheat, frost-free, subhumid lands in the United States siphoned away potential settlers.[61] It was not until the early 1900s that agricultural settlement on parkland developed its greatest momentum. The Peace River Block, a parkland outlier in the Peace River Valley of Alberta, was the last parkland region to be settled. Its development did not occur until after 1914.[62]

For settlers coming from agricultural experiences in humid or subhumid environments, parkland demanded little in the way of adaptation. Homes were built of wood, and wood for fuel was usually available within a reasonable distance. Nevertheless a major innovation in agricultural technique was accomplished in the development of early ripening varieties of wheat. The first of these varieties, Red Fife, was available during the 1870s.[63] This development foreshadowed later agricultural innovations that would take place on the treeless plains.

By the late 1860s the negative images of a barren, subarctic wasteland in the British Northwest were being reversed.

By 1875 Mennonite immigrants successfully demonstrated farming techniques on the open prairie, and by 1878 other settlements followed their example.[64] But the majority of settlers in Canada had little experience farming the treeless grassland. The decision in 1881 to construct a transcontinental railroad across the southern plains changed this situation. Agricultural pioneers in Canada during the 1880s confronted not only treeless grassland but the drier mixed grass community of the Great Plains.

The mixed grassland encountered by Canadian farmers in the 1880s and by U.S. farmers in the 1870s are found on the Great Plains of North America. This vast region is situated between the Rocky Mountains on the west, the central lowlands in the east, the upper Saskatchewan River in the north and the Rio Grande River in the south. The Great Plains landscape is predominantly flat. The vegetation consists mostly of the mid and short grass species. And the climate varies from subhumid in parts of the eastern plains to semi-arid in the western and southern plains.

The moisture deficiency of the Great Plains was a central factor shaping the experiences of agricultural pioneers on the plains. Unlike the prairie, the Great Plains could not accommodate agricultural techniques commonly used in the more humid east. Although the tall grass region of the prairie introduced the challenge of a level treeless environment, the region did not demand dry farming techniques. Farmers settling on the Great Plains faced the twin challenges of a treeless and dry environment.

Agricultural pioneers entered the plains through the mixed grass region, a broad transition zone which provides the vegetational cover for most of the Great Plains. The term mixed grass is used because the zone consists of grasses from both mid and short grass species.[65]

Settlers entering the plains through the mixed grass region barely noticed the transition. Unlike the abrupt change between forest and tall grass prairie, the transition between the tall and mixed grass regions is gradual. The eastern boundary of the mixed grass region roughly corresponds to a line beyond which rainfall does not exceed twenty inches. Both the 98th and 100th meridians have been used to designate this line.[66] During periods of prolonged drought or above-average rainfall the eastern boundary of the mixed grass plains may fluctuate. A series of dry years can cause the drought-resistant mixed grasses to invade areas formerly

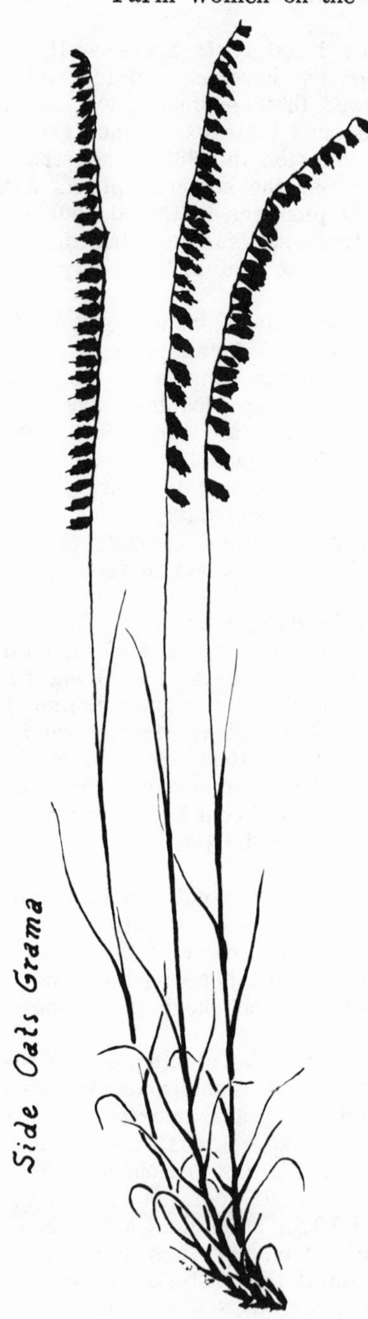
Side Oats Grama

populated by tall grasses. In the same way a number of above average years of rainfall can cause tall grasses to appear in areas formerly occupied by mixed grasses. However, these tall grasses are usually smaller than if found on the prairie.

The vegetation of the mixed grass region is characterized by mid grasses which reach heights of one to three feet, and, growing beneath these mid grasses, short grasses which reach heights of only three to seven inches. Common mid grasses found throughout the mixed grass region are needle and thread, sand dropseed, western wheat grass, and Junegrass.[67] Before widespread grazing little bluestem, porcupine grass, side oats grama, and prairie dropseed were also prominent.[68] In a region of level land and open sky all of these grasses bring pleasing variety to the landscape. The chameleon-like changes of little bluestem are an example:

> In early spring the grass stand is light green when you look with the wind, and dark green when you look toward the wind. In summer the grasses take on a reddish-brown hue and by autumn they show purple and copper tints....[69]

In areas where grazing is restricted, showy forbs, similar to those found in the tall grasses, appear among the grasses. Blazing star, Cut-leaved Goldenweed and Missouri Goldenrod are only a few of the many colorful forbs that may appear.[70]

But it is the short grasses, growing beneath the mid grasses which give the mixed grass plains a special character. Blue grama and buffalo grass are two of the most common short grasses. Even though the flower stalks of blue grama may reach as high as twenty inches, the bulk of the foliage of these grasses is only three to seven inches high.[71] Short grasses are good soil binders and they increase in areas where mid grasses and forbs are heavily grazed. Without the mid grasses, short grasses resemble a massive carpet spreading toward the horizon. This effect is especially apparent in parts of the semi-arid high plains where the land is primarily used for semi-arid grazing.

The shorter grasses of the mixed grass region are indicators of dry conditions. They are the most xeromorphic of the mixed grass species.[72] Precipitation, like the rest of the climate, is variable in the mixed grass plains. In

Blue Grama
MDS '82

general, precipitation ranges from ten to twenty inches and is classfied as semi-arid. Ecologists John Weaver and F. Albertson qualify this classification:

> The climate is one of extremes. It is commonly called semiarid but in some years it is humid and in others desert-like. It is not a permanently established climate but a dynamic one with large scale fluctuations and wet and dry trends....[73]

Fluctuations in precipitation are especially important to the soils of the mixed grass plains. These soils are primarily of the Dark Brown or Brown soil classification.[74] Precipitation is the critical factor determining their productivity.

The Great Plains region as a whole, like the prairie to the east, has no forest or land forms to block rapidly moving air masses. The result is often violent weather and intense drying winds. Rapid changes in the weather may bring about the early occurrence of frost, a more frequent hazard on the Great Plains than on the prairie. The frost-free or growing season in the mixed grass plains ranges from 120 days in the north to nearly 200 days in the south.[75]

Although the climate of the mixed grass plains has distinct disadvantages for agriculture, it does have some advantages. Richard A. Bartlett explains:

> Solar radiation and light intensity are beneficial to the crops, and the high altitude, low humidity, sparse cloud cover and winds that keep the air clean are distinct assets. The autumn season is usually dry and peaceful, which ensures good harvesting with modern machinery. Finally, the arid climate inhibits many types of plant diseases, especially fungi.[76]

Homesteaders entering the mixed grass plains in the 1870s were unaware of these benefits. In fact, as late as 1870 maps of the United States designated the plains with the legend "Great American Desert." The image of the plains as desert began early. In the 1690s Henry Kelsey, the first white man to explore the interior grasslands of Canada, described the plains as barren and as a desert.[77] These images were perpetuated down to the nineteenth century through the published accounts of numerous travelers and explorers. Major Stephen Long received credit for giving formal recognition to the image of the plains as desert. After an expedition through the central plains of the United States in 1820, Long described the country as "almost wholly unfit for cultivation, and of course uninhabitable by people depending upon agriculture for their subsistence."[78] A narrative of the Long expedition was published in 1823, accompanied by a map labeling part of the plains as a Great Desert. This map reappeared in numerous publications, including school textbooks, throughout the nineteenth century.

The impact of the literature regarding the Great American Desert was not limited to U.S. readers. John Warkentin argues that the desert image also affected the evaluation of the mixed grass plains in Canada. The same expeditions that recommended parkland as a fertile area, also identified an arid region unsuitable for agriculture. This region coincided with the southern portion of the mixed grass plains in Canada. This arid region, commonly called Palliser's Triangle, was considered the northern-most extension of the Great American Desert.[79]

Even though the boundaries of the Great American Desert were unclear, the desert image was based on at least three certain characteristics of the land. The land was treeless, subhumid and unoccupied by white men. Until the middle of the nineteenth century these characteristics affirmed the desert image. But by the late 1860s conditions had changed. Farmers in the United States were adapting to the treeless environment of the prairie, pockets of settlement were developing on the Great Plains, and expansionists were raising questions about the suitability of the climate for settlement.

The desire to reappraise the agricultural potential of the Great Plains surfaced even before the middle of the nineteenth century. In his book, Commerce of the Prairies, published in 1844, expansionist Josiah Gregg reflected the conflict between the desert image and expansionism. Gregg recognized the environmental basis for the desert image when he wrote:

> It will now readily be inferred that the Great Prairies from Red River to the western sources of the Missouri, are, as has before been intimated, chiefly uninhabitable--not so much for want of wood (though the plains are altogether naked), as of soil and of water; for though some of the plains appear of sufficiently fertile soil, they are mostly of a

> sterile character, and all too dry to be cultivated. These great steppes seem only fitted for the haunts of mustang, the buffalo, the antelope, and their migratory lord, the prairie Indian.[80]

Gregg continued by suggesting that "some favorable mutation" would be required "in nature's operations, to revive the plains and upland prairies."[81] Gregg tentatively proposed that the actions of men might induce such a mutation:

> The high plains seem too dry and lifeless to produce timber; yet might not the vissitudes of nature operate a change likewise upon the seasons? Why may we not suppose that the genial influences of civilization--that extensive cultivation of the earth--might contribute to the multiplication of showers.... At least, many old settlers maintain that the droughts are seeming less oppressive in the West.... Then may we not hope that these sterile regions might yet be thus revived and fertilized, and their surface covered one day by flourishing settlement to the Rocky Mountains.[82]

Gregg's proposal was a forerunner of the notion later popular in the United States that "Rain Follows the Plough." The fact that the U.S. plains experienced a series of wet years between 1878 and 1886 discouraged any successful challenge to this notion.[83]

During the 1880s a reassessment of the desert image also occurred in Canada. Throughout the 1870s popular conceptions of the Fertile Belt expanded to include not only the parklands but most of the mixed grass region as well. As a result, Palliser's Triangle came to mean only the most arid portions of the mixed grass plains in southwestern Saskatchewan and southeastern Alberta. Even this obstacle to agricultural settlement was challenged when John Macoun, a botanist and western expansionist, publicized the results of his expedition through the Canadian plains. Macoun argued that parts of Palliser's Triangle received adequate moisture for crops during the critical spring and summer months of the growing season. It was not important that the overall annual rainfall of the region was slight.[84] Few understood that Macoun's evaluation of Palliser's Triangle was made during a period of abundant rainfall on the plains.

Reassessments of the desert images in both the United States and Canada combined with social, political, and

Prairie Print No. 3 Dakota Sodhouse

economic forces to create expectations for a new agricultural frontier on the plains. Out of these expectations a different image emerged, instead of a desert the plains were a garden. Inspired by this image farmers in Canada and the United States confidently entered the mixed grass plains. The initial transition between the humid tall grass region and the subhumid mixed grass plains was made less difficult by fluctuating years of abundant rainfall, the rapid expansion of railroads and the passage of Homestead legislation.

In the United States substantial migration onto the plains began following the Civil War. Settlers, between 1870 and 1890, filled in the remaining areas of the prairie and ventured out into portions of mixed grass region in the central plains states of Kansas and Nebraska, the northern plains of the Dakotas and eastern Montana and the southern mixed grass region of eastern Colorado and Texas. Oklahoma, because it was reserved as Indian Territory, was the last mixed grass region opened for settlement.[85]

In Canada the first wave of settlement on the plains began with the construction of the Canadian Pacific Railroad in the 1880s. By 1886 settlement occurred as far west as Moose Jaw, Saskatchewan. Beyond this point, the semi-arid climate and more rugged terrain discouraged farmers.[86] But the real rush for the Canadian plains did not occur until after the supply of frost-free subhumid lands in the United States was exhausted.[87] This occurred about 1890. Beginning in 1900 a second wave of settlers rapidly filled in the remaining arable lands in both the mixed grass and parkland regions.

The process of making the mixed grass plains accommodate the needs of agricultural settlement was twofold. First, it required the utilization or modification of implements and techniques used in the prairie plains. This was especially true of problems related to the absence of easily available timber. For example, plains farmers developed the partial sod home of the western tall grass region into a true soddy. Warm in winter and cool in summer these homes were built almost entirely of sod cut from the soils of the grassland. To construct the home, furrows were ploughed in areas of tough sod. These furrows were then carefully marked off into even lengths. Using an axe the homebuilder separated the lengths of sod and loaded them on a wagon for transport to the construction site. A well-planned sod home followed a careful design. Evelyn Slater McLeod's family built an elaborate sod home near Consort, Alberta, in 1909. She described the construction process:

> The first row of sod slabs showed the outline of the house. They were placed side by side, grass side down, to make a rectangle whose outer dimensions were 49'4" and 21'4". After the first tier was laid, and carefully levelled by forcing chunks of soil into the cracks, the second course was placed and then the third, each with a different pattern. This procedure was then repeated to add stability. The overlapping of joints discouraged mice and snakes....
>
> When the sod walls were two feet high, the spaces for windows were left open, but the wall laying continued up to 6'8".[88]

Not all sod homes were this large, nor did they have the wood floor later described by Mrs. McLeod. Most settlers used only a thick mat of prairie grass for flooring. A few settlers could afford roofs made of wood, but most used a combination of willow or poplar poles, tar paper and sod. If built well these homes lasted for years. Mrs. McLeod lived in her family's sod home for twelve years. Many settlers converted their sod homes into barns or storage areas once they were able to afford a frame house or obtain logs for a log house.

The fact that the partial sod homes of the prairie were easily modified to fit the mixed grass plains environment suggests that the absence of trees was not a basic problem for farmers on the plains. Instead it was that farming itself was more complex on the plains. Gilbert Fite explains:

> ... the lack of readily available wood and water was a symptom of a basic problem and not the problem itself. It was not particularly difficult to use cow chips or twisted hay for fuel instead of wood, to put up a windmill rather than using the old hand pump, or to substitute barbed wire for the rail fence. The basic problem was one of working out and adapting proper farm organization patterns to fit natural conditions on the Great Plains.[89]

Developing proper farm organization was the second part of the process required to make the mixed grass plains meet the needs of agricultural settlement. Proper farm organization, according to Gilbert Fite, meant at least three things: the utilization of dry farming techniques, mixed grain and livestock farming and the maintenance of cash reserves.[90] Dry farming, defined as "agriculture without irrigation in regions of scanty precipitation,"[91] developed independently in the United States and Canada during the middle 1880s. It involves the selection of crops demanding lower quantities of moisture, such as wheat, and the use of summer fallowing techniques. Summer fallowing is the frequent working of fallow land in an effort to prevent loss of moisture from the soil. The second aspect of proper farming organization, mixed grain and livestock farming, was useful because the livestock provided an added source of income. Finally, the maintenance of cash reserves was insurance against hard times.

The utilization of proper farm organization came only after farmers endured a difficult period of trial and error on the mixed grass plains. During this period, which lasted well into the twentieth century, farmers in the United States and Canada developed an understanding of the plains environment. This understanding meant that farmers recognized the value of adjusting their farming operations to the environment. But it also meant, in some cases, farmers accepted that the land was unsuitable for agriculture. This was particularly true within the semi-arid short grass community. Semi-arid grazing was more appropriate in this region. In reality the mixed grass plains were neither desert nor garden. Perhaps, as the words of South Dakota homesteader Grace Fairchild suggest, the plains were somewhere in between these opposites. On the one hand she wrote, "Homesteading on the dry plains was a hard life...."[92] But on the other hand she concluded, "I made my bed in 1898 when I got married ... and moved to western South Dakota ... but when I look around ... I find the bed a good place to grow old in."[93]

By about 1920 the agricultural frontier within the grasslands of North America was largely settled. Most of the best agricultural land was already taken. The grasslands were not the first or last agricultural frontier in North America. Nevertheless, the environmental conditions encountered by agricultural pioneers in this region would not be duplicated on any other agricultural frontier in North America. The interior grasslands provided a distinctive arena for the expansion of agricultural settlement. Consequently the story of agricultural settlement in the grasslands is a unique chapter in the history of the land and the people of North America.

The experiences of agricultural pioneers varied, yet most settlers envisioned their individual portions of the grassland as places of material value. Settlers differed on how this vision could be achieved. Nevertheless nineteenth- and early twentieth-century agricultural economy required that farmers accomplish their vision, at least to some degree, through subjugation of the land. This task was radically different from tasks undertaken by previous inhabitants of the grasslands. For the most part earlier inhabitants had no desire to subdue the land, only to use it. Between no two social groups is this distinction more clear than between native Americans and farmers. Native American Robert Bunge explains:

> Traditional native-Americans scorn the white man's love--a love that wastes the land by "working" it; plowing, tilling, digging.... The white man, on the other hand, shrugs off Indian love, does not the Indian waste the land precisely because he does *not* "work" or "sink roots" in the land and merely wants the land over which to "roam."[94]

Indians were not the only inhabitants of the grasslands to use the land in this manner. Fur traders, miners and ranchers used the land to extract resources. Like the Indians their livelihoods did not depend upon subduing the land.

The distinction between using and subduing the land was especially important to farmers, both men and women. It meant that they would have to reappraise environmental conditions in view of their own needs. Their adaptations to environmental conditions within the grassland are part of the evidence that this occurred. Along the way they gradually discarded their earlier notions about the land. The grasslands were not subarctic, a desert, or a garden.

Women's experiences, part of this process, are surveyed in the following essays.

--S.B.S.

References

1. John L. Vankat, *The Natural Vegetation of North America* (New York: John Wiley and Sons, 1979), p. 159.

2. John E. Weaver, *North American Prairie* (Lincoln, Nebraska: Johnsen Publishing Company, 1954), pp. 7-12.

3. John E. Weaver and F.W. Albertson, *Grasslands of the Great Plains* (Lincoln, Nebraska: Johnsen Publishing Company, 1956), pp. 11-22.

4. F.B. Watts, "Climate, Vegetation, Soil," in *Canada: A Geographical Interpretation*, ed. John Warkentin (Toronto: Methuen Publications, 1968), pp. 94-95.

5. Weaver, p. 5.

6. Watts, "Climate, Vegetation, Soil," pp. 91-92, and H. J. Scoggan, The Flora of Canada (Ottawa: National Museums of Canada, 1978), p. 34.

7. Patricia Duncan, The Tallgrass Prairie (Kansas City: The Lowell Press, 1978), p. 5.

8. Father Louis Hennepin, Description of Louisiana, trans. Marion E. Cross (Minneapolis: University of Minnesota Press, 1938), p. 59.

9. Ibid., p. 62.

10. David Costello, The Prairie World (Minneapolis: University of Minnesota Press, 1969), p. 37.

11. Weaver, p. 6.

12. Ibid., pp. 22-38.

13. Patrick Shirreff, A Tour Through North America: Together with a Comprehensive View of the Canadas and United States as Adapted for Agricultural Emigration (Edinburgh: Oliver and Boyd, 1835), p. 195.

14. Costello, p. 40.

15. Weaver, pp. 53-67.

16. Costello, p. 42.

17. Weaver, pp. 123-133.

18. Rebecca Burlend, A True Picture of Emigration: or Fourteen Years in the Interior of North America; Being a Full and Impartial Account of the Various Difficulties and Ultimate Success of an English Family Who Emigrated from Barwick-in-Elmet, near Leeds, in the Year 1831, ed. Milo Milton Quaife (1848; reprint ed., Chicago: Lakeside Press, 1936), p. 84.

19. Caleb Atwater, "On the Prairies and Barrens of the West," American Journal of Science and Arts, 1 (1818): 124.

20. Atwater, p. 124.

21. Burlend, p. 84.

22. Costello, p. 63.

23. Weaver, p. 8.

24. Ibid., p. 7.

25. J. Wreford Watson, *North America: Its Countries and Regions* (London: Longmans, 1963), p. 38.

26. U.S. Department of Agriculture, *Yearbook of Agriculture 1941* (Washington, D. C.: Government Printing Office, 1941), p. 864.

27. Watson, p. 380.

28. Catherine Stewart, *New Homes in the West* (1843; reprint ed., Ann Arbor: University Microfilms, Inc., 1966), p. 53.

29. Costello, pp. 10-11.

30. John Macoun, *Manitoba and the Great Northwest* (Guelph, Ontario: World Publishing Co., 1882), p. 294, quoted in T.R. Weir, "Pioneer Settlement of Southwest Manitoba, 1889 to 1901," *The Canadian Geographer*, 8 (1964), p. 64.

31. Ray Billington, *Westward Expansion*, 3rd ed. (New York: The Macmillan Company, 1967), pp. 293-294.

32. J. Wreford Watson, "The Role of Illusion in North American Geography: A Note on the Geography of North American Settlement," *The Canadian Geographer* 13 (1), 1969: 10.

33. Billington, p. 307.

34. Douglas Owram, *Promise of Eden* (Toronto: University of Toronto Press, 1980), pp. 11-14.

35. Ibid., p. 16.

36. Hennepin, p. 63.

37. Douglas R. McManis, *The Initial Evaluation and Utilization of the Illinois Prairies, 1815-1840* (Chicago: University of Chicago, 1964), p. 90.

38. Shirreff, p. 250.

39. Allan G. Bogue, From Prairie to Corn Belt (Chicago: The University of Chicago Press, 1963), p. 68.

40. Ibid., p. 67.

41. Everett H. Dick, The Sod-House Frontier 1854-1890 (1937; reprint, Lincoln: University of Nebraska Press, 1979), p. 58.

42. Ibid., p. 110.

43. Bogue, p. 70.

44. Ibid., p. 70, and Shirreff, p. 445.

45. Readings in the History of American Agriculture, ed. Wayne D. Rasmussen (Urbana: University of Illinois Press, 1960), p. 78.

46. Costello, p. 214.

47. Bogue, p. 71, and Shirreff, p. 445.

48. John Woods, Two Years Residence in the Settlement on the English Prairie, in the Illinois Country, United States (London: 1823) reprinted in Early Western Travels 1748-1846, Vol. 10, ed. Reuben Gold Thwaites (Cleveland, Ohio: The Arthur H. Clark Company, 1904), p. 320.

49. Dick, p. 261.

50. Winchell and Upham, 1884, quoted in Costello, p. 40.

51. John Warkentin, "Mennonite Agricultural Settlements of Southern Manitoba," Geographical Review 49 (3), 1959: 352.

52. Leslie Hewes, "Early Fencing on the Western Margin of the Prairie," Annals of the Association of American Geographers 71 (4) 1981: 499-526.

53. Gilbert Fite, The Farmer's Frontier 1865-1900; Histories of the American Frontier (1966; reprint ed., Albuquerque: University of New Mexico Press, 1974), p. 35.

54. John Warkentin, "Western Canada in 1886," in Canada's Changing Geography, ed. R. Louis Gentilcore (Scarborough, Ontario: Prentice-Hall, 1967), p. 60.

55. J. Howard Richards, "The Prairie Region," in Canada: A Geographical Interpretation, ed. John Warkentin, pp. 403-404.

56. Captain John Palliser, Papers Relative to the Exploration of British North America, August 18th, 1860, p. 21 quoted in Henry Youle Hind, Narrative of the Canadian Red River Exploring Expedition of 1857 and of the Assinboine and Saskatchewan Exploring Expedition of 1855 (1860; reprint ed., 2 volumes, New York: Greenwood Press, 1969), 2:223.

57. Watts, "Climate, Vegetation, Soil," p. 119.

58. W.A. Mackintosh, Prairie Settlement: The Geographical Setting, Canadian Frontiers of Settlement, Vol. 1 (Toronto: The Macmillan Company of Canada Limited, 1934), pp. 89-94.

59. Hind, p. 234.

60. Owram, p. 149.

61. K.H. Norrie, "The Rate of Settlement of the Canadian Prairies, 1870-1911," Journal of Economic History, 35 (June 1975): 422-423.

62. Richards, pp. 410-413.

63. Ibid., p. 407.

64. James M. Richtik, "Prairie, Woodland, and the Manitoba Escarpment: Settlement and Agricultural Development in Carlton Municipality to 1877," Red River Valley Historian (Summer 1976): 17.

65. Weaver and Albertson, p. 16.

66. Walter Prescott Webb designates the boundary at the 98th meridian and Gilbert Fite places the boundary at the 100th meridian. See Webb, The Great Plains (1931; Grosset's University Library, 1973), p. 7, and Fite, p. 3.

67. Weaver and Albertson, p. 27.

68. Costello, p. 42.

69. Ibid., p. 46.

70. Weaver and Albertson, pp. 44-53.

71. Ibid., p. 59.

72. Watts, p. 94.

73. Weaver and Albertson, p. 12.

74. Ibid., p. 12, and Watts, pp. 96-97.

75. Ibid., p. 12.

76. Richard A. Bartlett, "The Land, Climate, and Living Things," in *The Great Plains Experience: Readings in the History of a Region*, eds. James Wright and Sarah Rosenberg (University of Mid-America, 1978), p. 21.

77. Henry Kelsey quoted in *The Western Interior of Canada: A Record of Geographical Discovery 1612-1917*, ed. John Warkentin (Toronto: McClelland and Stewart Limited, 1964), pp. 20-29.

78. Edwin James, *Account of an Expedition from Pittsburgh to the Rocky Mountains ...* (London, 1823); reprinted in *Early Western Travels*, Vol. 14, ed. Reuben Gold Thwaites (Cleveland, Ohio: The Arthur H. Clark Company, 1905), p. 20.

79. John Warkentin, "The Desert Goes North," in *Images of the Plains*, eds. Brian Blouet and Merlin P. Lawson (Lincoln: University of Nebraska Press, 1975), pp. 152-157.

80. Josiah Gregg, *Commerce of the Prairies* (1844; reprinted in 2 volumes, Ann Arbor, Michigan: University Microfilms, Inc., 1966), 2: 191-192.

81. Ibid., p. 192.

82. Ibid., pp. 202-203.

83. Fite, p. 96.

84. Owram, p. 159.

85. Billington, pp. 705-723.

86. Richards, p. 407.

87. Norrie, p. 427.

88. Evelyn Slater McLeod, "Our Sod House," *Beaver, A Magazine of the North*, 308 (1977): 12-13.

89. Fite, pp. 222-223.

90. Ibid., p. 222.

91. Mary Wilma Hargreaves, *Dry Farming in the Northern Great Plains 1900-1915* (Cambridge: Harvard University Press, 1951), p. 3.

92. Walter Wyman, *Frontier Woman: The Life of a Woman Homesteader on the Dakota Frontier* (River Falls: University of Wisconsin-River Falls Press, 1972), p. 2.

93. Ibid., p. 3.

94. Robert Bunge, "Land Is a Feeling," *Report of Papers Presented at the Spring Conference, April, 1979* (Vermillion: Institute of Indian Studies, University of South Dakota), pp. 2-3.

A USABLE PAST:

PIONEER WOMEN ON THE AMERICAN PRAIRIES

In 1819 a small party of United States government military men and their families halted on the Wisconsin prairie at Prairie du Chien while a woman gave birth to a child. That child, Charlotte Ouisconsin Van Cleve, spent her childhood at Fort Snelling where conditions were primitive. Supplies arrived from St. Louis at irregular intervals and infrequent mail deliveries provided an uncertain link with civilization. Indians justifiably resented the encroachment of whites and created tension. The doctor usually had to be "soaked" (to use Charlotte's word) before he was sober enough to help the sick and, although the government provided a teacher for the children, the spiritual needs of the garrison community were left in the hands of Charlotte's mother and the General's wife, Mrs. Snelling.

Thus Charlotte had an unusual apprenticeship for frontier life. Nevertheless, almost forty years after her birth on the Wisconsin prairie, she experienced intense despair while travelling across the Minnesota prairie to help found a new community in Long Prairie. In her memoirs she vividly recalled the night when the horses gave out within six miles of their destination and the travellers were forced to camp. While others slept, Charlotte watched over her baby in the wagon, thinking of the comfortable beds and close friends left behind. "These thoughts," Charlotte wrote, "kept my *heart* warmed and comforted, albeit I shivered with external *cold*."[1]

Charlotte had developed many mental and psychological resources for surviving on the frontier, yet the loneliness and discomfort she described makes us wonder why she and other women left their familiar homes, their families, and friends to settle in new lands which seemed hostile and

Prairie Print No. 4 Mealtime on the Overland Trail

desolate. How did they cope with their isolated circumstances and the new roles required of them? And what were the compensations and means of self-fulfillment which enabled Charlotte to look back on her five years in Long Prairie as happy years, "though not unmixed with trial and sorrow."[2] To what degree does she represent prairie women and their experiences? Through this study readers can discover a usable past, a variety of models for adapting to and surviving in new territories.

In an attempt to answer these questions I have drawn on the letters, diaries, and memoirs of women on the Illinois, Kansas, Nebraska, Iowa, Minnesota, and Dakota prairies. These were not ordinary women: they had the education, the energy, and a sense of their roles in history which enabled them to record their experiences for families and friends either day by day, or in retrospect. Because of their exceptional qualities, we cannot assume that they speak for the majority of prairie women. On the other hand, I do not think we should assume that their experiences were unique. The most important message inherent in these works is that women reacted in a variety of ways to the prairie frontier, and those variations will be the focus as I examine their role in deciding to go to the prairie, their reactions to the new environment, their responsibilities in settling the prairie, and the ways they found fulfillment as pioneer women.

In Frontier Women: The Trans-Mississippi West 1840-1880, the feminist historian Julie Roy Jeffrey raises a basic question: "Since emigration meant months of hard living, one wonders what motivated women to go west at all. Were they just dragged unwillingly by their men or did they participate in the decision? If they contributed to the decision, what were their reasons for doing so?"[3] Christine Stansell provides one answer:

> I have sampled ... some of the more than seven hundred diaries of men and women travelling to California and Oregon.... These indicated that the man usually initiated a plan to emigrate, made the final decision, and to a greater or lesser degree imposed it on his family. Men's involvement with self-advancement in the working world provided them with a logical and obvious rationale for going West.[4]

Another historian, Lillian Schlissel, examined the diaries of emigrating women between 1840 and 1860, and supports Stansell's conclusion: "The decision to make the journey was always a determination made by men."[5] However, the materials which provide a basis for the present study indicate that many prairie women actively participated in the decision-making process, although others actively rebelled. Let me begin with some of the more dramatic cases.

A Swiss immigrant woman told about one wife who was tricked into emigrating to the American prairies. The husband had gone to America to find land and, after a time, had written to his son to come and to bring his mother. The mother, who feared the sea, refused to go. The son secretly packed some of her possessions and had them placed on board ship. Then he asked her to come on board and see him off. He detained her and then endured her hysteria when she discovered she had been tricked. Fortunately, there was a happy ending. Once safe in New Orleans, "she praised him for his strategy" and proceeded to the prairie in good spirits.[6]

At the other extreme is the example of Anna Dalander, a widow who at the age of 44 emigrated to America with six children between the ages of fifteen and twenty-five. According to one account, Anna was responsible for organizing the 1846 party of forty-two emigrants with the intention of joining Västerlösa neighbors in their settlement at New Sweden, Iowa.[7] Anna was an emigration leader, not a reluctant follower.

Some young, single women aggressively sought means to emigrate. In an article entitled "Women Pioneers in Iowa," Glenda Riley quotes from a newspaper advertisement placed in an 1860 edition of the Waterloo Courier:

> A young lady ... in Central New York, is desirous of opening a correspondence with some young man in the West with a view to a matrimonial engagement.... She is about 24 years of age, possesses a good moral character, is not what would be called handsome, has a good disposition, enjoys good health, is tolerably well-educated, and thoroughly versed in the mysteries of housekeeping.... None but young men of good moral character and strictly temperate habits need address.[8]

As Riley notes, "Eastern women were aware of the matrimonial possibilities existing in Iowa"[9] and apparently preferred the prairies and matrimony to the east and spinsterhood.

Elsie Armstrong's move from Pennsylvania to Illinois was made in two stages; she was the major decision-maker in both. Her father had purchased land for her in Ohio and she persuaded her husband to make the first move, hoping to remove him from an environment where brandy flowed too freely. However, Mr. Armstrong bought a distillery in Ohio and pursued his former occupation and habits while Elsie and the older sons ran the farm. Finally, in 1829, Elsie grew weary of paying off Armstrong's debts, separated, and took her six sons (ages 15, 12, 11, 8, 6, and a baby not yet a year old) to Illinois where they joined the oldest son, who was learning the weaving trade, and her brother. She stayed with her oldest son and, whenever there was a free horse, rode over the country looking for a good claim which would provide enough timber for a house, fuel, and fences; a creek for cattle and sheep; and stone for a chimney. She settled in LaSalle County and prospered in spite of ague epidemics, Indian massacres, and pillaging soldiers.[10]

More conventional women emigrated for better health and for increased opportunities for their children; others emigrated out of obedience to their husbands. Both Charlotte Van Cleve and her husband believed that the Minnesota prairie would be a healthier place to live: "we turned our faces towards Minnesota, in the hope that that far-famed atmosphere would drive away all tendency to intermittent fevers and invigorate our shattered constitutions."[11]

Rebecca Burlend, a rural Yorkshire woman, described her resistance to the decision to go to the prairies: "Whatever may have been our success in America, I can attribute but little of it to myself; as I gave up the idea of ending my days in my own country with the utmost reluctance, and should never have become an emigrant, if obedience to my husband's wishes had left me any alternative."[12] However, she goes on to explain that they had not been able to provide their large family with a decent living on their Yorkshire farm, and emigration to Illinois in 1831 seemed the best solution. At times when Mr. Burlend's courage faltered, she assured him that he was making the right decision.

Many women agreed to go to the prairie because the men they had chosen to marry wanted to go west. A Vermont woman, Cynthia Hill, recalled that when she became engaged "it was agreed" that they would go west.[13] Gro Svendsen endured a painful wrenching from her native Norway and beloved family because she wanted to marry a man who had decided to go to the United States.[14] Grace Fairchild, born and raised in Wisconsin, had gone to South Dakota as a school teacher and married a widower. When he and his grown son wanted to go west of the Missouri for free land, she said that all she could do, with two babies, was to go along.[15] Shy Fairchild insisted on going into the "desolate unknown" when good farmland could have been obtained near settlements. Grace remarked: "Funny though it never occurred to me to act like a balky horse and refuse to go any farther."[16] At another point she says: "I have wondered many times why I ever followed him to South Dakota but then, I loved him."[17]

Other accounts are provided by young women in their late teens who emigrated with their parents. The Birkbeck daughters, though they never complained in their letters written to relatives in England, had no choice but to accompany their father to Illinois in 1817. Their biographer records a conversation among Mr. Birkbeck, one of his daughters, and an acquaintance. The acquaintance says to Miss Birkbeck: "Miss Birkbeck, take my advice: don't let anybody get you more than twenty miles from Boston, New York, Philadelphia, or Baltimore." Birkbeck supposedly replied, "Miss Birkbeck has a father, Sir, whom she knows it to be her duty to obey."[18]

Not all fathers were as authoritarian; some daughters apparently chose to go to the prairie. For example, eighteen-year old Jennie Osborn accompanied her parents to a variety of midwest locations when they decided to go into the hotel business and, when that failed, tried other means of gaining a livelihood. She saw the move as "a jumping off place" into new experiences.[19] Mollie Sanford turned down two marriage offers in Indianapolis and followed her parents to Nebraska; she felt it was her duty to her parents to go with them, especially to her mother who depended considerably on her assistance in managing the household and raising the younger children.[20]

From this sampling it appears, then, that not all women were dragged unwillingly to the prairies. Men did not, in all instances, make the decisions. Certainly many women obediently left the eastern or border states and European homes because husbands' and fathers' decisions were honored. Others, as we have seen, shared in the decision or even initiated emigration procedures.

Yet a prototypical painting of emigration by the popular nineteenth century artist Emmanuel Luetze reveals none of the optimism or enthusiasm expressed in women's writings. In the center background of Westward the Course of Empire Takes Its Way, ca. 1861, a woman has been laid out for burial. To the left, a woman seated on a rock ledge with a child in her lap rests in the shadow of the larger-than-life male figure and refuses to look in the westward direction toward which the man is pointing so eagerly. Slightly to the right, another woman driving horses puts hand to forehead in a gesture of despair as two men try to bring the excited horses under control. In the foreground, a fourth woman, walking, focuses all her attention on the child she is carrying, while a fifth woman--the only one facing westward--appears to be half rising from the wagon seat and gazing with mixed awe and fear toward the new territory. The painting reinforces dominant cultural myths that women were reluctant emigrants.

Women's reactions to the prairie landscape were as mixed as their attitudes toward emigration. Rebecca Burlend recalled that both she and her husband wept when they got off the boat at Philip's Ferry, on a November evening, and mistakenly thought there were no accommodations or people to help.[21] Grace Fairchild and Mollie Sanford represented another type. Although Grace, as we have seen, resented having to settle so far from a community, she delighted in the prairie and noted that "even in dry years the prairie was abloom in the early spring. Mother nature seemed to make every homesteader a bet: if we could survive the long hard winter, she would give us wonderful flowers in the spring. Even in the summer, the alfalfa looked like an ocean of blue and green over the fields, and this, too, was one of the joys of living west of the Missouri."[22] On May 4, 1857, Mollie Sanford recorded the following impression in her journal:

> [Father] took us all out for a ramble, out on the high prairie where we had a fine view of the country. The landscape was beautiful. The prairies look like a vast ocean stretching out until earth and sky seem to meet. We found many varieties

> of our cultivated flowers, growing in wild profusion. Father says we will love our new home. I already love the Nebraska prairies.[23]

Christiana Tillson, on the other hand, told her children that

> As it was my first introduction to the State which was to be my home I tried to make the dismal-looking bottom prairie through which we were passing look cheerful and homelike, merely because it was Illinois. Your father suggested that we should not make up our minds yet as to the beauty of a western prairie from what we saw of the 'bottom lands,' and as I could not find anything to admire.... I was willing to let the future take care of itself....[24]

Her sarcasm was carried over into her next impression where she described coming to an area called 'Hind's Prairie': "This was my first introduction to a real prairie, and I must say I was sorely disappointed.... Your father said, 'you never saw anything like this before.' I said 'no' but did not say I never saw anything more dismal."[25]

Gro Svendsen, who participated in all the major decisions regarding their farming venture, saw not just beauty but possibilities: "Our land is beautiful, though there are few trees. Trees, however, can be had and planted at the cost of from five to ten per acre. We have good spring water near by. Best of all, the land is good meadowland and easily plowed and cultivated."[26]

Women not only had to adapt to a new kind of landscape but to isolated living conditions as well. It is symbolic that Emma Mitchell New, when recalling her Kansas pioneer days, chose before anything else to describe how she felt the day she discovered she had a neighbor lady: "Many a homesick day I saw, many a tear was shed. I couldn't bear to go to the window and look out. All I could see everywhere was prairie and not a house to be seen. We had been there about three months when my two little children ... came rushing into the house so excited for they saw a woman coming over the hill."[27] She discovered that the neighbor's sod dugout had been obscured by a little hill and her joy in finding this woman was boundless.

Whether on isolated homesteads or in small settlements, women also felt vulnerable to Indian attacks in areas

Prairie Print No. 5 Pasque Flower

where Indians remained and were hostile to settlers. For example, Isabella Stone, age fourteen, arrived at her father's new homestead in Palo Alto County, Iowa, on March 9, 1857. A few days later travellers informed them of the March 8 massacre at Spirit Lake in Dickinson County. She wrote:

> I now came to that period of our pioneer history which seems to me to be the hardest and most tragical of anything we had encountered up to that time.... One morning we saw a man coming down from the north on foot. When he came he told my father all about the outbreak of the Indians and how they had captured and carried off with them four female captives.... You can readily imagine with what consternation we were struck on hearing of this most bloody and brutal murder. Spirit Lake was (I think) in or about 40 miles from where we lived, and we had no feeling of security for our own lives, not knowing how soon we and the other settlers might be the next victims.[28]

A Minnesota settler, recalling a similar period of stress, associated the death of a child by drowning with an Indian uprising, and the subsequent departure of many women neighbors. Cynthia Hill wrote:

> My second child, a boy named Earnest died.... It was the year of the Indian Massacre. I was so heart broken I thought I would soon follow but the Lord decreed otherwise. I staid much alone without fear until the Indian out break at New Ulm & word came for all settlers to leave so we went as far as Winnebago and forted for a few nights then the neighbors went back and turned the hogs into their corn fields and took the cattle and families as far as the Mississippi river where they left the women while the men went back to their homes and found everything all right so we loaded up and went back. Then was when I felt timid. The neighbor women all except myself and one other all went back East to their native homes so there were vacant houses or homes without housekeepers for miles around. I did wish to go but husband thought it not best so I staid.[29]

This account typically focuses on the fears of the whites. In retrospect women recalled only their own predicament without recognizing the plight of the Indians and their struggle to keep their lands. Even Melissa Moore's 1860s account, while describing a positive Indian-white relationship, failed to acknowledge the Indians' prior claim to the land. Moore noted that two hundred Osage Indians camped on "their" farm for two years. They were, she recalled, "a great protection to us against the murderous bands who infested our border."[30]

Memoirs serve as reminders that Indians were essential to the survival of white settlers in other ways. Dr. P.L. Scanlan, a Prairie du Chien historian, described a Sioux woman noted for nursing white settlers in the Prairie du Chien area in the early nineteenth century, describing her death as "a great loss to [the] village."[31]

Feminist historians grappling with women's responses to the prairie pioneer experience provide insights into white-Indian relationships. In a collection of essays, Women, Women Writers, and the West, Susan Armitage presents one perspective: "The frontier myth is a male myth, preoccupied with stereotypically male issues like courage, physical bravery, honor, and male friendship. While these are important themes, they by no means encompass the reality and complexity of the frontier experience."[32] Yet for writers and painters who wish to glorify this myth there is no better way for showing courage, bravery, and honor in males than by placing them beside helpless, fearful females.

Armitage goes on to say that the frontier, if we accept Frederick Jackson Turner's definition, was the boundary between savagery and civilization. Hence, "in the frontier myth, these two extremes are represented by the Indian, symbol of savagery, and the white woman, symbol of civilization. Usually, however, they remain secondary characters.... Because of this persistent focus on the white male, Indians and women rarely achieve full, authentic stature in frontier literature."[33] Armitage points out that when we turn to women's writings, however, we are more apt to find descriptions of Indian-white women confrontations ending peacefully rather than violently. Another historian, Glenda Riley, concurs in her study of Iowa women, Frontierswomen: The Iowa Experience: "The myth is that white women feared and hated Native Americans; that they were raped and carried off by Native Americans in vast numbers; and that they always chose to return to their homes rather than to remain with their captors."[34] Riley feels that widely circulated captivity narratives and the fictional works arising out of that genre strongly influenced attitudes about Indian-white women relationships. Riley notes that "the few scholars who have looked beyond captivity narratives have unearthed significant, but seemingly contradictory, views of Native Americans by white women."[35] Women who accepted their role as civilizers inevitably saw the Indians as inferior and savage. On the other hand, some women did not see themselves as civilizers but were as attracted to the wildness of the new lands as the men and even fantasized themselves as "white squaws." This, Riley observes, "might be a threatening concept for many Americans to consider, given their anti-Indian attitude."[36] Hence literature and history committed to maintaining traditional sex roles have ignored this particular female stance.

Two examples of women who wrote about the massacres of whites demonstrate the complexity of the female attitude in regard to Indians. Juliette Magill Kinzie's book, Wau-bun, The "Early Days" in the North-West (1856), included three chapters on the 1812 massacre at Chicago. Based on the experiences of her husband's parents, the material had been first published as a pamphlet in 1836 and undoubtedly was read with considerable curiosity by a wide variety of people. Kinzie's account notably acknowledged admirable and despicable qualities in both government officers and troops and among the Pottowattamies. Female readers of her pamphlet would have concluded that harmonious relations with Indians could be upset at any time; that some Indians would be helpful while others would be indifferent, vindictive, or murderous; that the government and military troops could not be relied on to defend whites; and, finally, that women and children were indeed wounded and scalped, but that many women fought valiantly, cunningly, and frequently successfully against their attackers.[37]

Fifty years after the Chicago massacre a Minnesota Territory woman, Guri Endreson, wrote a letter to her married daughter in Norway describing the Sioux massacre that had taken place four years earlier in 1862:

> To be an eyewitness to these things and to see many others wounded and killed was almost too much for a poor woman; but, God be thanked, I kept my life and my sanity, though all my movable

> property was torn away and stolen. But this would have been nothing if only I could have had my loved husband and children--but what shall I say? God permitted it to happen thus, and I had to accept my heavy fate and thank Him for having spared my life and those of some of my dear children.[38]

She concluded the letter by noting that some had encouraged her to sell the land, but she wrote: "I would rather keep it for a time yet, in the hope that some of my people might come and use it; it is difficult to get such land again, and if you, my dear daughter, would come here, you could buy it and use it and then it would not be necessary to let it fall into the hands of strangers."[39] This passage demonstrates Guri Endreson's attachment to the land in spite of the painful associations related to it, and her belief that her daughter's family would profit from emigration.

The subtext of this passage contains another need. Guri Endreson not only wants the land occupied by family; she also needs family near by to alleviate the loneliness which is undoubtedly the most pervasive ordeal for pioneer women. Most prairie women could say, like Cynthia York Hill, "I staid much alone." Men were often absent and women had to cope with children, animals, fowl, and crops during their absence. Men might be trapping, helping another farmer build a house or barn, taking grain to a mill, travelling long distances to stock up on supplies for the winter, rounding up signatures for the railroad right of way, campaigning for elections, organizing a school board--the list of male activities which required their absence from home seemed endless. And in their absence women had to cope with prairie fires, injuries, illnesses, premature childbirth, reduced food supplies from unexpected visits by neighboring Indians, stray cattle--this list, too, is endless.

All prairie women, in the first years, had to adjust to an existence without basic community services and support. After Mollie Sanford's brother was bitten by a rattlesnake and they had to take care of him without the help of a doctor--or their father--she wrote: "Poor Mother was perfectly prostrated after the fright was over. She sometimes feels wicked to think she is so far away from all help with her family. But it cannot be helped now."[40] The lack of school for children was another problem which distressed Mollie's mother: "My Mother's birthday--40 years old. I fear she is a little blue today. I do try so hard to be cheerful. I don't know as it is hard work to keep myself so, but it is hard with her. She knows now that the children ought to be in school. We will have to do the teaching ourselves.'[41] Gro Svendsen, whose father was a teacher and active citizen in Norway, articulated her concerns in a letter to him:

> The training of children is not an easy task. We are not all able to carry on as we should. When I think of our sacred duties as parents and the heavy responsibilities laid upon us, I often become sad and think it is best to do as Ole [her husband] once advised. He said we should rear the children to the best of our understanding and ability, and then leave the rest to him who said, "For of such is the Kingdom of Heaven.'[42]

This passage illuminates the religious obligation nineteenth-century women felt toward the education of their children. Gro was distressed by the lack of church and especially by the failure of what she called the "American settlers" to observe the Sabbath. She took much interest in the fund-raising for building a church and bringing a pastor to the community.

Needless to say, women also missed the "nice things" in life. Mrs. Orpen, in her Memoirs of the Old Emigrant Days in Kansas, 1862-1865, unconsciously juxtaposed the two symbols required for survival. She remembered a set of shelves where, at the very top, sat "the keg of gunpowder, and beside it, lonely, white, and beautiful, a small statue of Parian marble, representing Venus with a Dolphin ... the only thing of beauty in our Kansas house, and, I verily believe, in the whole wide prairie.'[43] The gunpowder was protection against any number of hostile forces, including belligerent settlers and wild animals. The Parian marble was protection against barbarism, a reminder of values and a way of life which must be preserved. Many women lovingly recalled the titles of the few books which provided their link with the art and ideas of the outside world; others found the family Bible-reading ritual sufficient.

Most of these prairie women seemed aware of the nineteenth-century norms for female behavior, although some found enforced deviation from the norms easier than others did. They generally seemed to believe that women should be feminine in appearance and manners if at all possible and accepted woman's role as nurturer of the bodies and souls of children and husband. Even the unmarried women assumed that they would marry and lead traditional lives.

Therefore, women were concerned about their feminine appearance--the face, the figure, the hands, the clothes they wore--and some of their most delightful accounts are related to their attempts to maintain feminine appearances. The sunbonnet symbolized woman's determination to remain fair-complexioned, a seeming denial of the fact that large portions of their responsibilities required outside work in the sun and the wind. At the same time, however, many women were good-naturedly resigned to the difficulty of maintaining the image of fair fragility in themselves or in their daughters. Eva Hill Fairbanks recalled that when her brother Jerm was old enough to herd cattle, she often accompanied him: "Mother would start me off with a sun bonnet tied under my chin. Very soon it came off my head and was tied around my waist. Upside down it made a fine bustle on my back. Sometimes they came untied and I lost them. Mother said there should be a fine crop of bonnets I sowed so many."[44] The matter could not always be treated this lightly. Miriam Colt was haunted by the sight of a barefooted woman settler lugging a sack of cornmeal: "I said to myself--'Is that what I have got to come to?'"[45] Nevertheless, when she had to drive oxen, lug water, and nurse a dying husband and son, she made bloomers and wore them in order to work more efficiently.

Mollie Sanford, under less stressful conditions, was able to laugh about the difficulty of looking feminine and attractive while performing basic duties. She did not complain about having to assume male responsibilities; she did complain about having to chase cows without the advantage of male attire, and described the repercussions from wearing her father's clothes:

> ... without letting anyone know of my project, I slipped out into the back shed, and donned an old suit of Father's clothes, pulled on an old cap over my head and started out on my pilgrimage. I was prowling thru the bushes calling, "Co, Boss, co, Boss, Co" singing the "Farmer Boy," feeling secure that no men folks were around. Coming out from a thicket of underbrush to a clear spot, what was my consternation to emerge into a camp of men, who were quietly seated on the ground eating

> their breakfasts! I could not scream nor faint as that feminine resource would certainly betray me, but thought "discretion the better part of valor" and that "he who runs away will live to fight another day," and the way I travelled through those woods to the house was a caution.[46]

She went on to describe her family's confusion when they thought an escaped lunatic was crashing in through the door: "When all was explained, it was very funny to all but Mother, who fears I am losing all the dignity I ever possessed. I know I am getting demoralized, but I should be more so, to mope around and have no fun."[47] The charm of this narration was undercut by the serious dilemma which it suggested: What price must be paid, eventually, for deviation from the feminine norms of behavior? The isolation of young prairie women allowed them to indulge in healthy rowdiness. However, females who identified with middleclass standards for behavior had to conform in order to become respectable women in the growing community.

In almost all instances, women were required to do outside work as well as fulfill their responsibilities within the domestic sphere. Mrs. Orpen insisted that "women never did the worst drudgery. They were too rare in the old emigrant days, and men still felt it their duty to lighten the load for them as much as possible."[48] I suspect both men and women wanted to believe this to be the case; however, many women, to survive, had to assume non-traditional roles. Even women who were spared "the worst drudgery" were saddled with awesome tasks. The nature of the pioneer experience required hard work from both men and women.

For example, Christiana Tillson was married to an affluent businessman and frequently had servants helping with her "inside" work. Like the wives of businessmen and small tradesmen in colonial times, Christiana performed two kinds of roles besides those of wife and mother: she was innkeeper and business partner. Because their house was relatively large and comfortable, there were extra people boarding with them almost continuously: a friend's daughter who needed a place to stay for a few weeks, travelling preachers and legislators, friends passing through, a neighbor suffering from ague who needed nursing, and her brother-in-law who lived with them on a permanent basis. Christiana reminded readers of the prairie housewife's dilemma: "The indescribable care devolving upon a housekeeper in that new and rough country and the ways and means to which one must resort in order to keep up a comfortable establishment absorbed not only the physical strength of a Yankee housewife, but all the faculties of the mind had to be brought into requisition in order to secure a comfortable living."[49]

Because of their affluence, the Tillsons were regarded with curiosity by neighbors who felt free to drop in on Sundays--as was the custom of the country--and to be fed ham and biscuits, with honeycomb for dessert.[50] Christiana also, on occasion, worked late into the night writing letters and bills related to Mr. Tillson's various business activities, and because Mr. Tillson was "the post office," she had to oversee postal shipments when he was absent. Thus it is not surprising that she recalls with amusement the gossiping neighbors who were "much perplexed to know what Tillson's wife found to do. She didn't spin nor weave, and had that little Dutch girl, and the men helped her to milk. They had heard [and here she mimics their dialect] that she got up nights to help Tillson write, but that wasn't much, no how; never seen her in the 'truck patch;' didn't believe she knowed how to hoe."[51]

Most women helped with the outside work to some degree, sometimes in emergencies and sometimes on a regular basis. Mrs. New told how she would "take a hand at the plow" whenever her husband was willing to take the time to saw soft rocks into bricks to strengthen the walls around the base of their cabin.[52] Mollie Sanford volunteered to climb up on the roof and help her father when it meant the difference between a dry house and healthy children or a damp house and sick children. She took pride in the fact that she could "put her hand to anything."[53]

Although Gro Svendsen never did any of the hard labor, she obviously participated in all the decisions: she knew the price of every piece of equipment purchased, the amount of their mortgages, and the profits or losses anticipated from the crops. When her husband left to fight in the Civil War, she ran the farm with the help of a young brother-in-law.[54]

Grace Fairchild gradually assumed complete control of the South Dakota homestead. Shy Fairchild had gone to short grass country to get rich growing horses but, according to Grace, he had absolutely no business sense. This is Grace's version of what happened: "While the family broke the sod, fought drought and grasshoppers, and made a home, Shy sat in the shade and complained about his aches and pains."[55] He not only couldn't make good decisions, he couldn't work! She goes on to say "Homesteading on the dry plains was a hard life even if everybody pulled together. It was harder doing it the way we did it. After many years we divided the property and Shy moved into a shack of his own. Things did not change much, but I could now run the homestead without having a husband around messing things up."[56] She sounds like an older, less feminine version of Mollie Sanford when she talks about helping build the new room: "Since the lumber was going to make another room twelve by fourteen on our house, I never minded doing a man's work, even some of the cussing needed to haul lumber over thirty miles of ruts and dust."[57] While Grace didn't stop to worry about being feminine, she was careful not to embarrass a man who might be sensitive to abnormal female behavior. One day when the stockman was having difficulty helping a cow give birth, Grace said, "'Charlie, if it doesn't bother you too much I'll go with you and we will see what can be done about it.' I took some small ropes and some wire with me. I pushed the [calf's] head back and tried to get hold of the calf's feet, but the feet were both backwards. There was nothing to do but cut off the calf's head. I took a knife and cut off the head, reached in and got a rope tied on to the feet and we pulled the calf out and we saved the heifer."[58] She proudly noted that word got around that Grace Fairchild was a pretty good veterinarian.

However, even Grace had regrets that she was required to perform masculine duties and to neglect her obligations as mother. One day when she was working out in the field, a nephew and her daughters were playing "coyote" with a loaded gun; one of her daughters shot and killed a little sister. Grace said: "I could never forgive [Shy] for putting off the wheat stacking so long that I had to be a hired hand and leave the young ones."[59]

Fortunately, the outside work required of most women allowed them to stay near the cabin. This work, viewed as traditional women's work, included such activities as raising chickens and hogs, milking cows, planting, weeding, and harvesting the produce from the garden, or shearing sheep. Daughters shared these tasks at home as well as working for other families when the money was needed. Mary Paulson King described the kind of work she did which included housework, sewing, threshing, and other odd jobs: "When the neighbors wanted help they would come after me, and I was glad to go. I used to be so tired some times that it seemed

I couldn't get up in the morning, but I always did. There would be corn husking, potato digging and sewing dresses, for even then I was handy with the needle."[60]

Jennie Stoughton Osborn, who emigrated with her parents to southwest Missouri in 1867, provided a portrait of herself as an adventurous young woman working at a variety of jobs over the five-year-period before her marriage. She held numerous teaching posts, but schools frequently ran for four-month periods; she had ample time to experiment with other kinds of work. On one teaching assignment Jennie made friends with a Miss Greeley, "a down East Yankee who had come west for her health,"[61] and the two of them went to a millinery establishment where they learned to cut and fit dresses and to trim hats. However, they didn't like the business and returned to the classroom. Two years later Jennie, at the request of her mother, accompanied her father on a trip to Texas to sell fruit trees: "mother always babied father; she was afraid he would get sick so far away from home."[62] The second year she volunteered to go by herself, insisting that she could do the job as well as her father could, and on this trip she sold merchandise which had been funded by Miss Greeley.

Here we have a portrait of a single woman as teacher, milliner, dressmaker, hauler of goods, and merchant. After marriage she worked with her husband raising sheep and chickens and growing wheat. Her matter-of-fact descriptions imply that she enjoyed the variety of tasks and found nothing unusual about working in both "inside" and "outside" spheres.[63]

While prairie women talked freely about the kinds of tasks they performed and their feelings about those tasks, they were typically silent on other subjects: illness, depression, menstruation, pregnancy, childbirth, birth control, abortion, or sexual relationships. Prostitution and infidelity were never hinted at in the sources used for this study. This is understandable when we consider that most of the women were writing to or for parents, children, and grandchildren and that nineteenth-century women rarely discussed these issues. The New England educator Catherine Beecher, writing in 1855, noted the reluctance of women to talk candidly about their health; women tended to describe themselves as "perfectly healthy," yet "on close inquiry, [women] would allow that they were subject to frequent attacks of neuralgia, or to periodic nervous headaches, or to local ailments to which they had become so accustomed, that they were counted as 'nothing at all.'"[64] The prairie women writers occasionally recorded accounts of depression, illness, even insanity in other women, but it is difficult to arrive at an accurate estimate of their own physical or mental health.

For example, in a discussion of women's depression Jeannie McKnight draws on a passage in Mollie Sanford's diary to illustrate what McKnight interprets as a reluctance on Mollie's part to express despondency. McKnight writes: "If Mollie harbors unacceptable wishes ... she seems to have to try to disguise them from herself.... 'I sit listlessly with dripping oars,' she writes. 'I am tired of rowing. But if I don't row, what horrible things will sweep me away? Despair would.'"[65] However, I would like to suggest that we can't take Mollie too seriously in this passage. She had aspirations as a poet (her first poems had just been published in the local paper) and a glance at a few nineteenth-century sentimental poems is enough to remind us that Mollie's metaphors and distress are part of a literary tradition with which she identifies. In this instance it is difficult to separate Mollie's true feelings from her persona as a poet. We need to look elsewhere for allusions to unhealthy mental states.

Gro Svendsen, in letters to her parents in Norway, seemed less restrained than most writers about discussing physical problems. She described the difficulties she had after the birth of her fifth son: "My eyes gradually grew stronger, but then my breasts became inflamed. We succeeded in getting the infection stopped, so that I escaped with not too much suffering and pain."[66] Eight years later she wrote: "Next month, if God wills it, I shall have another child. This will be my ninth confinement. It is difficult these last days because I am always quite weak but God, who has always been my help and comforter during my confinement, will surely help me this time, too."[67] From the tone of this letter we can see that she was apprehensive but uncomplaining. She died a year later at the age of thirty seven, shortly after the birth of a tenth child.

Grace Fairchild, one of the later homesteaders, lived far enough into the twentieth century to be able to speak more frankly about personal matters. She said she would have used birth control if she had known about it, and admitted to trying to induce an abortion:

> To have six children in less than eight years is something of a record. You would have thought I

> was in a race to see how fast we could get that new country settled. I decided it was time to call a halt and in the next four years I didn't have a child. Once during those four years I thought "oh, my God, I am pregnant again" and took a heaping table spoonful of quinine and went to bed. Pretty soon I began to feel queer. I staggered around the house trying to get my breath and wondered if my last day had come. After walking around for a couple of hours, I decided that after this I'd better quit bucking nature so I could be around to look after the family we already had.[68]

However, Grace doesn't tell us how she avoided pregnancy during those four years.

If we look for insights into the sexual relations of these women, we will seek in vain. Emily Gillespie, three months after her marriage to James, provided one glimpse: "guess James and me will never forget when we went to bed. how I chased him in the Hall and he fastened me out of the room. O, how pleasant. seems like spring. Jan. 3, 1863."[69] And Mollie Sanford wrote about missing her husband: "By [her husband's nickname] is gone on a business trip.... I miss him of nights."[70] We can only wonder if these entries are nineteenth-century codes for sexual feelings.

Although prairie women were silent about sexual issues and reticent about discussing physical and mental states, some of their doctors were not. Following are two representative entries from a medical journal kept by John Engstad who began practicing medicine in Grand Forks, North Dakota, in 1885:

> Mrs. Flalrud. $1.00.
> Aborted after two months pregnant. Worked next day. Was taken sick with fainting spells, improved after a time. Menses regular but with dysmenorrhoea [painful menses] and leukorrhea [vaginal discharge, white]. Is pregnant to the sixth month. Well nourished. Has had two children and first delivered by forceps. Appetite good. Bowels regular. Pain in back over last dorsal vertebra of a dragging bearing down character, and it more or less continues. Reflux from uterine disease. Iron, with sedatives for the pain.

*** *** ***

> September 4, 1890. Mrs. Martin le Aanes, McKenna. Age 29. Had four children, one dead, oldest eight, youngest five years. Seven years ago after the third confinement she was taken with cramps, constipation, and a general weakness. Had to wash her children on the second day. Up the second or third day. Had to work in the fields and in the house over her strength. Had to carry water up a steep hill rain or shine. No closet in farm. The husband a devil. Will not allow her to do any fancy work or anything that would be a pleasure to her. Cries a great deal and depressed. Very neat and attractive in her dress and appearance. Erysepelis lasted fourteen days. Vomits every morning. Belladonna and alum pills and solal for the pain.[71]

Dr. Engstad's entries demonstrate a holistic approach in treating women patients with an appropriate balance between objectivity and human concern.

In _A Prairie Doctor of the Eighties: Some Personal Recollections and Some Early Medical and Social History of a Prairie State_, Francis A. Long shares some of his Madison, Nebraska, experiences early in the 1880s. He talks about women's childbirth complications, illnesses, requests for abortion, and premarital sexual relations, thus providing a view of women that is missing from their diaries, letters, and memoirs.[72]

The diary of an Iowan, Emily Gillespie, offers one of the most honest and revealing accounts of a woman's feelings about marriage, children, and work during her years of marriage from 1862 to the late 1880s when she separated from her husband. A January 16, 1878, entry reveals a great deal about her state of mind, her aspirations, and her ambivalence about James, her husband:

> I am sad--do not know but tis foolish, but the tears will sometimes start, perhaps tis The Blues. I _did_ so want to go and hear Miss Susan B. Anthony lecture last Monday evening & _might_ have gone, only that it seems to be so much trouble to take me any where, that I am, seems to me, almost a hermit, tis the saddest of all things to give up, as it were, the Idea of being any higher in society than merely to be always at home, except sometimes to go when necessity compells us to.

> but I must not give up no no, my children are too noble, I must use every effort to help them to be what I might have been. tis my only pleasure to see them happy. yes & James too is ever so kind as one can be, ever ready to do anything to promote others happiness though it make himself miserable, therefore knowing as I do, I never let him know how great my desire is to go in public. no blame to him, he may sometime see differently. I hope still hope on as ever for a contented mind....[73]

Her diary entries during the next decade describe bouts with emotional depression and James's increasingly irrational and abusive behavior. As the editor of the diary notes, both Emily and her daughter, when preparing a typescript of the diary, remained true to the original manuscript and resisted the impulse to present a "nicer" version to the public.[74]

There is another facet of prairie women's lives that requires special consideration--the problems and concerns unique to immigrant women from Europe, east Europe, and Scandinavia. Many undoubtedly left stressful situations--a volcanic eruption in Iceland, a famine in Ireland, persecutions in Poland. Then, as Ardith K. Melloh reminds us in an article on immigrants in New Sweden, Iowa, the sea crossing was physically and emotionally hazardous:

> Death took its toll of immigrants. Steffanson's daughter died of cholera on a canal boat from Chicago to Peru, Illinois.... John M. Monson ... wrote that some days on the Erie Canal their boat had to stop 'almost every hour' to bury another cholera victim. One was his father.... The widows continued on to New Sweden with their children. They could do nothing else. In 1852 Olaus Svenson's little daughter died at sea.... Yet even those who escaped cholera had reason to be concerned about their health. Sailing ships of that day provided no food for immigrants and, according to Monson, every family had to provision itself for three months.... Immigrants were often exhausted and in poor physical condition when they reached their destination.[75]

At the end of the sea journey, illnesses persisted; there were also physical injuries and child births en route, ailing horses, and broken wagons. Some encountered dishonest merchants and land speculators; others lost their way on the trail.

Those making group settlements had the advantage of maintaining cultural and religious traditions. Although there were difficulties communicating and transacting business with the Americans, within the group the bonding of same-language individuals looking out for each other reduced the trauma of settling a new land. Many immigrants coming individually joined families or acquaintances who had emigrated earlier. As Dorothy Skårdal notes in The Divided Heart: Scandinavian Immigrant Experience Through Literary Sources, these "ties of kinship required that an older resident do all in his power to help the new arrival." Food, board, introductions, and possibly a job smoothed the way for newcomers.[76]

Nevertheless, all foreign-born immigrants faced prejudices in some form. In his essay, "The Middle West," John Fraser Hart insists that immigrants coming from western and northern Europe "by and large spoke the same languages, practiced the same religions, and shared the same social and political traditions as those who were already on the ground."[77] However, much of the literature by and about foreign-born immigrants indicates that both an Englishman and a German Mennonite from Russia confronted disconcerting prejudices, though certainly the Englishman to a lesser degree. Skårdal notes four typical stages leading to assimilation. At first the natives react with contempt and amusement. Then, as they see the outsiders becoming securely established and even prospering, they fear their growing numbers and are envious of their successes. Then they fear that the outsiders will become a political threat to the established community. In the final stage, when fears have been allayed, Americans accept the foreign-born as worthwhile citizens.[78]

When we consider the problems of both eastern and foreign-born women in adapting to a new land, to isolation, to roles which frequently required deviation from the norm, to raising children without supporting social institutions, medical care or female support groups, we might well ask why so many affirmed the pioneer prairie experience. What contributed to the happiness and sense of fulfillment which they so often expressed?

Many women could take pride in the fact that they had had a role in educating prairie children and in organizing the first schools. One woman estimated that "two thirds of the women of Kansas have taught school."[79] Some of the first school sessions were held in sod dugouts where women would teach fundamentals to their own children and two or three neighbors' children. Emily Biggs told how her mother transformed her kitchen into a schoolroom, unpacked her school books and bell and, several decades later, named a representative to the state legislature, a sheriff, and a district judge among her former students.[80]

Other women helped establish the first churches. During the early period of settlement, women opened their homes for services. When fundraising began for a church building, women organized their sewing circles to raise money. Then a circuit rider would be invited to preach, baptise, perform marriages and attend the sick and dying.[81] The memoirs of a Kansas woman provide insights into the life of a circuit rider's wife who had to manage her own household with very little assistance from her husband. May Woodburn Crane, the daughter of a circuit rider in Nemaha, Washington, and Jackson counties, recalled her mother "preserved a sweet spirit" about the donations her father brought home, and managed to raise eleven children with limited resources. Crane concludes: "Our home was used as a sort of hotel or wayside inn for friends and for strangers coming into the country. And with all the hard work and the privations of the new country, Mother kept her sweetness and her poise and dignity. She had a keen sense of humor which helped her over many drab places in life."[82]

Maggie Long found considerable satisfaction as a doctor's wife. She observed that "the doctor's wife was usually the center of [church] activities in the small town. She was held in high esteem by all, and much was expected of her."[83] When we read the descriptions of her responsibilities, we realize that Maggie paid a price for the "high esteem" that was accorded her. She kept the business records and had to deal with the prejudices of men who hesitated to transact business with women or, thinking a woman couldn't possibly understand the intricacies of payments and receipts, would try to trick her into providing a receipt without having made a payment.[84] Maggie was in charge of laundering the surgical linen, garments, bandages and towels; she scrubbed the office every day before patients arrived; she interrupted her housework to receive patients; she gave over her kitchen table to surgical operations when necessary. Above all, she noted her willingness to get meals for her husband at any hour--it gave her the sense of helping with "his" business.[85]

Nettie Bryson wrote about women as nurses and midwives, telling how "Mother Crampton," a neighbor woman with the gift of healing with herbs, came to the rescue of her mother after a complicated childbirth that the doctor couldn't cope with. She writes: "Doctor Gibbony was delighted to have Mother Crampton's help, and allowed her to go ahead and give Mother some of her home remedies. In an hour's time Mother was sleeping peacefully...."[86] In fact, Nettie's mother was also known for packing a basket and going throughout the community doctoring snake bites and delivering babies. One incident Nettie describes is particularly interesting because it deals with a mentally-ill woman: "A man came to Mother from the adjoining County, begging Mother to go to his house as he feared his wife was losing her mind. I was afraid of insane persons and pleaded with Mother not to go, but she went. More than that, she brought the woman home, sent for the doctor, nursed her a few weeks, and the patient recovered....[87]

Several images emerge from these anecdotes. Nettie Bryson's description of her mother provides an image of the traditional prairie angel--the nurturer and healer. Grace Fairchild, working a 1440-acre ranch, represents the prairie plow-woman. Gro Svendsen, teaching Norwegian children in the neighborhood and writing articles for the Norwegian-language newspaper, Emigranten og Faedrelandet, represents the prairie culture-bearer. Each role brought satisfaction to a different type of woman.

Relationships with other women were another source of pleasure. Mary Paulson King recalled that "When the other children were outdoors playing, Mother and I would sit and sew and I remember this as one of the happiest times of my life."[88] Eva Hill Fairbanks remembered that "There was a very active C.E. [Christian Education] society in our church and a live W.C.T.U. These gave me much comfort; also the ministers." When she thought of her women's Sunday school class she wrote, "How I love to think of our hours together." She was also delighted with breaks in the daily routine: "It was the neighborhood custom to look across the prairie and if some one saw Lornes Pung [a neighbor] going to another house they too would hitch up and follow: perhaps three or four families would spend the day together unexpectedly."[89]

Young girls found opportunities for heroism. Nine-year-old Doaty Orpen's father and other men in the neighborhood were away fighting the Civil War when settlers received word that Indians might attack. Doaty was the only one left who knew where the ford was in Big Sugar Creek: "My knowledge of prairie tracks and river currents was their only hope, and the skill I possessed in managing horses at difficult moments, in doubling teams and driving the lot through deep water, might be their only chance."[90]

Many of the older women were also aware of their heroism, although some generously gave their husbands most of the credit. Maggie Long said that women's strength and perserverance "made it possible for the men to develop this new country."[91] However, Grace Fairchild, looking over the ranch that she had finally made pay, would have thought Maggie Long gave the men more credit than they deserved.

In concluding, I must emphasize again that most of the writings referred to in this study represent the situations and attitudes of women who were remarkable in their sense of self and their role in developing a new land, yet typical in their confrontation of common problems. Even the most optimistic remembered the droughts, the death of a child, the devastating prairie fires, the grasshoppers, the loneliness, the hard work, and the deprivations. But most would share Charlotte Van Cleve's view of the prairie experience:

> [Life on Long Prairie] had taught us much. We felt our hearts stronger and richer for its lessons, and we all look back on that memorable time as something we would not willingly have missed out of our lives, for we learned that one may be reduced to great straits, may have few or no external comforts, and yet be very happy, with that satisfying, independent happiness which outward circumstances cannot affect.[92]

Like that earlier American farmer who affirmed the pioneer experience, propagandist St. John de Crèvecoeur, these women found "satisfying, independent happiness" on the prairie.

As propagandists, pioneer women writers accomplished three important things. First, they provided raw materials for re-writing the cultural text of American history even though that revision was not acknowledged until the 1970s when feminist historians began publishing their radical perspectives on the prairie pioneer woman's history.

Second, the letters, diaries, and memoirs of prairie

women challenged images of pioneer women created by powerful male image makers. For example, Alexis de Tocqueville's Democracy in America, based on his 1832 travels in America, impressed generations of Americans with his observations of people and institutions; his impression of the frontier woman would have been noted by many. De Tocqueville wrote:

> I find the following passage in my travel diary, and it will serve to show what trials are faced by those American women who follow their husbands into the wilds. The description has nothing but its complete accuracy to recommend it.
>
> *** *** ***
>
> A woman was sitting on the other side of the hearth, rocking a small child on her knees. She nodded to us without disturbing herself. Like [her husband], this woman was in the prime of life; her appearance seemed superior to her condition, and her apparel even betrayed a lingering taste for dress; but her delicate limbs were wasted, her features worn, and her eyes gentle and serious; her whole physiognomy bore marks of religious resignation, a deep peace free from passions, and some sort of natural, quiet determination which would face all the ills of life without fear and without defiance.[93]

This image of the frontier woman is pervasive in frontier letters, journals, diaries, memoirs, poems, paintings, popular songs, fiction, travel books, and illustrations, and there is no reason to doubt its accuracy; however, what many women writers insisted is that there were other images. They wanted to juxtapose the images of women who were energetic, strong, self-sufficient, inventive, and far-sighted against the traditional image represented by de Tocqueville's pioneer woman.

Third, these writers have provided women in the 1980s with a usable past. As Adrienne Rich observes in Of Woman Born, "The most important thing one woman can do for another is to illuminate and expand her sense of actual possibilities."[94] Above all, this is what pioneer women's letters, diaries, and memoirs have done. Today, women experiencing hard times, limited resources, confining roles, or reduced circumstances can gain inspiration from their foremothers. Women on the threshold of new experiences can find courage to act independently and to take risks. Eighty-seven year-old Jennie Osborn, just learning to type, expressed some uncertainty about her reasons for writing her Memories. She said, "All this I have written may not be interesting to some who may chance to read it in years to come, but it is a part of the memories stored away in my brain for over eighty years, for what purpose, I do not know." We can picture her writing this sentence, then pausing, the tips of her fingers resting on the keys. Then she makes up her mind, recognizing that she indeed had a message for her readers: "Perhaps it is to show that, with good health and energy, we can conquer most any hardship if we have the stick-to-it-iveness in our constitution. This is required. Well, we stuck."[95]

--C. F.

References

1. Charlotte Ouisconsin Van Cleve, "Three Score Years and Ten": Life-Long Memories of Fort Snelling, Minnesota, and Other Parts of the West (Minneapolis: Harrison & Smith, 1888), p. 133.

2. Ibid., p. 157.

3. Julie Roy Jeffrey, Frontier Women: The Trans-Mississippi West 1840-1880 (New York: Hill & Wang, 1979), p. 29.

4. Christine Stansell, "Women on the Great Plains 1865-1890," Women's Studies 4 (1976), p. 90.

5. Lillian Schlissel, "Women's Diaries on the Western Frontier," American Studies 18 (Spring 1977), p. 88.

6. Elise Dubach Isely, Sunbonnet Days (Caldwell, Idaho: Caxton, 1935), pp. 29-30.

7. Roberta Anderson Smith, "The Dalander Colony at Swede Point, Iowa," The Swedish Pioneer History Quarterly 30 no. 3 (1979).

8. Glenda Riley, "Women Pioneers in Iowa," Palimpsest 57 no. 2 (1976), pp. 35-36.

9. Ibid., p. 35.

10. James Elder Armstrong, Life of a Woman Pioneer (Chicago: J.F. Higgins, 1931), pp. 19-30.

11. Van Cleve, p. 130.

12. Rebecca Burlend, A True Picture of Emigration (Chicago: Lakeside Press, 1936), p. 7.

13. Cynthia York Hill, unpublished manuscript.

14. Gro Svendsen, Frontier Mother: The Letters of Gro Svendsen. Trans. and ed. by Pauline Farseth and Theodore C. Blegen (Northfield, Minn.: Norwegian-American Historical Assoc., 1950), p. 3.

15. Walker D. Wyman, Frontier Woman: The Life of a Woman Homesteader on the Dakota Frontier (River Falls: University of Wisconsin-River Falls Press, 1972), p. 7.

16. Ibid., p. 13.

17. Ibid., p. 18.

18. Gladys Scott Thomson, A Pioneer Family in Illinois 1818-1827 (London: Jonathan Cape, 1953), p. 15.

19. Jennie Stoughton Osborn, Memories (Medicine Lodge, Kansas: Barber County Index, 1935), p. 17.

20. Mollie Dorsey Sanford, Mollie: The Journal of Mollie Dorsey Sanford in Nebraska and Colorado Territories, 1857-1866 (Lincoln: University of Nebraska Press, 1959), p. 2.

21. Burlend, pp. 143-144.

22. Wyman, pp. 108-109.

23. Sanford, p. 21.

24. Christiana Tillson, A Woman's Story of Pioneer Illinois, ed. Milo Quaife (Chicago: R.R. Donnelly, 1919), pp. 51-52.

25. Tillson, pp. 65-66.

26. Svendsen, p. 44.

27. Emma Mitchell New, "'Years Came Along One After the Other....'" *American Heritage* 28 no. 1 (1976), p. 5.

28. Isabella Stone, unpublished manuscript.

29. Hill, n.p.

30. Melissa Genett Moore, *The Story of a Kansas Pioneer, Being the Autobiography of Melissa Gennett Anderson,* intro. Melvin Gillison Rigg (Mt. Vernon, Ohio: Manufacturing Printers Co., 1924), pp. 36, 38.

31. Lillian Krueger, *Motherhood on the Wisconsin Frontier* (Madison: State Historical Society of Wisconsin, 1951), p. 23.

32. Susan Armitage, "Women's Literature and the American Frontier: A New Perspective on the Frontier Myth," in *Women, Women Writers, and the West,* L.L. Lee and Merrill Lewis, eds. (Troy, N.Y.: Whitson, 1979), p. 5.

33. Ibid.

34. Glenda Riley, *Frontierswomen: The Iowa Experience* (Ames: Iowa State University, 1981), p. 177.

35. Ibid.

36. Ibid.

37. Juliette Augusta Kinzie, *Wau-bun, the "Early Days" in the North-west* (New York: Derby & Jackson, 1856), pp. 157-193 passim.

38. Theodore C. Blegen, trans. "Immigrant Women and the American Frontier: Three Early 'American Letters,'" in *Norwegian American Studies and Records,* vol. V (Northfield, Minn.: Norwegian American Historical Association, 1930), pp. 27-28.

39. Ibid., p. 29.

40. Sanford, p. 49.

41. Ibid., p. 50.

42. Svendsen, p. 137.

43. Mrs. Orpen, Memories of the Old Emigrant Days in Kansas, 1862-1865 (Edinburgh & London: William Blackwood & Sons, 1926), pp. 17-19.

44. Eva Hill Fairbanks, unpublished manuscript.

45. Miriam Colt, A Heroine of the Frontier: Miriam Davis Colt in Kansas, 1856. Extracts from Mrs. Colt's Diaries, ed. J. Christian Bay (Cedar Rapids, Iowa: Private Printing for the Friends of the Torch Press, 1941), p. 20.

46. Sanford, p. 53.

47. Ibid.

48. Orpen, p. 45.

49. Tillson, pp. 56-57.

50. Ibid., p. 85.

51. Ibid., p. 102.

52. New, p. 5.

53. Sanford, p. 58.

54. Svendsen, pp. 53, 71-72.

55. Wyman, pp. 1-2.

56. Ibid., pp. 2-3.

57. Ibid., p. 17.

58. Ibid., p. 67.

59. Ibid., p. 77.

60. Mary Paulson King, "Memories of a Prairie Girlhood" (typed manuscript, Chippewa Valley Historical Museum Archives, Eau Claire, Wisconsin, n.d.), pp. 34-35.

61. Osborn, p. 23.

62. Ibid., p. 25.

63. Ibid., pp. 46-47.

64. Quoted in *Root of Bitterness: Documents of the Social History of American Women*, ed. Nancy F. Cott (New York: E.P. Dutton, 1972), p. 264.

65. Jeannie McKnight, "American Dream, Nightmare Underside: Diaries, Letters and Fiction of Women on the American Frontier," in *Women, Women Writers, and the West*, L.L. Lee and Merrill Lewis, eds. (Troy, N.Y.: Whitson, 1979), p. 38.

66. Svendsen, p. 98.

67. Ibid., p. 134.

68. Wyman, p. 29.

69. Judy Nolte Lensink et al., "'My Only Confidant'--The Life and Diary of Emily Hawley Gillespie," *Annals of Iowa* 45 (Spring 1980), p. 298.

70. Sanford, p. 151.

71. Elizabeth Hampsten, comp., *To All Inquiring Friends: Letters, Diaries and Essays in North Dakota* (Grand Forks: Department of English, University of North Dakota, 1979), pp. 182, 190.

72. Francis A. Long, *A Prairie Doctor of the Eighties: Some Personal Recollections and Some Early Medical and Social History of a Prairie State* (Norfolk, Nebr.: Nebraska Home Publishing Co., 1937).

73. Lensink et al., pp. 304-305.

74. Ibid., p. 289.

75. Ardith K. Melloh, "Life in Early New Sweden, Iowa," *The Swedish Pioneer Historical Quarterly* 32 (April 1981), p. 124.

76. Dorothy Burton Skårdal, *The Divided Heart: Scandinavian Immigrant Experience Through Literary Sources* (Lincoln: University of Nebraska Press, 1974), p. 91.

77. John Fraser Hart, ed. Regions of the United States (New York: Harper & Row, 1972), p. 263.

78. Skårdal, p. 91.

79. Joanna L. Stratton, Pioneer Women: Voices from the Kansas Frontier (New York: Simon & Schuster, 1981), p. 169.

80. Emily Biggs quoted by Stratton, p. 158.

81. Stratton, pp. 179-180.

82. May Woodburn Crane quoted by Stratton, pp. 180-181.

83. Long, pp. 163-164.

84. Ibid., p. 169.

85. Ibid., pp. 168-170.

86. Nettie Korb Bryson, Prairie Days (Los Angeles: Times-Mirror, 1939), p. 104.

87. Ibid., p. 124.

88. King, p. 30.

89. Fairbanks, n.p.

90. Orpen, p. 161.

91. Long, p. 166.

92. Van Cleve, p. 147.

93. Alexis de Toqueville, Democracy in America, trans. George Lawrence (Garden City, NY: Doubleday Anchor, 1969), pp. 731, 732.

94. Adrienne Rich, Of Woman Born: Motherhood as Experience and Institution (New York: W.W. Norton, 1976), p. 246.

95. Osborn, p. 42.

FARM WOMEN ON THE CANADIAN PRAIRIE FRONTIER: THE HELPMATE IMAGE

> 'Poor girl!' say the kind friends. 'She went West and married a farmer'--and forthwith a picture of the farmer's wife rises up before their eyes; the poor, faded woman ... hair the color of last year's grass, and teeth gone in front.[1]

In the case of farm life on the grassland frontiers of western Canada there is little argument that life was difficult for women. Nevertheless, women were part of the earliest efforts to establish agricultural settlements on the prairie and plains of the western interior of Canada. What were the experiences of these women, and how did they respond to pioneer life in the grasslands?

Previous attempts to answer these questions have not revealed women's experiences in all their variety. Instead what has emerged are images that obscure differences between individual women's experiences. Responding to these images, this study examines, from the perspective of women themselves, one image of pioneer farm women on the Canadian prairies--that of pioneer farm women as helpmates.

In her analysis of the helpmate image for frontierswomen in the United States, Beverly Stoeltje writes, "the primary defining feature of [helpmates] was their ability to fulfill their duties which enabled their men to succeed, and to handle crises with competence and without complaint."[2] Carl Dawson and Eva R. Younge, in Pioneering in the Prairie Provinces: The Social Side of the Settlement Process, expresses this image when they use this description to depict the experiences of pioneer farm women in Canada:

> As for the pioneer woman, what shall we say? When her man was at home she stood shoulder to shoulder with him in the conduct of the day's affairs. When he was absent ... she cared for the family, she looked after the stock, she took upon her lone shoulders burdens which were none too light for husband and wife to bear.[3]

Because a pioneer woman's experiences were tied to the needs of her husband and family she, as June Sochen explains in her study of frontier women, "is not the prime mover in her life. She does not determine her own individual destiny."[4] This image is taken to its gloomy extreme in the following interpretation of prairie women's lives:

> A prairie woman's life was defined by the needs of her family. When her children left, the habit of working remained. Tasks which once were necessary for survival now had no point, yet they had become so much a part of her that only death could bring release.[5]

Another dimension of the image of pioneer women as helpmates is the notion that farm work for pioneer women was drudgery. A recent study of Canadian prairie women describes farm life for pioneer women in dreary terms:

> For the typical pioneer woman, life was a hectic chorus of mend, weed, pump, chop, churn, bake and scrub. If she had children--and families tended to be large in those days--they added their giggles and howls.[6]

The monotony of pioneer life was intensified by the isolation of the prairie frontier. Women stoically endured these hardships because, as prairie pioneer Nellie McClung explained, they were just too busy to complain.[7]

But Nellie McClung also observed "that people love to generalize; to fit cases to their theory, they love to find ... farmers' wives shabby, discouraged and sad."[8] Women's writings challenge these images and generalizations. Autobiographies, letters, journals, and reminiscences recount the experiences of women as wives, mothers, daughters, and single women on the frontier. They are some of the sources used in this essay. These women are not representative of pioneer farm woman as a whole. Instead they are a small group of women who had the ability and the inclination to record their experiences and attitudes. In some cases women wrote contemporary accounts, in others they relied upon memory. Regardless of these distinctions and limitations, women's writing still clearly reveal a rich variety of experiences which are useful in examining images of pioneer farm women in the grasslands.

Most Canadian pioneer women came to the grasslands in one of two migrations. The first wave began about 1870 and lasted until the late 1890s. Prior to 1870 the grasslands were part of Rupert's Land, a broad expanse of territory, controlled by the Hudson Bay Company. Its boundaries lay between the Red River in the east and the Rocky Mountains in the west. In 1870, the Canadian government acquired Rupert's Land from the Hudson Bay Company and the grasslands began to be recognized for its agricultural potential. Settlers from various parts of Ontario, the United States, and Europe trickled into the grasslands.

By the late 1890s, a second, larger migration began. Promising free homesteads and assisted passages, the Canadian government and the Canadian Pacific Railway launched vigorous advertising campaigns to encourage agricultural settlement within the grasslands. Partially as a result of these campaigns, significant numbers of settlers from the United States, Great Britain, the Balkans, the Ukraine, and Russia immigrated to the grasslands of Canada. The rapid influx of settlers during this second migration lasted until about World War I. The pioneer experiences of most women cited in this study fall between 1870 and 1914.

The beginnings of the first migration to Canada coincided with the passage of Homestead legislation in 1872, which provided settlers with 160 acres of land for a ten dollar fee, providing they plowed the land, built a shelter, and lived on the property for six months out of a year for three years. The lure of cheap land, the chance for economic independence, captured the imaginations of women as well as men. Sarah Roberts, an early twentieth-century Alberta pioneer, remembered that land was a major factor influencing her family's decision to move from Illinois to Canada, "We had lived for years in Illinois where land is priced at one hundred dollars per acre. No doubt the thought of receiving 480 acres 'free' made more of an appeal to us than was justified."[9] It is important to note that Sarah Roberts included herself as part of the decision-making process to move west. Her participation in this process is contrary to the notion that women did not affect decisions concerning their futures and the futures of their families.

In fact, women were sometimes the first to recognize the opportunities inherent in western land. In 1880 Letitia McCurdy Mooney persuaded her husband that the future of their children depended upon their opportunity to acquire fertile land. Letitia's daughter, Nellie Mooney McClung, recalled her mother's persuasive argument to move west:

> "We'll have to go some place, John," she said one night to my father. "There's nothing here for our three boys. What can we do with one-hundred-and-fifty stony acres? The boys will be hired-men all their lives, or clerks in a store. That's not good enough!"
>
> Father was fearful! There were Indians to consider, not only Indians, but mosquitoes. He had seen on the Ottawa what mosquitoes could do to horses; and to people too. No! It was better to leave well enough alone.[10]

Clara Goodwin, another late nineteenth-century Manitoba pioneer, remembered "my mother had visited Winnipeg the year before and was very much taken with the West. I remember quite distinctly her saying to my father, 'Richard, you MUST go to that country! That's the place to live!'"[11]

Sometimes it was not just the economic opportunities that persuaded women to suggest moving their families to the west. Letters from friends and family exerted a strong influence. Lulu Beatrice Wilken recalled that her mother was persuaded to go west to Saskatchewan by her brother Edward:

> So he wrote to her to try to persuade Father to move his family West and to take up land also.
>
> I am sure that it did not take long to convince Father of the advantages to be obtained in such a move, and, in the spring of 1891, Mother took her three small children and joined her brother.[12]

For Muriel Parsloe it was not enticements from family members, but a sense of adventure that caused her to initiate her family's move to Swan Lake, Manitoba. After reading an advertisement for western Canadian land she said,

"We've tried Australia, let's take a trip to Canada and see how we get on there."[13]

A more conventional reason brought Kathleen Strange to the grasslands. It was because of their doctor's recommendation that Kathleen Strange and her husband purchased a farm in the remote area of Fenn, Alberta, in 1920. The active outdoor life of a farm in the west was their doctor's prescription for an injury received by Kathleen's husband in World War I.[14]

Unmarried women also came to farms in the grasslands. Western farmland offered these women a means for achieving economic independence. Land was not "free" for these women. Women could not obtain "free" homesteads unless they were the sole support for their families. Qualified women took advantage of this opportunity. A women's column in a 1914 issue of the Grain Grower's Guide carried this appeal:

> Dear Miss Beynon: I am writing to ask for a great favor for a very deserving widow with children. She wants to homestead and has not the wherewithal to look about.... perhaps some of the kind sisters know of one suitable for mixed farming....
>
> Intending Homesteader[15]

A notable example of a successful woman homesteader during this period is Georgina Binnie-Clark. For a period of about five years between 1909 and 1914, Binnie-Clark owned and operated her own wheat farm in the Qu'Appelle Valley in Saskatchewan. In her book Wheat and Woman, Binnie-Clark detailed her farming experiences and argued the case for farming as a means of achieving economic independence for women.[16]

Unmarried women came to farms in the grasslands for other purposes as well. In 1886 the Canadian Pacific Railway issued a questionnaire asking women about their lives in the Northwest Territories. One of the questions read, "Can hard-working honest girls easily obtain situations at good wages on farms or [in] households in the North-West...." A concise reply came from Mrs. T. D. Elliott in Alexandria. She answers, "1. Good girls can get plenty of good places at good wages then marry good young men with good farms."[17] Opportunities for women in farm homes as domestics or home-helps promised gains for women in other ways besides wages. The shortage of females on the frontier was a prominent theme in appeals for female immigrants to the west. This theme was evident in the MacLeod Gazette of May 15, 1896:

> "Do you know" remarked W.D. Scott to a Toronto newspaper reporter, "one of the greatest needs in the North West at the present time? It is women, simply women. Married men with their wives are contented enough out there, but single men on farms are apt to get lonely. If girls could only be persuaded to go out there they would be sure of good situations, and I tell you it would not be long before they would get married."[18]

Educated middle-class women from the British Isles were prime targets for these appeals. At the turn-of-the-century the British Isles found itself saddled with an oversupply of single, middle-class women unable to find suitable jobs. Employment and marriage opportunities in the Canadian west offered relief to these women. In her book West-Nor'-West, published in 1890, Jessie Saxby, herself a middle-class British widow, expressed this concern:

> In Britain one of the most urgent social difficulties is what to do with our surplus women--how to provide for them, how to find remunerative employment for them. In Canada one of the most urgent social difficulties is how to persuade women to come there.... In Quebec, in Winnipeg, in Regina, everywhere, I was told the same thing. "Oh, if respectable women from the old country would come out West!"[19]

To assure the successful adaptation of British emigrant gentlewomen to the west, emigration societies and training schools were established to provide information about the west and to instruct women in necessary domestic skills.

Women did not always have a choice of whether to stay in their present circumstances or to take a chance in a new land. Edna Jaques' family migrated from Ontario to Moose Jaw, Saskatchewan, in 1902. She remembered her father announcing they would leave for Moose Jaw:

> His name was Robert Jaques. He came to visit dad one day in January 1902. They were in the

> parlor talking and laughing together.... Suddenly the folding doors between the two rooms opened and dad stood in the doorway (I can see him yet) and loudly announced to my mother, "We're leaving Collingwood." Taking a long breath he said, "We're going homesteading in the Northwest Territories...."
>
> My mother fainted.[20]

Nevertheless, after the initial shock some women adapted to the idea, as did Jessie Raber's mother. Jessie Raber remembered that even though it was her father's idea to take up a homestead near Lacombe, Alberta, in 1895, her mother soon recognized the economic and social advantages of the move.

> Mother said perhaps she had been selfish in not being anxious to move to a farm in Canada before, for she knew that a growing family did need plenty of room. The milk, fresh eggs and the wonderful vegetables one could grow in Canada: for she did want us all to grow up into strong and healthy men and women, with good educations.[21]

Other women remained unconvinced of the advantages of a westward move. Clara Middleton "had no urge to go adventuring," but went along because "Homer was bent on it [and] that was enough for me."[22] Laura Salverson simply resigned herself to the inevitable, "And now George had the grand vision of the independent life of a landowner.... There was nothing to be done about it, except to let the disease run a swift unhindered course."[23]

Without the satisfaction that comes from participation in an important decision and without the confidence that comes from belief in the promise of a new land, women's journeys to Canada could be painful experiences. Maria Adamowska's family emigrated from the Ukraine to Alberta in 1899. She recalled her mother's sad experience:

> Mother, on the other hand, was tenderhearted. Of all the trials that had been her lot in life, this one was the most bitter. Whenever father had mentioned going to Canada, she had started to cry. And she cried all the way on the train and missed seeing the lovely sights in God's good world.[24]

The experience of this unhappy emigrant woman fits one aspect

Prairie Print No. 6 Ukrainian Church, near Tolstoi, Manitoba

of the helpmate image. That is, in this instance, Maria Adamowska's mother did not determine her own future. However, clearly this is not true for all women on the frontier. Women came to the grassland frontiers for themselves, as well as for others, and when they did come for others, they were energetic, as well as reluctant, pioneers.

Whatever their reasons for coming to the grasslands, women worked when they arrived. As prairie homesteader Georginia Binnie-Clark observed "On a prairie settlement the women work ... I owe one debt to my life on the prairie and that is a fair appreciation of my own sex."[25] For married women, the home was the hub of pioneer farm women's work. In her study of frontier women's work, Susan Armitage identifies two categories of household work. The first category, household maintenance, involves routine activities, such as cooking and cleaning.[26] The lack of mechanical aids made their chores time consuming. The experience of Laura Salverson's mother, an Icelandic immigrant, illustrated this fact, "Mama was forever busy. She had a passion for keeping things scoured and scrubbed.... When you carried water from a pump half a block away or melted snow after the winter set in, all this washing and cleaning consumed a lot of time."[27] In another example, Kathleen Strange remembered a dreaded chore, wash day:

> Washing! What a job that always was. Usually it took me the entire day. In summer I washed outside; in winter, down in the basement. The boiling, sudsy water had to be carried in pails from the stove to wherever my tubs were set. More than once I burned myself severely, spilling water on unprotected hands and legs.[28]

Nevertheless, some women found satisfaction in these routine chores. Edna Jaques recalled the "glow" on her mother's face as the wash emerged "whiter than white."[29] Lulu Beatrice Wilken remembered the pride her mother felt in the polished appearance of the floor in their sod shack. Years of washing with hot sudsy water made it smooth and white.[30]

It was not just the lack of conveniences that made chores time consuming. It was also the number of people requiring women's care. Because children were potential laborers, large families were an asset. Women often had several children to tend, in addition to housekeeping chores. Jessie Raber, daughter of immigrant parents who homesteaded in Alberta during the early 1900s, remarked on her mother's experience, "Mother often wished she could bundle us all off to school or somewhere. Just think, seven [children] under her feet all day and every day. Such patience she must have had."[31]

The number of people in a household was enlarged in other ways as well. Hospitality was an integral part of frontier life and an important social custom. Saskatchewan pioneer Harriet Neville remembered "No stranger was ever refused meals or shelter night or day at our home."[32] Sometimes women turned this custom to profit by taking boarders and earning a wage.

It should be noted here that daughters, like their mothers, worked on the family farm. Often they assumed their mother's chores, thereby reducing their mother's overall workload. For example, as a teenager, Jessie Raber assumed responsibility for much of the cooking and for care of the younger children.[33] In some cases daughters' chores as surrogate mothers came at an early age. Because both her parents worked outside the home, Veronica Kokotailo, even though she was only five years old at the time, took care of the younger children![34] Daughters also worked as field hands. Nellie McClung recalled overseeing the cattle rather than going to school.[35]

Daughters contributed to the family's economic well-being in other ways. In some cases they worked as home-helps, a term applied to domestic help, to earn wages to assist their parents. Ukrainian immigrant Anna Farion remembered her work as a home-help. "My work was harder than the year before as there were four children, and four or five hired men to look after. But I stuck it out, as I wanted to help my parents as much as I could."[36] In another way Anna's experience illustrates the hardships some immigrant girls and women experienced. Earning only a few dollars a month, Anna requested a raise. Her employer "brushed me off with the rejoinder that she had trained me for the job and, besides, she had paid Kolessar $5.00 for me. Her words hurt me deeply. Evidently, I had been sold...."[37]

Not all immigrant girls and women working as home-helps encountered discriminatory treatment of this kind. In an effort to evaluate employment opportunities for British women, Elizabeth Keith Morris travelled throughout western

Canada during the early part of the twentieth century. She considered the position of home-help suitable employment for capable British women:

> The position of home help is a safe, cheap and sure way of earning capital to start in other work, of learning Canadian methods and requirements, and of feeling one's feet in a new country; but the work is hard and heavy including washing, ironing, baking, scrubbing, ... therefore, only to be undertaken by the robust.[38]

The second category of frontier women's work was household sustenance. Armitage defines household sustenance as "work which contributed directly to family economy by making cash expenditure unnecessary."[39] Farm women were manufacturers in their own homes. Harriet Neville used skins to make "hoods, mittens, muffs and necks" as well as spinning wool to make clothing, bed mattresses and quilts.[40] The daily entries of Mrs. Seward St. John revealed she made butter and raised chickens to use in trade for other goods.[41] Lulu Wilken remembered "Soap making is an art, ... The fat and lye water had to be boiled to the right stage, and the proper proportions of water and grease maintained or they would separate and it became a failure."[42] Mrs. Emma Phair remembered that her mother manufactured the fuel necessary for their cooking stove. "She knew just how many twists of straw it took to heat the oven for baking.... It took one hundred and twenty five twists to heat the oven; four bags altogether to heat the oven and bake the bread."[43]

Women's contributions to sustenance reached beyond the domestic sphere. They worked as field hands. Late nineteenth-century homesteader Harriet Neville drove the oxen while her husband pitched hay.[44] Another Saskatchewan pioneer, Mrs. Edward Watson, noted that she and her children built their sod barn,[45] and Sarah Roberts helped to brand cattle.[46] Some women, like Georgina Binnie-Clark preferred outdoor work. She wrote:

> I worked hard through June at the stoning, and started to harrow ... From the beginning I was perfectly happy working on the land, only I wished it was someone else's turn to get those tiresome three meals a day.[47]

Sarah Roberts, on the other hand, said of her branding job:

"I stayed with my job until it was done, and I am glad that I never had to do it again. I think that it is not a woman's work except that it is everyone's work to do the thing he needs to do."[48] Veronica Kokotailo's mother must have agreed. For two weeks she worked for a neighbor plastering his barn. Her payment was a pail of potatoes.[49]

Aside from their responsibilities as homemakers, home manufacturers, field hands, and wage earners, women performed other important functions. They were nurses and doctors for their families and neighbors. In a letter written to her grandmother from her family's Saskatchewan homestead, Maryanne Caswell described picking herbs for medicinal purposes.[50] Ukrainian immigrant, Maria Adamowska remembered, "As I was reaping with a sickle, I cut my finger. The gash was so deep that the finger dangled, just barely held on by the skin. Mother managed to splice it somehow, and the wound healed."[51] Even in the prairie town a woman's medical skills were relied upon. As late as 1930, Fredelle Maynard, a young resident of the town of Birch Hills, Saskatchewan, recalled that a doctor's responsibilities were limited to declaring quarantine and delivering babies.[52] In more isolated areas women acted as midwives, even if they were inexperienced. Clara Middleton described such an experience:

> We got home about midnight and at one o'clock came Mr. Barnes. His wife was in labour, and would I come? I protested that I wouldn't be any good, that I knew nothing.... No; his wife wanted me.
>
> "It's up to you," said my husband, but I knew by his tone that he had no doubts. I could almost hear him thinking, "You're a woman and you're needed."[53]

The thoughts of Clara's husband are a fitting description of women's work on the prairie. Women performed whatever work was needed. Regardless of training or experience women were expected to be self-reliant. Sometimes the responsibilities of self-reliance could soften women's adjustment to the isolation of the frontier. For example, Clara Middleton remembered that women acted as morticians as well as doctors. The ritual of preparing a body for burial provided women the opportunity to support and comfort one another.[54] In another example, Harriet Neville, finding herself isolated from nearby schools during the winter of 1884-1885, ordered textbooks from Toronto and kept regular school hours for her children. Of this experience she said, "One thing these things did for me. I never had a moment to be lonely to feel the lack of neighbors. I slept well and did not dream so much about old friends."[55]

Nevertheless, the challenge of self reliance proved too great for some women. On their way to their homestead in Manitoba, Nellie McClung remembered encountering a family returning from the prairie. The wife, dressed in a silk dress and flimsy shoes, was sobbing. She tearfully explained, "She hated the country ... it was only fit for Indians and squaws...." In an effort to comfort the woman, Nellie's mother suggested that perhaps the woman would be more comfortable travelling in simple clothes. The roads were muddy, sturdy shoes and gingham dresses were more practical. The woman did not sew, her mother had always done her sewing. "Mother's zeal began to flag, 'Take her back,' she said to Willard, 'she's not the type that makes a pioneer.'"[56]

The confining nature of women's work was a different source of discontent for women. Peace River pioneer Ida Scharf Hopkins articulated this frustration:

> Much as the woman becomes completely involved in the homestead life many of the challenges become repetitive....
>
> We women were never unhappy, but sometimes life was a bit dull. There was so little variety in the day-by-day routine. So much necessary work to be done there was little time or energy left for anything else. We had to keep the homefires burning.[57]

But women did appreciate their vigorous lives on the frontier prairie. Saskatchewan pioneer Alice Rendell illustrated this when she wrote to a friend in 1904:

> I would never advise anyone to come out here who is the least afraid of work. They are better off at home. There is plenty of room to breathe in this country and if the work is hard the freedom, which is the indispensable attribute of life here, makes one far less susceptible to physical fatigue.... Here one feels that each week's work is a step onward whilst in the old country oftentimes a year's toil brought nothing but disappointment and additional anxiety.[58]

Prairie Print No. 7 Prairie Couple

Kathleen Strange, like Alice Rendell, appreciated freedom. For Kathleen, pioneer life offered a new opportunity to work as a full partner with her husband. She missed this partnership in her later, less rigorous role of a city wife:

> My own life, on the other hand, is almost completely changed. And, most important of all, I am deprived of one particularly vital thing. On the farm I was a real partner with my husband, sharing with him in almost every detail of his daily work. Now his work is carried on in a downtown office, with professional help. There is little I can do to assist him.[59]

Prairie farm women like Kathleen Strange were, indeed partners with their husbands, not only because they shared in their husbands' day-to-day work, but also because of their own day-to-day responsibilities. Farm women's roles as homemakers, home manufacturers, field hands, wage earners, doctors, morticians, and teachers meant that women made substantial contributions to the business of farming. These contributions receive inadequate recognition when interpreted from the perspective of women as helpmates. Viewed as ancillary to the work of farm men, our conception of prairie farm women's work loses equality within the economic structure of the farm, an equality which is justified given women's roles as providers of valuable goods and services.

In a similar way the diversity of prairie farm women's experiences is lost when they are assigned the blanket role of helpmate. Women in this study reveal that it is a mistake to assume that all women on farms were wives and mothers. Single women were farmers in their own right, and they worked on farms as home-helps or domestics. Women's experiences also reveal that contrary to the image of women as obedient helpmates, some women did affect the decision-making process which led to their pioneer experiences in the grasslands. Some women actively participated in the decision-making process, others made the decision solely on their own.

Women's experiences differed in other important ways as well. Although women's responsibilities on the farm meant hard work, prairie women did not unanimously agree that their work on the farm was drudgery. The notion of universal drudgery, more than any other aspect of the helpmate image, deprives women of any possibility of joy or fulfillment in the process of pioneering. Prairie women's experiences reveal that although some women found their chores monotonous and confining, others felt obvious pride in their accomplishments. Some even found their responsibilities to be useful buffers between themselves and the loneliness of the frontier. Others appreciated the freedom and opportunity resulting from their work. As Kathleen Strange perceptively observed, "Drudgery! That is a word with many connotations. What is drudgery to one person may not be drudgery at all to another."[60]

The image of the stoic, hardworking helpmate not only homogenizes prairie women's experiences, it leaves some experiences out altogether. What about the women who could not cope with frontier life on the prairie? What factors made the difference between success and failure? We lose part of the story of women who stayed, when we ignore those who left.

The experiences of women in this study raise more questions than they provide answers. Yet the diversity of experiences revealed in women's writings admonish us to look more closely at our images of pioneer farm women on the Canadian prairie.

--S. B. S.

References

1. Nellie McClung, In Times Like These (1915; reprint ed. Toronto: University of Toronto Press, 1972), p. 109.

2. Beverly Stoeltje, "'A Helpmate for Man Indeed': The Image of the Frontier Woman," Journal of American Folklore 88 (January-March 1975): 32.

3. Gerald Willoughby, Retracing the Old Trail (Saskatoon, 1933) quoted in C. Dawson and E. R. Younge, Pioneering in the Prairie Provinces: The Social Side of the Settlement Process, Canadian Frontiers of Settlement Series, Vol. 8 (Toronto: The Macmillan Co. of Canada Ltd., 1934), p. 19.

4. June Sochen, "Frontier Women: A Model for All Women?" South Dakota History 7 (1), 1976: 36.

5. The Corrective Collective, Never Done: Three Centuries of Women's Work in Canada (Toronto: Canadian Women's Educational Press, 1974), p. 54.

6. Linda Rasmussen, et al., A Harvest Yet to Reap: A History of Prairie Women (Toronto: The Women's Press, 1976), p. 42.

7. Ibid., pp. 42-43.

8. McClung, p. 109.

9. Sarah Ellen Roberts, Alberta Homestead: Chronicle of a Pioneer Family, Lathrope E. Roberts, ed. (Austin: University of Texas Press, 1971), p. 4.

10. Nellie McClung, Clearing in the West (New York: Fleming H. Revell Company, 1936), p. 32.

11. Audrey Peterkin and Margaret Shaw, Mrs. Doctor: Reminiscences of Manitoba Doctors' Wives (Winnipeg: The Prairie Publishing Company, 1976), p. 2.

12. Lulu Beatrice Wilken, "Homesteading in Saskatchewan," Canada West Magazine 7 (Spring 1977): 27.

13. Muriel Jardine Parsloe, A Parson's Daughter (London: Faber and Faber Ltd., 1935), p. 220.

14. Kathleen Strange, With the West in Her Eyes (Toronto: George J. McLeod, Ltd., 1937), p. 8.

15. "Sunshine," The Grain Grower's Guide, 11 March 1914, p. 20.

16. Georgina Binnie-Clark, Wheat and Woman (1914; reprint ed. Toronto: University of Toronto Press, 1979).

17. Canadian Pacific Railway, What Women Say of the Canadian Northwest (n.p. 1886), p. 32.

18. MacLeod Gazette, 15 May 1896 quoted in Rasmussen, et al., p. 14.

19. Jessie M. E. Saxby, West-Nor'-West (London: James Nisbet and Company, 1890), p. 100.

20. Edna Jaques, *Uphill All the Way: The Autobiography of Edna Jaques* (Saskatoon, Saskatchewan: Western Producer Prairie Books, 1977), p. 14.

21. Jessie Browne Raber, *Pioneering in Alberta* (New York: Exposition Press, Inc., 1951), p. 10.

22. Clara and J.E. Middleton, *Green Fields Afar* (Toronto: The Ryerson Press, 1947), p. 12.

23. Laura Salverson, *Confessions of an Immigrant's Daughter* (London: Faber and Faber Ltd., 1939), p. 480.

24. Maria Adamowska, "Beginnings in Canada," in *Land of Pain; Land of Promise: First Person Accounts by Ukrainian Pioneers 1891-1914* trans. Harry Piniuta (Saskatoon, Saskatchewan: Western Producer Prairie Books, 1978), p. 54.

25. Georgina Binnie-Clark, *A Summer on the Canadian Prairie* (London: Edward Arnold, 1910), p. 278.

26. Susan Armitage, "Household Work and Childrearing on the Frontier: The Oral History Record," *Sociology and Social Research* 63 (3): 469.

27. Salverson, p. 37.

28. Strange, p. 220.

29. Jaques, p. 105.

30. Wilken, p. 28.

31. Raber, p. 67.

32. Harriet Johnson Neville, "Pioneering in the North-West Territories," Harriet Purdy and David Gagan, eds. *Canada: An Historical Magazine* 2 (June 1975): 42.

33. Raber, pp. 136-137 and 140-141.

34. Anne B. Woywitka, "A Roumanian Pioneer," *Alberta History* 21 (4) 1973: 22-23.

35. McClung, *Clearing in the West*, p. 116.

36. Anna Farion, "Homestead Girlhood," in _Land of Pain; Land of Promise_, p. 92.

37. Ibid., p. 91.

38. Elizabeth Keith Morris, _An Englishwoman in the Canadian West_ (Bristol: J.W. Arrowsmith or London: Simpkin Marshall, 1913), p. 188.

39. Armitage, p. 469.

40. Neville, pp. 48-51.

41. Seward T. St. John, "Mrs. St. John's Diary," _Saskatchewan History_ 2 (Autumn 1949): 25 and 29.

42. Wilken, p. 29.

43. Isabel M. Reekie, _Along the Old Melita Trail_ (Saskatoon, Saskatchewan: Modern Press, 1965), p. 49.

44. Neville, p. 20.

45. Mrs. Edward Watson, "Reminiscences of Mrs. Edward Watson," _Saskatchewan History_ 5 (Spring 1952): 67.

46. Roberts, p. 226.

47. Binnie-Clark, _Wheat and Woman_, p. 151.

48. Roberts, p. 226.

49. Woywitka, p. 22.

50. Maryanne Caswell, _Pioneer Girl_ (McGraw-Hill Co. of Canada Ltd., 1964), 10th letter.

51. Adamowska, p. 67.

52. Fredelle Bruser Maynard, _Raisins and Almonds_ (Toronto: Doubleday Canada, Ltd., 1972), p. 16.

53. Middleton, p. 48.

54. Ibid., p. 51.

55. Neville, p. 30.

56. McClung, Clearing in the West, p. 58.

57. Ida Scharf Hopkins, To the Peace River Country and On (Richmond, British Columbia: The Author, 1973), pp. 118-119.

58. Alice Rendell, "Letters from a Barr Colonist," Alberta Historical Review (Winter 1963): 24-25.

59. Strange, p. 292.

60. Ibid., p. 276.

WOMEN AND THEIR VISIONS:

PERSPECTIVES FROM FICTION

A popular prairie poet from Saskatchewan, Edna Jaques, closes her collection Prairie Born, Prairie Bred (1979) with a poem entitled "To the Next Generation" wherein she raises the question:

> Will they, too, love these dear brown fields
> And call them home ... and sing?[1]

These lines from one of the last poems of an eighty-year-old woman are intriguing because they imply that Jaques' whole generation loved the prairies and felt at home there. Yet anyone who has read some of the literature and history about the Canadian or American prairies knows that this is not always the case; often women have been portrayed as hard-working and long-suffering, living out their lives on isolated homesteads, growing up on bleak farms or in dreary towns. However, historian Glenda Riley points out in her 1980 essay, "Women in the West," that prominent male writers like Garland and Rölvaag and historians--even feminist historians--have relied too much on traditional images--Gentle Tamers, Pioneers in Petticoats, Saints in Sunbonnets, Madonnas of the Prairies, Pioneer Mothers, Light Ladies, Calamity Janes and Fighting Feminists.[2] "The problem with all these interpretations," Riley notes, "is that they rely on stereotypical rather than on factual materials. Such portraits tend to give birth to legends rather than to accurate insights."[3] She goes on to say that the time has come to put aside the myths and stereotypes inherited through history and to let women speak for themselves.[4]

The purpose of this essay is to let the voices of women writing fiction mingle with the voices of the women described in chapters two and three. In fact, the images embedded in prairie women's fiction, long overlooked, will be useful to historians because they demonstrate the complex roles and multi-dimensional images of frontier women. From the literature we can glean new facts and perspectives. As Russel B. Nye has pointed out in his essay "History and Literature: Branches of the Same Tree," "Both historian and literary artist begin with the 'fact' (however we define that term), with the raw material from which the creative process starts and out of which it shapes something new.... A literary fact is an imaginative event; but it is no less usable or real for all of that."[5] Thus I have turned to fiction for some answers to the following questions: First, what was the vision of the pioneer woman who left Ontario or western Pennsylvania or the Ukraine to settle on the North American prairies? Secondly, what was the effect of that vision on the daughter--how does she ultimately react to a way of life which, in many instances, makes rigorous physical and psychological demands? Thirdly, what is the response of the contemporary female to her homeplace, now that the tall swaying grasses are mostly a memory? The stories, representing one hundred years of prairie fiction writing, are located in Illinois, Iowa, Kansas, Nebraska, Dakota Territory, Manitoba, Saskatchewan, and Alberta. While the emphasis is on women's writings, four male authors are included for making comparisons and for showing the respect and sympathy that many male writers had toward the kinds of females portrayed in their works.

Settling the Prairie: Catherwood and Garland

In the last quarter of the nineteenth century two writers, Mary Hartwell Catherwood and Hamlin Garland, presented unromantic views of pioneer farm life. In "The Monument to the First Mrs. Smith," (1878), Catherwood describes a woman who has worked herself to death, going without basic necessities while her husband gets the farm paid for and saves money for a house big enough to fit his image of himself--"Not one of your cheap frames, but a brick, and all new-fangled like them town houses, you know!"[6] However, Susan Smith died before the house was built, and it is the young second Mrs. Smith who reaps the benefits of the selfless, hard-working first wife. Catherwood concludes the story with a warning: "MORAL--Girls, if you must marry Mr. Smith, don't take him on the first ballot--i.e.: wait till the monument is built, and then enter as the second Mrs. Smith."[7]

Susan Smith, however, is only one kind of pioneer Catherwood observed on the Illinois prairie. An 1880 story by Catherwood, "The Career of a Prairie Farmer," explores the lives of the more affluent settlers who emigrated with adequate financial resources so that neither man nor woman had to suffer the kinds of deprivations described in the first story. Catherwood speculates about the vision of the farmer: "Perhaps the farmer saw with prophetic eye the whole sloping plain of Illinois, with its wooded stream-courses and tufted groves, turned into a stock-paradise, with pasture-land depended upon by half a continent."[8] His young wife and sister also are enthusiastic--they "found the situation novel. They watched the prairie flush--there is no other word to express its sudden overspreading with tender shades of green...." They delighted in the prairie-hen, the long-legged sandhill cranes, the wild rose-bushes and Indian moccasins and pale-yellow sensitive plants.[9] The women's lives, over the years, are comfortable and secure. Yet Catherwood points out that the pioneer experience takes its toll. The way of life is monotonous, the farmer becomes more interested in making money than in pursuing some of his former literary interests; his wife and sister have had every possible convenience and hired help, but the prairie still leaves its mark: "A shoreless river of wind rushed through space. Its roar was terrible to inexperienced ears. But in time the farmer's wife and sister became so steeped in this constant flow, teasing in summer, sweeping and icy in winter, that they received a rich meer-schaum tint, which the ague diligently infused with saffron."[10]

This story includes other cameos. There is Allie Jennings, the pretty, refined schoolteacher who has to board in overcrowded homes until the affluent farmer's sister rescues her. When asked how she likes the prairie, Allie responds: "It presses me down, and chokes me. But maybe I shall get used to it." The farmer's sister replies, "Why, how can you feel so? When I first saw it I wanted to fly, it was so wide and free."[11] Old Mary comes to Trail City as a domestic servant but eventually finds security as the preacher's wife. The final portrait of the story, however, is a disturbing one. Catherwood describes the shabby, hollow-faced woman who descends from the railroad platform one day and begins asking if anyone knows a man named Thomas Nolan. She is told that the very first person buried in the new graveyard was a Thomas Nolan who had died the week before:

> They were startled by her head bumping the

> platform. When she came out of her long fainting-fit, surrounded by compassionate strangers, there was no bright ending to her story, such as writers are able to give their tales of separation and suffering. He was dead, and under a hummock in the new cemetery. She found some work and melted silently into the new community.[12]

The story may not have a happy ending, but the fact that Mrs. Nolan could find a place for herself in the community is in itself significant.

Hamlin Garland's 1891 story, "A Prairie Heroine," contains elements similar to those found in Catherwood's two stories: the life is hard on everyone, but particularly hard for some women. While Catherwood places a great deal of responsibility on men like Mr. Smith for creating unnecessary hardships due to their selfish visions,[13] Garland feels the political system is responsible for the suffering of women like Lucretia Burns, his prairie heroine. Garland begins the story with a description of her: "Lucretia Burns had never been handsome, even in her days of early girlhood, and now she was middle-aged, distorted with work and childbearing, and looking faded and worn as one of the boulders that lay beside the pasture fence near where she sat milking a large white cow."[14] Her husband, Sim Burns, is described as "a type of the prairie farmer and his whole surrounding was typical"--a mortgaged farm, unpainted box-like house, ragged children, and over-worked horses. He was known by his neighbors as "a hard-working cuss, and tollably well fixed."[15]

The irony Garland points to is that even "tollably well-fixed" farmers live sub-human lives. Through one of the town characters, Garland describes the system that alienates farm couples, pushing women like Lucretia Burns to consider suicide. He offers a solution: "The abolition of all indirect taxes. The state control of all privileges, the private ownership of which interfered with the equal rights of all. He would utterly destroy speculative holdings of the earth. He would have land everywhere brought to its best use, by appropriating all ground rents to the use of the State, etc. etc...."[16]

Lucretia Burns's heroism lies in her ability to go on, even without a vision, because she owes it to her children, because her husband finally admits that he's been "cussed," because the young schoolteacher and Sim's sister both offer sympathy and understanding. But as things stand, Garland insists, farm families will continue to live out their lives as automatons, "lives but little higher than their cattle"[17] despite the fact that they live in the midst of a glorious landscape.

Prairie Matriarchs: Gates, Donovan, Cather, and Roy

Eleanor Gates's portrayal of a pioneer prairie woman in The Plow-Woman (1906) departs radically from the images found in Catherwood and Garland. In this novel, Dallas Lancaster's father is a railway section man disabled on the job, so he and Dallas decide to homestead in the Dakota Territory. They choose a site near a fort where Indians are garrisoned, and the story line is dominated by the kinds of intrigues typical of prairie romances--blizzards, illegal homesteading practices, Indian uprisings, and love stories. One of the more interesting plots involves Dallas's friendship with Squaw Charley, an Indian outcast. However, underlying all of these situations is the true substance of the novel: it is the story of a woman who loves the land, does the plowing, "proves up" the homestead, and refuses to marry unless she can continue farming. At the end of the novel she tells her lover, "Outside work is fine.... Better than cooking over a hot stove or breaking your back over a tub. Men have the best half of things--the air and the sky and the horses. I don't complain. I like my work. Let it make me like a man."[18] Her lover assures her she is too womanly ever to look like a man and, he says, "I don't ask you to chain yourself up in a house. There's a big future in the cow business. We'd take my share of the Clark herd--you'd ride with me--we'd be partners."[19]

Josephine Donovan's 1930 novel, Black Soil, describes the relationship of a woman to the prairie over a long period of time. Initially, Nell Connor reacts negatively to the prairie: "Direction? ... There was no direction. The prairie stretched to the end of the world.... Why had Tim selected land so far, far from any signs of life?" However, her little girl interrupts these thoughts by shouting "Fowers! Fowers! Everything is Fowers!"[20]

These details--the endless, directionless prairie and the flowers--symbolize the duality of the prairie which Nell eventually accepts. One scene shows Nell standing at the

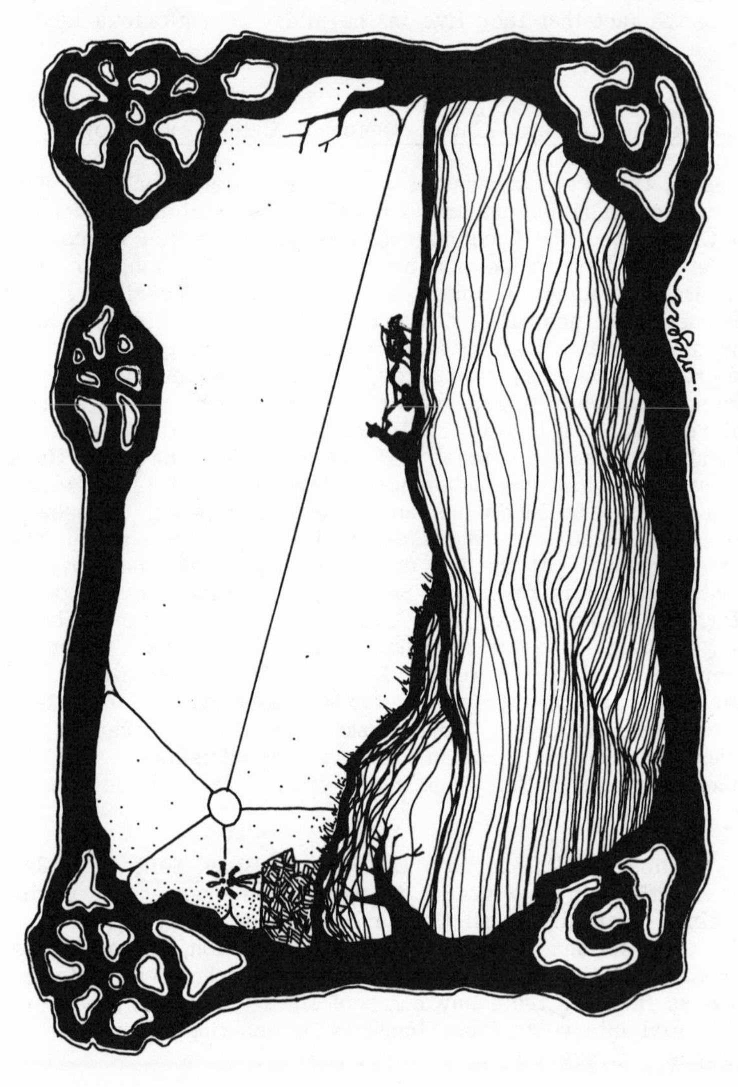

Prairie Print No. 8 Plow-Woman

window. She sees, one moment, a destitute land which holds no promise for her children. The next moment the prairie becomes transformed into a fruitful land: she and other women will transplant the heritage of the East in the prairie soil and in the hearts and souls of prairie children.[21] On the other hand, her husband Tim sees the spirit of the prairie--not eastern culture--as the force that will enter and enrich the lives of the children.[22]

Although the views presented in Black Soil seem, at times, to be naïvely optimistic, they remind us that there were, surely, parents like Nell and Tim who lived and worked on the prairie and saw their children flourish "like sturdy stalks of corn, well rooted in black soil."[23] The ending of the novel suggests that the visions of both Nell and Tim become realities. Plans have been made for the oldest son to go East for his education; he will become a doctor and return to care for the sick. His sister, in another year, will go East to prepare for teaching prairie children. The spirit of the East is blended with the spirit of the West in Donovan's prairie youth.

Although both Josephine Donovan and Eleanor Gates emphasize hardships on the prairie homestead, their stories conclude with a sentimentally optimistic view of the pioneers. Nevertheless, their portraits of prairie women should not be disregarded for this reason. As George Woodcock points out in his discussion of prairie pioneers,

> It was a life whose harshnesses women and men shared in equally, for the women who settled on the prairies had to do everything that their predecessors in Ontario had done, in addition to enduring greater remoteness....
>
> Yet despite all the dangers and discomforts, and largely because of a survival code of cooperation and mutual support, the settlers converted the Prairie provinces in a surprisingly short time from a harsh frontier to a more-or-less suitable agricultural economy....[24]

In O Pioneers! (1913) and My Ántonia (1917), Cather provides more realistic descriptions of prairie matriarchs than those found in Gates and Donovan; in addition, each novel presents the attitudes of a mother and a daughter, thus enabling us to make comparisons and understand the different visions of pioneer families. Mrs. Bergson in O Pioneers!

"had never quite forgiven John Bergson for bringing her to the end of the earth; but, now that she was there, she wanted to be let alone to reconstruct her old life in so far as that was possible."[25] However, Mrs. Shimerda in My Ántonia was the dominant decision-maker. Ántonia tells Jim Burden that her father had not wanted to emigrate: "My mamenka make him come. All the time she say 'America big country; much money, much land for my boys, much husband for my girls.' My papa, he cry for leave his old friends what make music with him.... But my mama, she want Ambrosch for be rich, with many cattle."[26]

In O Pioneers! Alexandra, rather than her brothers, has the intelligence for successful farming and the love of the land which brings prosperity and the fulfillment of her father's vision. She makes sacrifices and leaves personal desires unfulfilled in order to develop the farm, but she finds compensation in the land itself. One passage in particular illuminates her feelings: "For the first time, perhaps, since the land emerged from the waters of geologic ages, a human face was set toward it with love and yearning. It seemed beautiful to her, rich and strong and glorious. Her eyes drank in the breadth of it, until her tears blinded her."[27]

Ántonia, like Alexandra, loves the land in spite of the sacrifices it requires. To emphasize Ántonia's singular love of the land, Cather places Jim Burden's view next to Ántonia's. True, Jim comes to love the prairie, but the sharpness of his first feelings is never quite nullified by the remaining events of the novel and he chooses a way of life which is dissociated from the prairie. Jim recalls that as a ten year-old boy he "had the feeling that the world was left behind, that we had got over the edge of it, and were outside man's jurisdiction.... Between that earth and that sky I felt erased, blotted out."[28]

When Jim Burden returns briefly to Nebraska after several years' absence, Ántonia tells him "I'd always be miserable in a city. I'd die of lonesomeness. I like to be where I know every stack and tree, and where all the ground is friendly. I want to live and die here."[29] At the end of My Ántonia, twenty years have lapsed and Jim is visiting Antonia again. Ántonia still affirms life on the prairie: "I belong on a farm," she says. "I'm never lonesome here like I used to be in town."[30] Jim now sees her

as a woman who has lent herself to immemorial

> human attitudes which we recognize by instinct as universal and true. I had not been mistaken. She was a battered woman now, not a lovely girl: but she still had that something which fires the imagination, could still stop one's breath for a moment by a look or gesture that somehow revealed the meaning in common things. She had only to stand in the orchard, to put her hand on a little crab tree and look up at the apples, to make you feel the goodness of planting and tending and harvesting at last. All the strong things of her heart came out in her body, that had been so tireless in serving generous emotions.
>
> It was no wonder that her sons stood tall and straight. She was a rich mine of life, like the founders of early races.[31]

In this passage we see Ántonia through Jim's eyes as the archetypal prairie matriarch, rooted and flourishing spiritually in a land which had been harsh and deadly to other settlers, female and male. She is linked with the cycles of nature, with images of growth and fruition. We need only recall Mrs. Shimerda's vision of the land for her sons to grasp Cather's message: in the late nineteenth century the American dream could be grasped by some women--not just by Ántonia, but by the other hired girls as well: the three Marys, Tiny Soderball, and Lena Lingard all succeeded despite failed expectations and reversals along the way.

One more example will round out the discussion of prairie matriarchs. In Gabrielle Roy's story, "Garden in the Wind," the narrator is driving along a rural road when she sees "under the enormous sky, against the hostile wind and among the tall grasses, this little garden, fairly bursting with flowers."[32] Despite the fact that so many stories have already been told about the prairie and pioneering, the narrator decides one more needs to be told--the story of Maria Marta Yaramko who emigrated from the Ukraine about 1920. We discover that it was Marta, not Stepan, who wanted to emigrate, "for he was frightened by the long journey toward the unknown. She was the one who had swept him along in the ardour of her faith in this still undiscovered country...."[33] The Yaramkos and the other Ukrainian immigrants failed to establish a prosperous community on the Alberta prairies; the droughts defeated them year after year, and many left, including Marta's children. However, the situation that the narrator felt compelled to record was

Marta's relationship with the landscape. Living without speaking with a bitter, alienated old husband, Marta continued to find "inexhaustible consolation" in the prairies.[34] The vision that led her from the Ukraine to Canada has never diminished: "Once again the thought crossed her mind that the plain was deep in a great dream of things to come, and was singing of patience, with promise that all things, in their time and place, would be accomplished."[35]

Prairie Patriarchs: Ostenso, Rölvaag, and Grove

The portraits of matriarchs--Dallas Lancaster, Nell Connor, Alexandra Bergson, Ántonia Shimerda, and Marta Yaramko--need to be placed beside those of prairie patriarchs in Martha Ostenso's Wild Geese (1925), Rölvaag's Giants in the Earth (1927), and Grove's Fruits of the Earth (1933).

In Wild Geese Ostenso describes the father, Caleb Gare, standing on a ridge and looking over his land: "He could hold all this, and more--add to it year after year--add to his herd of pure-bred Holsteins and his drove of horses--raise more sheep--experiment with turkey and goose for the winter markets in the south--all this as long as he held the whip hand over Amelia."[37] Because Caleb equates land with money and power, his passion for the land is perverted:

> There was a transcendent power in this blue field of flax that lifted a man above the petty artifices of birth, life, and death.... Caleb would stand for long moments outside the fence beside the flax. He would creep between the wires and run his hand across the flowering, gentle tops of the growth. A stealthy caress--more intimate than any he had ever given to woman.[38]

Caleb is removed from essential life forces which are, from his perspective, "petty artifices"; he is not sexually aroused by woman but by the flax which represents a full harvest and large sums of money.

His wife, Amelia, is ill-fitted to her environment. She tries, in vain, to keep linen napkins and lace doilies--remnants of her former life--in place. While she doesn't share Caleb's goals, she serves them in order to protect her first son, born out of wedlock and fathered by another man, from what she fears would be the disgrace of exposure. This is the "hold" that Caleb has over Amelia and, indirectly, over their four children.

The two daughters in Wild Geese respond differently to the situation. Ellen is passive, obedient and, symbolically, half-blind. She prides herself on "her stoic endurance of physical pain."[39] As one of the brothers observes: "Ellen was like a pea-pod that had ripened brittle, but could not burst open. Then he realized that he, too, was a closed pea-pod--they were all closed pea-pods, not daring to open."[40] The reader soon discovers, however, that the other daughter, Judith, dares to open and to defy Caleb; she recognizes that under Caleb's rule her brothers will know nothing but work, her sister Ellen will go blind, and she will go crazy. She says, "'He's got to quit thinkin' we're animals he can drive around.'"[41] The tension of the novel is built upon the conflict between father and daughter: Caleb's determination to build a flourishing farm and Judith's determination to be free.

Although Judith rebels against her father, she does not, at first, reject the land. She responds intuitively to the fecundity of the soil in the patch of woods--a place which has not been violated by Caleb's plow--as demonstrated in the following passage:

> Judith took off all her clothing and lay flat on the damp ground with the waxy feeling of new, sunless vegetation under her. She needed to escape, to fly from something--she knew not what. Caleb ... Ellen ... the farm, the hot reek of manure in the stable when it was close as today. Life was smothering, overwhelming her, like a pillow pressed against her face....
>
> Oh, how knowing the bare earth was, as if it might have a heart and a mind hidden here in the woods. The fields that Caleb had tilled had no tenderness she knew. But here was something forbiddenly beautiful, secret as one's own body. And there was something beyond this. She could feel it in the freeness of the air, in the depth of the earth.[42]

However, Judith equates her father's sinister qualities with the soil and becomes firmer in her determination to leave the farm.

At the end of the novel Caleb is sucked under in the marsh that borders the field of flax while plowing a fireguard to protect his crop. The family is freed from his control, but only Judith leaves. In her mind, the land is too closely associated with her father. Therefore that portion of her self which could have loved the prairie is thwarted; she chooses a way of life which will prevent her from exploring a quality in the land she once divined was forbiddingly beautiful and free.

Per Hansa, the hero of Rölvaag's Giants in the Earth, is perhaps a more typical example of a prairie patriarch than Ostenso's Caleb Gare. Per Hansa envisions a "new kingdom" on the prairie; he is intoxicated with the enormous quantities of rich land and with the sense that he is going to do something remarkable "which should become known far and wide."[43] He envisions a royal mansion which he and his sons will build for Beret, his wife, and her "little princess" Anna. Even after his first year, Per Hansa continues to be exhilarated by the possibilities for life on the prairie and clings to the belief that he is "both prince and king, the sole possessor of countless treasures."[44]

Beret fails to share his vision. She sees only the desolation and loneliness of the prairie. As her sense of alienation increases, her religious fanaticism increases as well; she is convinced she is being punished for her sexual desires and for becoming pregnant before marrying Per Hansa. In addition, she feels she deserted her parents when they had offered to care for her and to raise the baby in Norway. She looks at the prairie which is to be her new home and asks: "How will human beings be able to endure this place? ... There isn't even a thing that one can hide behind!"[45] Initially Per Hansa ignores this attitude of Beret's and persists in his belief that she has the courage, physical stamina, and intelligence to aid him in his quest. However, Beret's response is conservative, cautious, and destructive in contrast to Per Hansa's joyful, vigorous, and ingenious assault upon the new land. Eventually he recognizes her inability to adapt and turns more and more to his sons for support and assistance.

But what of the daughter, Anna? Rölvaag has carefully developed the characters of Per Hansa and Beret, their sons, the neighbors--Syvert and Kjersti, Hans Olso and Sorrina, Sam and Henry Solem. Yet he remains strangely silent on the subject of daughters. Anna is seen sleeping, chattering, tugging on her mother's skirts and patting her mother's face on the Christmas morning when Peder Victorious, the new baby, is born. Her role as girl-child is limited and she has no function in the plot.

Perhaps the clue to Rölvaag's treatment of girls can be found in Peder Victorious, the sequel to Giants in the Earth. We are told this about Peder:

> As he grew older he felt an increasing desire to move things about and to re-arrange them to suit himself.... Oh, how could grown people behave so stupidly! Here went Anna Marie, his sister, never giving so much as a thought to the future. Didn't she realize that she was almost grown up, and that she ought to get married and have a husband and children to look after? That's what happened to all women who were any good.[46]

According to Peder, Anna is not fulfilling her destiny as a woman and lacks the assertiveness to pursue her musical aspirations. Other young women in the novel fare no better: the teacher is a gushing, sentimental patriot on the lookout for a husband; the widow's daughter becomes pregnant by an itinerant hired hand, lets the baby die of exposure, and hangs herself; the other young girls are sketched in a variety of girl-roles. Perhaps this lack of well-rounded girl characters reflects Rölvaag's view: prairie wives are a major factor in the success of the male settlers; sons are the means of building and maintaining the dream; daughters may be little princesses--a means of exhibiting wealth--but the welfare and the future of the family is not affected by them to any measurable degree. They only acquire significance as wives and mothers in new family units. Rölvaag does not see the daughter as participating in any active way in the fulfillment of the father's vision.

In Frederick Philip Grove's Fruits of the Earth the character development of the daughters is sketchy in the first part of the novel, but intentionally so. Grove too has created a portrait of a prairie patriarch and intends to show that a prairie empire is meaningless if a man loses his children in the process of making his vision come true. In contrast to settlers such as those represented by Per Hansa, Abe Spalding, the protagonist of Grove's novel, has no romantic notions about nature. He knows that his nearest male neighbor on the Manitoba prairie has become "half-crazed with work and isolation." Nevertheless, Abe believes that hard work gets results: "He would conquer this wilderness; he would change it; he would set his own seal upon it."[47] And one day he would raise a white mansion as symbol of his conquest over nature. As in Wild Geese and Giants in the Earth, the wife, Ruth, fails to share her husband's optimism. She is the daughter of a small merchant in Brantford, Ontario, and like the wife in Wild Geese yearns for a finer way of life than the prairie can offer for quite some time. Abe admits that "he had been in love with a face and a figure rather than a mind or soul,"[48] yet he hopes she will become reconciled to his vision and work patiently by his side. When the children are born, she becomes absorbed in their growth and development, ignoring Abe's accomplishments. Exhausted by the farm work, Abe has no energy left for the family. He rationalizes about his priorities: "the 'kids' were still small; he would take them in hand later; let him build up that farm first, an empire ever growing in his plans."[49] One day Ruth asks him why he works so hard. What he's doing seems meaningless to her. When she tells him that the country isn't fit to live in, he says: "Exactly.... I am making it a country fit to live in. That is my task. The task of a pioneer. Can't you see that I need time, time, time? In six years I've built a farm which produces wealth. Give me another six years, and I'll double it. Then I'll build you a house such as you've never dreamt of calling your own."[50]

Eventually Abe realizes that he may build a great estate, he may have the school district named for him as the first settler in the area, he may bring law and order to the community during a period in office as reeve, but he has lost his children in the process--although not, strangely enough, Ruth. At some point she comes to accept his goals and to admire him for his accomplishments when others on the prairie failed. Perhaps the comfort and status of the new house helped. Perhaps the bank account which he established in her name gave her a sense of security and made her feel more of a partner in the farm.

Nevertheless, there is no "happy ending." Abe Spalding realizes that "his life had been wrong.... He had lived to himself and had had to learn that it could not be done."[51] His son Charlie is killed because Abe needed a driver to haul grain to town and allowed Charlie to take on a task which should have been done by a man. His other son, Jim, chooses to be a mechanic rather than to run the farm. One

Prairie Print No. 9 Harvest

daughter marries a lawyer and assumes an entirely different way of life in town. The final crisis is brought about by the younger daughter, Frances: "Like so many others she had grown out of hand. She did not rebel or disobey; but she lived a life of her own, admitting no one into her confidence."[52] Abe and Ruth are disturbed by her style of dress, by her friends, by her inattentiveness to school work, by her attitude and activities, yet it is not until she becomes pregnant that they are forced to recognize the degree of Frances' alienation. Abe Spalding has successfully, even heroically, used mind and body to conquer nature. He has enjoyed a rich harvest of fruits from the earth; however--to extend Grove's metaphor--the fruits of his marriage have not been tended and he must pay the consequences. Earlier Ruth had asked him, "What is it all for?" At that time, Abe had an answer. Now he viewed his situation differently: "He had worked and slaved: what for? His great house was useless: the three people left in it would have had ample room in the patchwork shack. Soon he and Ruth would be alone, lost in that structure which, from behind the rustling wind-breaks, looked out over that prairie which it had been built to dominate."[53]

Some biographical criticism becomes useful at this point. Grove's vignettes in Over Prairie Trails and other autobiographical writings show that there is much of Frederick Grove in Abe Spalding: both the writer and the fictional character are exhilarated by matching intellect and physical endurance against blizzards and flooded rivers and runaway horses. However, Grove's affection for his wife and his grief over the early death of his daughter are in sharp contrast with Abe Spalding's feelings about family. Grove ends the novel without providing for a reconcilation between Spalding and his daughter; in this way Grove implies that a man who has invested in material success and prestige rather than in a child deserves rejection. The tragedy is that the children become so alienated from the parent that they never develop a sense of belonging to the land at a time and a place when life on the prairie could have brought material and emotional rewards.

Ostenso, Rölvaag and Grove, in their portraits of male patriarchs, emphasize the insensitivity of the male and, as Mary Frances Engels points out, the "inability to perceive what his pursuit of his dream is doing to those around him." However, Engels goes on to say that her survey of realistic settlement fiction reveals that "the lot of women is depicted as a lonely, tedious, and often alienating existence, over which the woman has no control."[54] However, even if we disregard the romance adventures by Gates and Donovan, we still have the works of Cather and Roy to demonstrate that female characters with a consuming vision (with the exception of Mrs. Shimerda) seek to fulfill not only their own needs but those of their families as well.

The Prairie-Born: Hudson, Parsons, and LeSueur

The next group of narratives are semi-autobiographical. They focus on the 1920s and 1930s, representing another era in prairie history--the bleak years of droughts and crop failures. In Upon a Sagebrush Harp (1969), Nell Parsons talks about her father's dreams and the realities of life near Lang, Saskatchewan:

> That was a pattern of prairie life ... windbreak ... firebreak ... backbreak ... heartbreak. But a homesteader dreamt on. Oh, next year would be great!
>
> Dreams differed from quarter section to quarter section. Some dreamed of making a "pile" quickly, and returning with a fortune to the place from which they had come to the raw land. Some planned on moving into town to live in idleness. Papa dreamed of staying on his land forever, of building for Mama that big house with a fireplace.
>
> Ah, the dreams were as different as the people, four dreams to each section.[55] (Ellipses in original.)

For the Parsons family there was no big house or prosperous farm. After a decade of failures, they became tenants on a farm further north where the land was better. By this time Nell, who had graduated from normal school, was teaching in a prairie school south of the Dirt Hills. At the end of the story she comes to terms with her feelings about her father's vision and their prairie homestead: "I still felt tightly bound to that homestead where Mama and Papa lived. I had seen the fields carved out of raw prairie. I knew every stone on the land, knew where each remaining sagebrush grew."[56] She recalls how her mother had hated the prairie, especially at first. Yet she sang morning, noon, and night, although Nell cannot decide how much of her singing came from a determination to be gay and how much from real contentment.

Nor can the mother share Nell's delight in the prairie. Nell remembers running to her mother with a sagebrush in her hand: "'Pretty? What's pretty about that?' responded Mama." Nell replies, "'Why, the ... the way it leans against the wind ... the way it grows, flat-like ... and.... I could not put my feeling into exact words. Everything was beautiful. The veil of twilight, the pale green afterglow of sunset. The ground under my bare feet seemed to pulsate."[57]

Lois Phillips Hudson describes the late 1920s and 1930s when the droughts and depression forced her parents from their Dakota farm. While dust and defeat are dominant images throughout the work, they are intermixed with images of greenness and survival. Looking back, Hudson sees herself as

> a prairie child, walking in the loneliness of great spaces, absorbing familiarity with eternity. In that enduring loneliness I might have existed through centuries of freedom and bounty, when the grass rose to the shoulders of the buffalo and the grass and the buffalo fed each other, and the land and the grass held each other against wind and drought. This eternity of abundance had spread a feast for the bread-hungry world and for the soul of the farmer.[58]

But, she adds, "the farmer's soul had been too small to cherish the immense heritage."[59] Ignorant, irresponsible farmers, exploitative landlords, the wind, and the drought had brought an end to the golden age of the prairie. Although the North Dakota prairie no longer resembles the Garden of the World entered and occupied by the Indians and the first settlers, its memory remains with Lois and she envisions the possibility of bringing back at least the fertility of the land.

Meridel LeSueur's "Corn Village" reveals the feelings of a young woman who stayed on the prairie farm despite years of crop failures. In the opening sentence the narrator says, "Like many Americans, I will never recover from my sparse childhood in Kansas. The blackness, weight and terror of childhood in mid-America strike deep into the stem of life. Like desert flowers we learned to crouch near the earth, fearful that we would die before the rains, cunning, waiting the season of good growth."[60] This is another side of the prairie experience--its ability to inflict what the narrator calls "mysterious wounds." Perhaps she chooses the word mysterious because the land sends forth contradictory signals represented by two similes: the Kansas prairie is like "a strong raped virgin"; it is also like "an idiotic lost peasant ... scattering incredibly tiny flowers" after the winter's thaw.[61] The images of the strong virgin and the flower seeds suggest fertility, yet LeSueur points out that after the pioneer generation passed, there was nothing left to conquer, no spirit left in the people, no community to bind them together; all around, she observes, "the land lies desolate like a loved woman who has been forgotten ... misused through dreams of power and conquest."[62]

Yet the narrator in "Corn Village" stays in Kansas although, as she tells the prairie, she has the option to leave: "Not going to Paris or Morocco or Venice instead staying with you, trying to be in love with you, bent upon understanding you, bringing you to life. For your life is my life and your death is mine also."[63] Like Hudson, LeSueur envisions a renewable prairie.

Departures and Arrivals: Stockwell, Laurence, and Van Herk

Three recent works explore the relationships between home-place and identity in female characters: Nancy Stockwell's Out Somewhere and Back Again: The Kansas Stories (1978), Margaret Laurence's The Diviners (1974), and Aritha Van Herk's Judith (1978).

In Stockwell's Kansas stories, the prairie is no longer an antagonist nor a threat to physical survival; in fact, the land and the historical events enacted there provide key images and metaphors which enable the narrator to describe her feelings about life and her situation as a lesbian.

In the title story, "Out Somewhere and Back Again," the narrator is on a Sunday afternoon ride with her easy-going, good-natured father and her grandparents. Her grandfather had surveyed and mapped the territory through which they are riding. He had charted the pipelines; he had "ordered" the land and made it safe for journeys out and back. Nancy's father also knows the land. He has grown up in the area and has apparently found it a comfortable, secure place in which to live. There's no indication that he is haunted by crop failures or by windstorms. As they drive along, he says,

> "No one needs to worry here," my father began, starting talk that might just go on and on if anyone cared to pick up the thread of it. "All the roads go a mile one way and a mile back the other way, it's as simple as that. There's nothin' very hard to figure out in this world, is there, Mother?"[64]

However, the narrator remembers that after a long pause her grandmother replied, "No, but doin' it's a different matter."[65] The ritualistic Sunday afternoon drive on the prairie becomes a metaphor for the journey through life. Life, like the prairie landscape, appears simple, but "doin' it" is, indeed, a different matter, as shown in the last story of the collection, "John Brown's Lookout."

In this story it becomes apparent that there are new kinds of roads through territories which haven't been mapped--territories which Nancy's grandfather never suspected and which her mother (who has found security in traditional prairie town values) views with horror. Nancy says:

> My mother gets angry at me ... the way my hair curls or does not curl, the way I talk, the way I will or will not live my life, the waste she imagines, about her fears, how she needs me, clutches, has tried to trap me, does not want me to go back to Boston, does not want to think about the woman there, wants me to get a good job as a school teacher, use my education, make a stable, secure life for myself, become something, write during a spring recess if I really have to write, or during the two summer months--isn't that what they give school teachers a vacation for she said--but write uplifting things, be good, have a nice apartment, don't dream, don't live in an imaginary world.[66]

Nancy has gone out somewhere--Boston--and has come back again for a visit during which old struggles with her mother are renewed. Once again Nancy insists that she can't stay in Myola, Kansas, and be the typical Kansas girl. She says to her mother: "I'm going back to Boston. I can't be the things you imagined or hoped or pretended I'd be. I'm someone else and you refuse to know me."[67]

For a few hours Nancy escapes from town and drives to John Brown's Lookout where she experiences a oneness with the topography and with the forces that formed the land.

She recognizes parallels between the land and her experience of loving a woman:

> In the trauma of the land there is, finally, an evenness, a sameness which is like symmetry thought of differently, as if two bodies sharing similar parts are doubling, stretching, curling and folding in many mutual ecstasies....
>
> I stand and look down--from the only hill southeast of Lawrence--imagining that I have inherited something here. I look at it, through it and at the distance it represents; that is all I can think of to know about it now, and as I stand here, it puts its arms around me, like a woman, like the only woman, I think, the one my life is saturated with, the idea of her, the all I want and the all I see, all that is in every way precious, the land like a body lying changed in many positions, always naked, and I hold her in my imagination, thinking of all she is.[68]

There is a strong sense of the land and of her love relationship as evolving, vital forces.

Also, the spirits of past pioneers surround her. She identifies with "Osawatomi" Brown and, to a greater degree, with the Pioneer Woman whose paintings and statue she has probably seen at the State Capitol:

> I rise to a standing position like a hardened prairie woman standing on a hill facing the wind, the blowing skirt solidified in bronze like my arms, the patina green, clashing, fighting, withstanding everything just to stand here, arms stretched out wide, wild like the rebel waving a rifle and a book. I know it has been a great, long flight to reach her and another place, frantic, frenzied, wild, jaded, scratched, heaved up, battered, whirled, bruised, going faster than desire to move towards her and myself, always reaching, wanting more and more, and still more....[69]

For Nancy, the Kansas prairie houses the spirits of men and women who fought not only for survival but for dignity and freedom. She is the grateful inheritor of that legacy.

In contrast to Nancy, Morag Gunn, the narrator of

Laurence's The Diviners, feels she has no legacy and is haunted for years by the sense that she came from nowhere. Her parents died of polio when she was five years old and she was taken from their prairie farm to live in town with her father's World War II buddy, Christie Logan, and his wife Prin. They raised her with all the care they would have given to their own child had he lived. Christie has no illusions about the quality of life in this little Manitoba town called Manawaka. He supposedly despises the town and the people because he daily witnesses the worst side of life as he hauls away the garbage and the liquor bottles and the excrement and the human fetus in the paper bag. Christie is "the Scavenger"--the garbage collector. He tells Morag: "You get the hell out of here, Morag, you hear, and you make something of yourself."[70] When Morag is eighteen she follows his advice and leaves Manawaka and the "goddamned prairie dust."[71] Later, after Morag has graduated from the university and marries her English professor, Christie brushes away her excuses for not inviting him to the wedding: He tells her "it's a bloody good thing you've got away from this dump. So just shut your goddamn trap and thank your lucky stars."[72] Morag replies. "Do you really think that Christie?" He replies, "I do.... And I also don't. That's the way it goes. It'll all go along with you, too."[73] Morag objects. She doesn't intend to let any of the Manitoba prairie go along with her.

More than two decades later Morag discovers that Christie was right. Manawaka is part of her even though she has tried to believe that all of Christie's stories about her famous Scots ancestor Piper Gunn represented her true heritage and that her real roots were in Sutherland, Scotland. After several years in a sterile marriage, she leaves her husband and lives with Jules Tonnerre, a Métis from Manawaka with whom she had gone to school. She allows herself to become pregnant, then leaves for Vancouver to live her own life and to raise her little girl.

Morag has inherited Christie's love of words and story-telling and eventually makes enough money to live in London where she hopes to find an intellectual home. In many ways she does feel at home, but she knows she will never really belong there. From London she goes to Scotland, but when a few miles from Sutherland she realizes where her real home is--Manawaka, of course. She had tried to deny Manawaka only to discover that "the whole town was inside her head"[74] for as long as she would live.

Although she still doesn't return to Manawaka, she settles in an equally small town in Ontario.

It is her daughter, Pique Gunn Tonnerre, who goes home to the prairie, not to the town but to Galloping Mountain where her father's people are trying to re-establish themselves. There she can explore the people and the place of her parents' pasts. From her mother, Pique has heard Christie's tales of Piper Gunn and the Scot rebels. Her mother has also told her everything she knows and remembers about the Tonnerre family; and over the years Jules has visited her and sung her the songs about his grandfather's role in the 1885 Riel Rebellion and his father's determination to raise his children even though he was "king of Nothing" and drank too much. Thus Pique claims not only her Scot ancestry and her Métis forebears, but also the Manitoba prairie.

Nancy (Out Somewhere and Back Again) and Morag (The Diviners) recognize the influence of their prairie ancestors and accept--even affirm--the effects of history and land on their identities. Nevertheless, they choose to live elsewhere. Aritha Van Herk, in a 1978 novel entitled Judith, shows a character who eventually adopts the lifestyle of her parents. Judith had a secure, almost idyllic, childhood during which she felt equally comfortable working with her mother in the house or helping her father with the pigs. However, after graduating from high school she rejects the farm and goes to Edmonton where she becomes a secretary and a metropolitan in her clothes, lifestyle, and values. When her parents ask her to come home and take over the farm, she refuses. Although growing more and more discontent with her city existence, she hasn't reached the point of nausea for herself and her role.

After her parents die in a car accident, however, she buys a farm in the Wetaskiwin area. This is where the action of the story begins, and the novel covers the first fall, winter, and spring as she pours all of her energy and money into the pigs. As she gains confidence in herself as a farmer, the pressure of her father's benevolent paternalism lessens; she becomes "her own father" in the sense that her decisions are self-determined rather than dictated by what she thinks her father would want her to do. In fact, she shows signs of becoming a matriarch in the tradition of Alexandra in O Pioneers!--equally comfortable in house and barn, ready for a relationship with a male who respects and supports her enterprise and need to be self-sufficient.

After witnessing the first birthing of one of her pigs, Judith emerges from the barn, walks the slope to the house, stops, and views the scene:

> She stood still, looking around her glowing world: the white, self-effacing house, the vibrant red barn, the jewelled celebration of the snow.
>
> Carefully she walked to a smooth patch, flopped down on her back and swung her arms through the snow high above her head and down to her sides, then spread her legs and brought them together in a convulsive act of love.[75]

This rite of angel-making, patterned after a childhood response to the freshness and beauty of a new snowfall and inspired by the satisfactory delivery of the first pigs, reflects her exhilaration in farming. Her vision shows promise of becoming a reality.

This survey of prairie fiction demonstrates that there is no simple yes or no answer to Jaques' question, Will the prairie-born love the prairie as she and her pioneer generation did? Many of the writers try to show different reactions to the prairie in both the pioneer generation and subsequent generations. However, two distinct patterns emerge from the fiction. First, male writers tend to show males who accept and work harmoniously in the prairie landscape and females who feel alienated from it. On the other hand, women writers describe the positive and powerful feelings females have for the land even during bad times. Although they too have visions of prosperity and security for their families, the land offers compensations even when the crops fail.

This brings us to the second difference. In an essay entitled "Empty as Nightmare: Man and Landscape in Recent Canadian Prairie Fiction," Laurence R. Ricou notes that the wasteland image predominates in fiction of the 1950s and 1960s. The prairie is "flat," "bleak," "inscrutable and unsmiling," "dreary," "unchanging," "without point or meaning," "godless," "blighted and withered," "unyielding," "barren," and "debilitating"--to use a few of the words and phrases he finds in novels by male writers.[76] Some of these descriptions appear in women's fiction over the hundred-year period we've been looking at. Yet the characters who find the prairie, from first sight to last, an unmitigated wasteland are almost without exception minor female characters or males. Words like "rolling," "level," "vast," "solitary" and "wild" frequently are used objectively. The words women have used to describe the prairie include "beautiful," "flushed," "spacious," "fruitful," "rich," "untouched," "young," or "covered with wondrous growth."

Thus when we turn to the most widely read stories ever written about the prairies, we should not be surprised to find what I believe to be archetypal male and female responses to the prairie landscape. Remember Dorothy and Uncle Henry and Aunt Em who lived on the Kansas prairies? Most of us have probably forgotten the description on the opening pages of The Wizard of Oz as Dorothy stands in the doorway of the farmhouse and looks around:

> She could see nothing but the great gray prairie on every side. Not a tree nor a house broke the broad sweep of flat country that reached to the edge of the sky in all directions. The sun had baked the plowed land into a gray mass.... Even the grass was not green, for the sun had burned the tops of the long blades until they were the same gray color.... Once the house had been painted, but the sun blistered the paint and the rains washed it away, and now the house was as dull and gray as everything else.

Then we are shown the effects of the prairie on Aunt Em and Uncle Henry: "When Aunt Em came there to live she was a young, pretty wife. The sun and wind had changed her, too. They had taken the sparkle from her eyes and left them a sober gray.... Uncle Henry never laughed. He worked hard from morning till night and did not know what joy was. He was gray also."[77]

Now consider Laura Ingalls Wilder's description in Little House on the Prairie: "Kansas was an endless flat land covered with tall grass blowing in the wind. Day after day they traveled in Kansas, and saw nothing but the rippling grass and the enormous sky. In a perfect circle the sky curved down to the level land, and the wagon was in the circle's exact middle." Later on in the story, after the Ingalls have settled on their homestead, Laura points out that she liked "the High Prairie best. The prairie was so wide and sweet and clean."[78] Readers of Wilder's series will agree that Laura's prairie remained green, metaphorically speaking, into her adult years. She needed no Oz to escape to. Wilder and innumerable other women writers in this study have been conscientious and, to a remarkable degree, objective in recording their experiences and observations of the people around them on the prairie. By letting these writers speak for themselves we can respond in part to Edna Jaques' question--yes, the prairie-born females love those dear brown fields, call them home, and, through their stories, sing.

--C.F.

References

1. Edna Jaques, Prairie Born, Prairie Bred: Poetic Reflections of a Pioneer (Saskatoon, Sask.: Western Producer Prairie Books, 1979), p. 84.

2. Glenda Riley, "Women in the West," Journal of American Culture 3 (Summer 1980), p. 311.

3. Ibid., p. 312.

4. Ibid., pp. 313-314.

5. Russel B. Nye, "History and Literature: Branches of the Same Tree," in Essays on History and Literature (Columbus: Ohio State University Press, 1966), pp. 145-146.

6. Mary Hartwell Catherwood, "The Monument of the First Mrs. Smith. A True Story of Today by 'Lewtrahl.'" Weekly Dispatch (Kokomo, Indiana), 7 November 1978, n.p.

7. Ibid., n.p.

8. Catherwood, "The Career of a Prairie Farmer," Lippincott's Magazine 25 (June 1880), pp. 706-707.

9. Ibid., p. 707.

10. Ibid., p. 709.

11. Ibid., p. 710.

12. Ibid., p. 713.

13. See A Son of the Middle Border in which Garland describes his father's vision: "He began to look away to the west as a fairer field for conquest.... Beneath the sunset lay the enchanted land of opportunity." Garland felt that his mother did not share this vision and simply made the best of things: "I began to understand that my mother had trod a ... slavish round with never a full day of leisure, with scarcely an hour of escape." (1917; reprint ed. New York: Macmillan, 1961), pp. 153, 365-366. Garland's attitude is the same as Catherwood's in this work.

14. Hamlin Garland, "A Prairie Heroine," Arena 1 (July 1891), p. 223.

15. Ibid., p. 227.

16. Ibid., p. 238.

17. Ibid., p. 229.

18. Eleanor Gates, The Plow-Woman (New York: Grossett & Dunlap, 1906), p. 300.

19. Ibid.

20. Josephine Donovan, Black Soil (Boston: Stratford, 1930), p. 2.

21. Ibid., p. 32.

22. Ibid., pp. 32-33.

23. Ibid., p. 319.

24. George Woodcock, The Canadians (Cambridge: Harvard University Press, 1979), p. 181.

25. Willa Cather, O Pioneers! (Boston: Houghton Mifflin, 1913), p. 30.

26. Willa Cather, My Ántonia (Boston: Houghton Mifflin, 1917), pp. 89-90.

27. Cather, O Pioneers!, p. 65.

28. Cather, My Ántonia, pp. 7-8.

29. Ibid., p. 320.

30. Ibid., p. 343.

31. Ibid., p. 353.

32. Gabrielle Roy, "Garden in the Wind," in Garden in the Wind, trans. Alan Brown (Toronto: McClelland & Stewart, 1977), p. 125.

33. Ibid., pp. 142-143.

34. Ibid., p. 141.

35. Ibid., p. 146.

36. According to Peter E. Rider, Wild Geese was co-authored by Ostenso and Douglas Durkin. See Rider's introduction to Durkin's The Magpie (Toronto: University of Toronto Press, 1974).

37. Martha Ostenso, Wild Geese (Toronto: McClelland & Stewart, 1961), p. 19.

38. Ibid., p. 119.

39. Ibid., p. 50.

40. Ibid., p. 143.

41. Ibid., p. 27.

42. Ibid., p. 53.

43. Ole Rölvaag, Giants in the Earth (New York: Harper & Row, 1965), p. 5.

44. Ibid., p. 107.

45. Ibid., p. 29.

46. Ibid., Peder Victorious (New York: Harper, 1929), p. 20.

47. Frederick Philip Grove, Fruits of the Earth (Toronto: McClelland & Stewart, 1965), p. 22.

48. Ibid., p. 20.

49. Ibid., p. 45.

50. Ibid., p. 48.

51. Ibid., p. 264.

52. Ibid., p. 231.

53. Ibid., p. 227.

54. Mary Frances Engels, "Bankrupt Dreams: The Isolated and the Insulated in Selected Works of Canadian and American Prairie Literature," Ph.D. dissertation, Kent State University, 1978, p. 75.

55. Nell W. Parsons, *Upon a Sagebrush Harp* (Saskatoon, Sask.: Western Producer Prairie Books, 1969), p. 128.

56. Ibid., p. 141.

57. Ibid., pp. 143-144.

58. Lois Phillips Hudson, *Reapers of the Dust: A Prairie Chronicle* (Boston: Little, Brown, 1957), p. 11.

59. Ibid.

60. Meridel LeSueur, "Corn Village," in *Corn Village* (Sauk City, Wisc.: Stanton & Lee, 1970), p. 15.

61. Ibid., p. 28.

62. Ibid., p. 18.

63. Ibid., p. 29.

64. Nancy Stockwell, *Out Somewhere and Back Again: The Kansas Stories* (Washington, D.C.: Women in Distribution, 1978), p. 9.

65. Ibid., p. 10.

66. Ibid., p. 94.

67. Ibid., p. 97.

68. Ibid., pp. 85-86.

69. Ibid., p. 86.

70. Margaret Laurence, The Diviners (New York: Bantam, 1975), p. 162.

71. Ibid., p. 28.

72. Ibid., p. 207.

73. Ibid.

74. Ibid., p. 353.

75. Aritha Van Herk, Judith (Toronto: McClelland & Stewart-Bantam, 1979), p. 72.

76. Laurence R. Ricou, "Empty as Nightmare: Man and Landscape in Recent Canadian Prairie Fiction," Mosaic 6 no. 2 (1973), pp. 144-157.

77. L. Frank Baum, The Wizard of Oz (New York: Scholastic Book Service, 1958), pp. 1-2.

78. Laura Ingalls Wilder, Little House on the Prairie (New York: Harper & Row, 1953), pp. 13, 112.

PART II: ANNOTATIONS

Prairie Print No. 10 Swainson's Hawk

HISTORY AND BACKGROUND

These annotations cover a wide range of subjects, but the emphasis is on the environment, homesteading, and homemaking. A few items have been included because they perpetuate stereotypes or have deceptive titles.

ALLEN, DURWARD. The Life of Prairies and Plains. New York: McGraw-Hill, 1967.
This book, richly illustrated with maps, photographs and drawings, is a useful introduction to the ecology and the ecological history of the North American grasslands.

ALLEN, RICHARD, ed. A Region of the Mind. Regina: Canadian Plains Study Center, University of Saskatchewan, 1973.
This collection consists of eleven research papers concerning the western Canadian plains region. Papers on the geography, historiography and literature of the Canadian plains are especially useful in providing background material for the study of prairie women.

ARMITAGE, SUSAN. "Household Work and Childbearing on the Frontier: The Oral History Record." Sociology and Social Research 63 (April 1979): 467-474.
This study focuses attention on the gap in our historical knowledge about household work on the frontier. Based on data from interviews with twenty pioneer women from the United States, the author examines the nature of frontier women's daily housework, its economic value, and its relationship to childbearing.

BEECHING, ELSIE. "Farm Women on the Canadian Prairies." Women of the Whole World 1 (1977): 53-55.
The significance of women's work on the prairie farm is the

theme of this brief article. Using her mother's experiences as an example, the author describes farm and household chores performed by pioneer farm women. She argues that women's work contributed to the formulation of capital. Nevertheless farm women's work received little recognition or reward. The author concludes by briefly discussing activities of modern farm women.

BERCUSON, DAVID. Opening the Canadian West. Focus on Canadian History Series. Toronto: Grolier Ltd., 1980.
Designed for young readers, this book is a concise history of western Canada to 1905. The book is illustrated with maps and photographs. The appendix includes brief biographies of notable western Canadians as well as an annotated bibliography of books concerning western Canada.

BILLINGTON, RAY ALLEN. Land of Savagery Land of Promise: The European Image of the American Frontier in the Nineteenth Century. New York: W.W. Norton, 1981.
The following sections are of special relevance to prairie research: the chapter on "Pioneer Farmers: Unsung Heroes" (pp. 175-194); responses to the prairies in the section "The Prairies and the Plains" (pp. 90-95), and the treatment of women on the frontier (pp. 258-261). An extensive bibliographic note is included.

________. Westward Expansion: A History of the American Frontier. New York: Macmillan, 1949.
Especially useful in research on prairie women are the introductory chapter in which he provides a portrait of the pioneer farmer and Chapter 35, "The Farmer's Frontier 1870-1890."

BLACKBURN, JOHN H. "A Woman's Work is Never Done." In Land of Promise, pp. 169-175. Toronto: Macmillan of Canada, 1970.
One chapter in this chronicle about homestead farming in central Alberta during the early twentieth century pays tribute to the work of pioneer women on the farm. The author details chores performed by his wife on their pioneer homestead. He recognizes the amount of physical labor involved in women's work, and he is sympathetic to women's long work hours.

BRAITHWAITE, MAX. The Western Plains. The Illustrated Natural History of Canada Series. Toronto: Natural Sciences of Canada, Ltd., 1970.

Written in a readable fashion, this natural history of the western plains of Canada is richly illustrated with useful maps, photographs, and diagrams.

BROADFOOT, BARRY. The Pioneer Years 1895-1914: Memories of Settlers Who Opened the West. Toronto: Doubleday Canada Ltd. and New York: Doubleday, 1976.
This book is a collection of stories compiled from edited interviews of pioneers who lived in the west between 1895 and 1914. The author does not identify names or locations of his informants. As a result, it is not always possible to determine where a story took place, or whether the story came from a man or a woman.

CAMPBELL, MARJORIE WILKINS. "Free Land, White Women and Wheat." In The Saskatchewan. Rivers of America Series, pp. 269-288. New York: Rinehart, 1950.
Although this chapter acknowledges that white women were part of the settlement process in the Saskatchewan River country after 1870, it presents only a limited picture of women's experiences. The author depicts women as wives of farmers. She uses flower and vegetable gardening, and bread baking as illustrations of their work.

THE CORRECTIVE COLLECTIVE. Never Done: Three Centuries of Women's Work in Canada. Toronto: Canadian Women's Educational Press, 1974.
One section of this book presents a general outline of pioneer women's work on the prairies.

COSTELLO, DAVID F. The Prairie World. Minneapolis: University of Minnesota Press, 1969.
This study is a readable introduction to the ecology and ecological history of the grasslands of North America. The contents include a map, photographs, and a bibliography.

DICK, EVERETT. "Sunbonnet and Calico: The Homesteader's Consort." Nebraska History 47 (March 1966): 3-13.
This essay perpetuates the stereotype of women as reluctant emigrants. The way of life on the prairie is discussed in terms of housing (emphasizing fuel and eastern women's reluctance to use cow chips), childbirth, "grinding poverty" and the ability of some women to survive with their families by selling the garden produce. Loneliness is contrasted with views of social life (especially the dances). The portrait of the defeated woman is balanced with one of the "valorous"

woman working beside her "hardy helpmate." There's no recognition that some men were not suited to pioneering.

DUNCAN, PATRICIA D. Tallgrass Prairie: The Inland Sea. Kansas City: Lowell Press, 1978.
Approximately one hundred photographs illustrate plants, animals, birds, the people, and the buildings of the prairie. The text is organized according to seasons and provides descriptions and information about major prairie sites. It includes a map, bibliography, and prairie information sources.

EAGER, EVELYN. "Our Pioneers Say." Saskatchewan History 6 no. 1 (1953): 1-12.
Men and women pioneers reveal miscellaneous information about their lives on the Saskatchewan frontier through their responses to a questionnaire entitled "Pioneer Experiences: A General Questionnaire." Responses reveal women's view of various circumstances of pioneer life including their impressions of the journey west, the prairie landscape, life on the farm, and local Indians.

EMMONS, DAVID M. Garden in the Grasslands: Boomer Literature of the Central Great Plains. Lincoln: University of Nebraska Press, 1971.
This is a survey of the literature on the Great American Desert theory and the counter theories that insisted the central plains were not a barrier to the manifest destiny ideal.

FARAGHER, JOHN MACK. Women and Men on the Overland Trail. New York: Yale University Press, 1979.
Faragher's central problem is "the reconstruction of the relationships between men and women in marriage in the mid-nineteenth century Midwest" through the analysis of 169 narratives of emigrants on the overland trail between 1843 and the 1870's. Feminist in perspective, the study examines women's work on the farm and on the trails, social life, and character traits, with special attention to the issue of femininity. More than eighty diaries and recollections by women are identified in the bibliography.

FITE, GILBERT. The Farmer's Frontier 1865-1900. New York: Holt, Rinehart & Winston, 1966.
Chapters concerning the history of agricultural settlement on the prairie and plains frontiers of the United States provide useful background material for the study of prairie women. The final chapter depicts pioneer life for western farmers. The study includes bibliographic notes and a bibliographic essay.

FOWLER, WILLIAM W. Woman on the American Frontier: A Valuable and Authentic History of the Heroism, Adventures, Privations, Captivities, Trials, and Noble Lives and Deaths of the "Pioneer Mothers of the Republic." 1879; reprint ed. New York: Source Book Press, 1970.
The introduction acknowledges that passages have been culled from works by Mrs. Ellet, Mrs. Van Alstine, Mrs. Slocum, Mrs. McCalla, Dicey Langston, and Deborah Samson. The author notes that "A large portion of the work is, however, composed of incidents which will be new to the reader." The emphasis on the extreme situation and the lack of documentation render the book almost useless as an historical resource.

GARLAND, HAMLIN. A Son of the Middle Border, 1917 reprint ed. New York: Macmillan, 1961.
Garland traces his family's travels between 1864 and 1892 from "a little Wisconsin coulee" to Iowa (where they lived for a brief time in a village), then to the Land of the Dakotas. He continuously expresses concern for his mother and sisters, pondering the effects of frequent moves on females. His discussions about his development as a realistic writer of the middle border are of particular interest.

GRAY, DOROTHY. Women of the West. Millbrae, Calif.: Les Femmes, 1976.
An essay on "Women of the Farm Frontier" (pp. 135-145) tries to place Miriam Davis Colt's disastrous immigration experience in Kansas in its historical context, but no attempt is made to present situations showing individuals who homesteaded and succeeded. The second half of the essay focusses on Mary Elizabeth Lease and her work with farmer activists in the late 1800s.

GRAY, JAMES H. Boomtime: Peopling the Canadian Prairies. Saskatoon, Sask.: Western Producer Prairie Books, 1979.
One chapter of this pictorial history focuses on the lives of women in the rural west. The middle of the nineteenth century to World War I is the time period.

HAMPSTEN, ELIZABETH. Read This Only to Yourself: The Private Writings of Midwestern Women, 1880-1910. Bloomington: Indiana University Press, 1982.
In an effort to reveal women's experiences from their point of view, Elizabeth Hampsten critically analyzes diaries and letters to and from rural women in North Dakota between 1880 and 1910. She identifies common themes in their

writings, and she discusses the relationship between women's social classes and their styles of writing. Her discoveries include the fact that common themes in women's writings transcend regional boundaries, that women wrote about sexuality and death, and that women's friendships were important aspects of their lives.

HARGER, CHARLES MOREAU. "The Prairie Woman: Yesterday and To-Day." Outlook, 26 April 1902, pp. 1008-1012.
Harger refutes the notion of easterners, that women on the prairie are martyrs. After acknowledging that the first years of homesteading are indeed harsh, Harger points out that sod houses are soon replaced by frame houses furnished with organs and carpets. Modern prairie women are educated, cultured, and well-travelled with busy social lives. The prairie town is remarkably like the East in appearance and activities.

HARGREAVES, MARY W.M. "Homesteading and Homemaking on the Plains: A Review." Agricultural History 47 no. 2 (1973): 156-163.
Reminiscences by Lewis, Roberts, and Fairchild are placed within the context of frontier history and compared with other versions of homesteading.

HEALY, W.J. Women of Red River. Winnipeg: Women's Canadian Club, 1923; Centennial ed., Winnipeg: Peguis Publishers, 1967; reprinted with index, 1977.
Based on interviews with pioneer women from the Red River region, the author depicts life in that region from a female perspective. The account consists of recollections to 1873.

JACKEL, SUSAN, ed. A Flannel Shirt and Liberty British Emigrant Gentlewoman in the Canadian West, 1880-1914. Vancouver: University of British Columbia Press, 1982.
At the turn of the century the British Isles experienced an oversupply of unemployed middle-class women. Advertisements encouraged these women to emigrate to western Canada for both employment opportunities and marriage possibilities. This book is a collection of contemporary articles, and extracts from contemporary books which describe these opportunities and examine conditions of life for British gentlewomen in western Canada.

JACKSON, J.B. "The Westward-Moving House: Three American Houses and the People Who Lived in Them." Landscape 2 (Spring 1953): 8-21.

Part II, "Pliny's Homestead," describes the prairie homestead of Pliny Tinkham near Illium in southern Illinois during the 1850s.

JEFFREY, JULIE ROY. Frontier Women: The Trans-Mississippi West 1840-1880. New York: Hill & Wang, 1979.
Over two hundred women's journals, reminiscences, letters and interviews form the basis for this study of women on the agricultural and mining frontiers; Mormon women; and women's organizations on the "urban" frontier. An extensive bibliographic essay is included.

KEYWAN, ZONIA. "Women Who Won the West." Branching Out, Nov./Dec. 1975, pp. 17-19.
This brief history surveys the experiences of Ukrainian pioneer women in western Canada. The author emphasizes the strength and courage demonstrated by Ukrainian pioneer women as they confronted the harsh conditions of the Canadian frontier. The article includes discussions about women's work and childbirth.

KRAFT, STEPHANIE. No Castles on Main Street: American Authors and Their Homes. Chicago: Rand McNally, 1979.
Two chapters are devoted to the homes of prairie women writers--Willa Cather's and Laura Ingalls Wilder's. However, Kraft does more than describe the houses; there are details about the writer's feelings toward the prairie and the community. People and places in the fiction are equated to their real-life equivalents. There is also a chapter on Sinclair Lewis' hometown, Sauk Center, Minnesota.

LAPP, EULA. "When Ontario Girls Were Going West." Ontario History 60 (June 1968): 71-80.
Using entries from her mother's 1904 diary, the author describes preparations for marriage and relocation from Ontario to Red Deer, Alberta. The entries reflect a young woman's perceptions of the climate and weather in western Canada, as well as her perceptions of the needs of a housewife on the urban prairie. The entries also highlight the social activities of the author's mother in Dresden and Forest, Ontario.

LeSUEUR, MERIDEL. North Star Country. New York: Book Find Club, 1945.
This history focuses on Minnesota and surrounding portions of the Midwest. "Woe to My People!" analyzes the lives of

Indians; the first portion of "Thunder On, Democracy" focuses on the settlers' lives in new country with some emphasis on women's experiences.

MacEWAN, GRANT. Between the Red and the Rockies. Toronto: University of Toronto, 1951; reprint ed., Saskatoon, Sask., 1979.

This book is a readable account of the settlement of the Canadian prairies and the development of western Canadian agriculture.

________. ... and Mighty Women Too: Stories of Notable Western Canadian Women. Saskatoon, Sask.: Western Producer Prairie Books, 1975.

This book, a companion volume to Grant MacEwan's Fifty Mighty Men, is a collection of thirty-two biographical sketches of notable western Canadian women of the nineteenth and twentieth centuries. The sketches recognize accomplishments in several fields, including art, journalism, literature, politics, and medicine. Several of the sketches relate to pioneer life and western Canadian agriculture.

MACKINTOSH, W.A. and W.L.G. JOERG. Canadian Frontiers of Settlement. Toronto: Macmillan of Canada.

This series, in nine volumes, is a study of frontier settlement in western Canada. Volume titles and their dates of publication are listed below:

I. MACKINTOSH, W.A. Prairie Settlement: The Geographical Setting. 1934. II. MORTON, A.S. and CHESTER MARTIN. History of Prairie Settlement and Dominion Lands Policy, 1938. III. McARTHUR, D.A. and W.A. CARROTHERS. History of Immigration Policy and Company Colonization. n. a. IV. MACKINTOSH, W.A. Economic Problems of the Prairie Provinces, 1935. V. MURCHIE, R.W. Agricultural Progress on the Prairie Frontier, 1936. VI. DAWSON, C.A. The Settlement of the Peace River Country: A Study of a Pioneer Area, 1934. VII. ________. Group Settlement: Ethnic Communities in Western Canada, 1934. VIII. ________ and E.R. Younge. Pioneering in the Prairie Provinces: The Social Side of the Settlement Process, 1940. IX. LOWER, A.R.M. and H.A. INNIS. Settlement and the Forest and Mining Frontier, 1936.

MADSON, JOHN. Where the Sky Began: Land of the Tallgrass Prairie. Boston: Houghton Mifflin Co., 1982.

Madson surveys the ecology, and history of the tall grass

prairie in the United States, at the time of agricultural settlement in that region. Subjects discussed include prairie vegetation, soil, and weather, as well as subjects concerning the attitudes and experiences of pioneer farmers. He presents a limited view of women's experiences, when, in a brief section, he recognizes women for their roles as helpmates. The appendix includes selected references and a list of prairie preserves located in the United States.

MELLOH, ARDITH K. "Life in Early New Sweden, Iowa." The Swedish Pioneer Historical Quarterly 32 (April 1981): 124-146.
The author describes the settlement of New Sweden, Iowa (Jefferson County), by Swedish immigrants in 1849 and the years following. Of particular interest is his analysis of special problems encountered by Swedish immigrants and the kinds of adaptations they had to make to succeed in America.

MORGAN, E.C. "Pioneer Recreation and Social Life." Saskatchewan History 18 (Spring 1965): 41-54.
The author presents a survey of pioneer recreation and social life using responses from 287 Saskatchewan pioneers to a questionnaire about their social lives on the frontier. The article contains information relevant to the study of women's social activities on the prairie frontier.

MYRES, SANDRA L. Westering Women and the Frontier Experience 1800-1915. Albuquerque: University of New Mexico Press, 1982.
This book, part of the Histories of American Frontier Series, focuses on the lives of women on the U.S. frontier. The author discusses the experiences of Indian, Mexican, French, and black women, as well as the experiences of Anglo-American women. Using both primary and secondary sources, the author examines, among other topics, images of frontier women, women's views of the Indians and the frontier, women's journeys westward, female frontier homemaking and women's participation in community building on the frontier. Women's experiences on the prairies and plains are parts of this history. The author's bibliographic notes are extensive.

ODDIE, EMMIE. "Western Women in Agriculture." In Development of Agriculture on the Prairies: Proceedings of Seminar, pp. 30-34. Ed. J.H. Archer. Regina: University of Regina, 1975.
In an effort to illustrate the role of women in prairie agriculture the author presents descriptions of women's work on

the farm. Her descriptions are drawn from historical accounts of pioneer farming on the prairie, her mother's pioneer farming experiences in Saskatchewan, and her own recollections of farming during the twentieth century. The article is not an in-depth study.

PHILIP, CATHERINE. "The Fair Frail Flower of Western Womanhood." In Frontier Calgary, pp. 114-123. Eds., Anthony W. Rasporich and Henry Klassen. Calgary: University of Calgary, McClelland & Stewart West, 1975.
To depict life for pioneer women in Calgary the author juxtaposes the late nineteenth and early twentieth century images of the sheltered female against descriptions of the often harsh social, political, and economic conditions confronted by women in frontier Calgary. She describes women as reluctant pioneers who brought change to the frontier through their role as culture-bearers.

POLOWY, HANNAH. "The Role of Pioneer Women in Family Life." Ukrainian Canadian, March 1972, pp. 20-21.
This brief article outlines Ukrainian pioneer women's responsibilities within the home and their role in the preservation of Ukrainian cultural identity.

RASMUSSEN, LINDA, L. RASMUSSEN, C. SAVAGE, and A. WHEELER. A Harvest Yet to Reap: A History of Prairie Women. Toronto: The Women's Press, 1976.
White women's experiences during the early years of agricultural settlement on the Canadian prairies are the subjects of this photographic and documentary history. Contemporary photographs and excerpts from documents pertaining to women's experiences on the prairies are grouped chronologically into chapters. Each chapter is introduced by an explanatory essay. The appendix includes a collection of short biographies about notable western Canadian women and a bibliography of sources concerning women in western Canada.

REEKIE, ISABEL M. Along the Old Melita Trail. Saskatoon, Sask.: Modern Press, 1965.
This is a history of settlement along the Melita Trail in southwestern Manitoba. The author uses information gleaned from interviews with Melita pioneers and their descendents to depict late nineteenth- and twentieth-century pioneer life in this area. In chapters such as "Homes are Built Along the Trail," "Home Life Along the Old Melita Trail," and "Community Life," the author presents information concerning life in rural Manitoba.

REITER, JOAN SWALLOW. The Women. Alexandria, Va.: Time-Life Books, 1978.
Brief discussions of several prairie women include Agnes Freeman and Mary Luella Nesmith White of Nebraska; Cary Nation, Estella Reel, Susanna Salter of Kansas; and Anna Webber of Kansas and Nebraska.

RICHARDS, HOWARD K. "The Prairie Region." In Canada: A Geographical Interpretation, pp. 396-437. Ed. John Warkentin. Toronto: Methuen, 1968.
This chapter contains an overview of the physical environment of the western Canadian plains and an outline of settlement patterns in that region.

RILEY, GLENDA. Frontierswomen: The Iowa Experience. Ames: Iowa State University Press, 1981.
The first two chapters analyze the pioneer experience: reasons for emigrating, responses to the new land, establishing the home, and varieties of work roles. Other chapters examine European immigrants, black settlers, women's lives during the Civil War, and women's educational and political activities. It includes a bibliographic essay.

_______. "Women in the West." Journal of American Culture 3 (Summer 1980): 311-329.
Riley challenges stereotypes of frontierswomen's experiences, and she calls for "serious research" in the area of frontierswomen's studies. Using source materials which allow women to "speak for themselves," Riley questions, among others, stereotypes of frontierswomen as reluctant pioneers and culture bearers.

ROBERTSON, HEATHER. Salt of the Earth. Toronto: James Lorimer & Co., 1974.
The author uses contemporary photographs and excerpts from autobiographical accounts to document the experiences of the late nineteenth- and early twentieth-century rural settlers in western Canada.

ROSS, NANCY WILSON. Westward the Women. New York: Alfred A. Knopf, 1945.
The overland trip and the far western experience are emphasized. It is intended for general reading audiences, hence the materials are not footnoted.

ROWLES, EDITH. "Bannock, Beans and Bacon: An Investigation of Pioneer Diet." Saskatchewan History (Winter 1952): 1-15.

Pioneer diet is discussed using information contributed by over two hundred Saskatchewan pioneers who set up housekeeping between 1880 and the early decades of the twentieth century. Information concerning the preparation, storage, and merchandising of food is relevant to the study of women's work on the frontier prairie.

SAUER, CARL O. "Homestead and Community on the Middle Border." Landscape 20 (Winter 1976): pp. 44-47.
This reprint of a 1962 Landscape article surveys the following aspects of midwestern life: the Indian legacy, the first wave of settlers, the migration from the north in the 1830s, the distinguishing characteristics of the prairie homestead, community developments.

SCHLISSEL, LILLIAN. "Diaries of Frontier Women: On Learning to Read the Obscured Patterns." In Women's Places: Female Identity and Vocation in American History, pp. 53-66. Ed. Mary Kelley. Boston: G.K. Hall, 1979.
The author demonstrates ways to use diaries and journals to find information about frontier women's lives. She does this by identifying patterns evident in the diaries and journals of women who followed the Overland Trail between 1840 and 1870. The patterns she identifies pertain to generational conflicts along the trail, instabilities of family life during the journey, and the effects of women's responsibilities on their overall response to pioneer life on the trail.

________. Women's Diaries of the Westward Journey. New York: Schocken Books, 1982.
Using diaries and letters from women travelling west between 1841 and 1867, the author examines the experiences of white women on the Overland Trail from a female perspective.

SHANKS, WILLIAM F.G. "The Great American Desert." Lippincott's Magazine 49 (May 1892): 735-742.
Shanks summarizes some of the widely published notions by explorers and visitors to the prairie who misrepresented the prairie as desert. He argues that what was once a "prairie wilderness" has become populated by an "enterprising race" which has conquered the "savages" and "subdued and overcome" nature. He then provides population statistics and discusses significant developments in numerous prairie cities.

SIGFORD, ANN E. Tall Grass and Trouble: A Story of Environmental Action. Minneapolis: Dillon Press, 1978.

This work introduces young people to the prairie, providing information on plant, animal, bird, insect and reptile life; the Indians and the first white settlers. One chapter tells how to make a prairie.

SILVERMAN, ELIANE. "In Their Own Words: Mothers and Daughters on the Alberta Frontier." Frontiers 2 no. 2 (1977): 37-44.
The author uses interviews from 130 women who came to Alberta between 1890 and 1929 to explore the relationships between mothers and daughters on the Alberta Frontier. Excerpts drawn from the interviews illustrate daughters' perceptions of their mothers.

SILVERMAN, ELIANE LESLAU. "Preliminaries to a Study of Women in Alberta, 1890-1929." Canadian Oral History Association Journal 3 no. 1 (1978): 22-26.
Based on interviews of 130 women, Eliane Silverman identifies patterns present in the lives of women in the late nineteenth and early twentieth centuries in Alberta. These patterns pertain to the effects of class distinctions on frontier women's lives, the existence of a women's culture on the frontier and the identification of significant events in frontier women's lives. The author's findings, though preliminary, suggest new ways of looking at women's frontier history.

SMALLEY, E.V. "The Isolation of Life on Prairie Farms." Atlantic 72 (September 1893): 378-382.
Smalley argues that isolation could be reduced considerably if prairie settlers would abandon their isolated farmhouses, draw together in villages, and work the land in a manner established by Russian peasants and imitated by the Mennonites in the Red River Settlement.

SMITH, MARGOT and CAROL PASTERNAK, eds. Pioneer Women of Western Canada. Toronto: Ontario Institute for Studies in Education, 1978.
Newspaper articles, extracts from books, memoirs, and photographs are the sources used in this book to illustrate the wide range of activities pursued by women in western Canada. Sources pertaining to women's accomplishments in the fields of agriculture, law, politics, medicine, literature, and social work are included as well as a handful of sources pertaining to conditions of life for pioneer women. Much of the book focuses on the activities of Alberta women between 1900 and 1940. The appendix includes a bibliography of materials about women in western Canada.

SMITH, ROBERTA ANDERSON. "The Dalander Colony at Swede Point, Iowa." *Swedish Pioneer History Quarterly* 30 no. 3 (1979): 162-171.
This is an account of Anna Dalander's trip from Sweden in 1846 which traces the route taken, and the decision to settle Swede Point (present-day Madrid) rather than join acquaintances at New Sweden on the Skunk River.

SOCHEN, JUNE. "Frontier Women: A Model for All Women?" *South Dakota History* 7 no. 1 (1976): 36-56.
Sochen notes that frontier women "offer us diverse examples of women as adapters and women as resisters to the dominant cultural patterns for women." Nevertheless her analysis of women's experiences affirms stereotypes of frontier women. She depicts frontier women as reluctant pioneers, culture bearers, and helpmates.

SPRAGUE, WILLIAM FORREST. *Women and the West: A Short Social History.* Boston: Christopher Publishing House, 1940.
Chapter II, "Hardships of Women on the Timber-Prairie Frontier," analyzes "The Journey Westward," "Their Tasks and Dangers on the Farms," "The Ravages of Disease."

STANSELL, CHRISTINE. "Women on the Great Plains 1865-1890." *Women's Studies* 4 (1976): 87-98.
Stansell notes that "in many frontier regions, women failed to reinstitute their own sphere. Without a cultural base of their own, they disappeared behind the masculine preoccupations and social structure which dominated the West. Despite their numbers, women were often invisible, not only in the first two decades of family settlement but in successive phases as well." The essay sketches "some ways of understanding how the fact of this masculine imperium affected women's experiences in the great trans-Mississippi migrations."

STOELTJE, BEVERLY. "'A Helpmate for Man Indeed': The Image of the Frontier Woman." *Journal of American Folklore* 88 (January-March 1975): 25-41.
The author analyzes three images of frontier women: refined ladies, helpmates, and bad women. She argues the helpmate image emerged as the dominant symbolic image for frontier women because it proved the most adaptable to the demands of the frontier.

STRATTON, JOANNE. *Pioneer Women: Voices from the Kansas Frontier.* New York: Simon & Schuster, 1981.

Eight hundred pioneer reminiscences form the basis of this study of Kansas women: the pioneer journey, settling the farm, working, relationships with Indians, social life, childhood, schools and teachers, church, and town. Other chapters discuss a British community, the war, and the temperance and suffrage movements.

TAGGART, KATHLEEN M. "The First Shelters of Early Pioneers." Saskatchewan History 11 no. 3 (1958): 81-93.
Based on responses to a questionnaire concerning the first or temporary homes of Saskatchewan pioneers, this article presents information about the design, construction, and cost of various styles of pioneer homes built between 1876 and 1916.

THOMSON, GLADYS SCOTT. A Pioneer Family: The Birkbecks in Illinois 1818-1827. London: Jonathan Cape, 1953.
The letters of Morris Birkbeck and his daughters describe the activities and goals of an upper middleclass Quaker family from Surrey, England, as they establish a utopian colony forty-five miles from Shawneetown, Illinois. Elizabeth and Prudence Birkbeck cheerfully record their early impressions of the growing community, of their acquaintances and relationships, of the social life that they value so highly. As the years pass, Birkbeck's enthusiasm is tempered by difficulties with his son and with other members of the community.

TURNER, ALLAN R. "Pioneer Farming Experiences." Saskatchewan History 8 no. 2 (1955): 41-55.
This article is a collection of responses from late nineteenth- and early twentieth-century pioneers to a questionnaire concerning pioneer farming in Saskatchewan. It includes miscellaneous information about pioneer farming which is useful for an understanding of everyday life in rural western Canada.

WARKENTIN, JOHN. "Time and Place in the Western Interior." Arts Canada, Early Autumn 1972, pp. 20-38.
This study examines changes in the cultural landscape of the western interior of Canada using illustrations from the architecture and land surveys of agricultural settlement within that region. It explains the design and function of various types of land surveys and of various architectural styles for homes, churches, and farm buildings. The study is amply illustrated with photographs.

WOMEN'S WRITINGS (NON-FICTION)

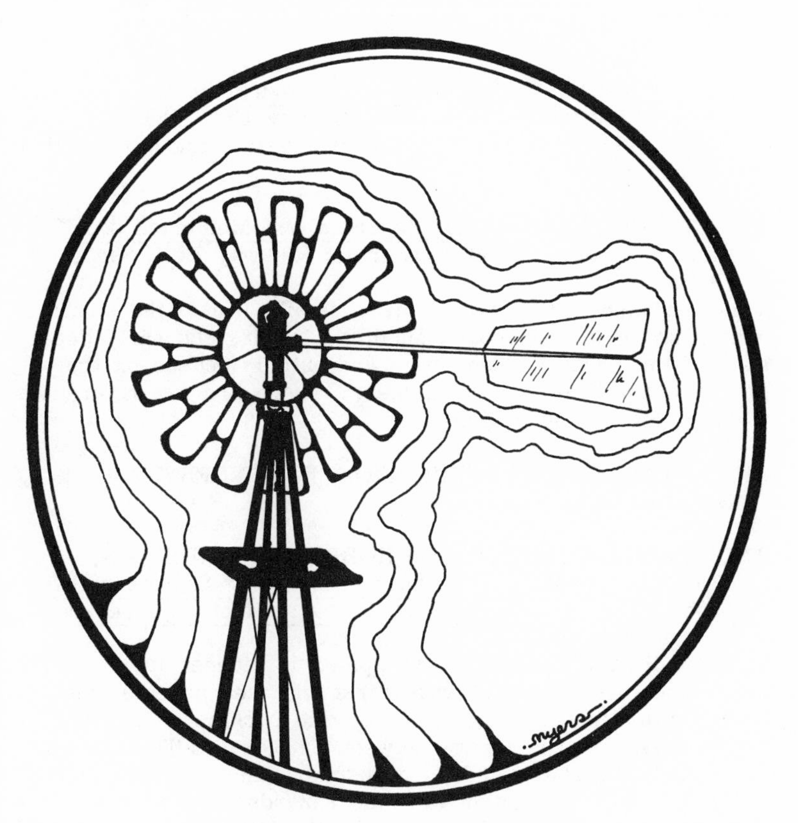

Prairie Print No. 11 Windmill

Canada

These annotations are a representative sample of women's writings about everyday life in rural western Canada. The books and articles annotated below are primarily biographies and autobiographies of late 19th- and early 20th-century farm women on the Canadian grasslands. Also included are women's observations of rural living conditions and of employment opportunities in the Canadian west. Sources not relevant to farm women but with titles which may suggest otherwise are also annotated to assist researchers.

ADAMS, HARRIET. A Woman's Journeyings in the New Northwest. Cleveland, Ohio: B-P Printing Co., 1892.
The northwestern United States is the setting for most of this travel memoir.

ALLAN, IRIS. Mother and Her Family: Memories of a Railway Town. Cobalt, Ontario: Highway Book Shop, 1977.
This reminiscence is a portrait of family life in the small prairie town of Transcona, Manitoba, during the early decades of the twentieth century. The author focuses on the domestic activities of her mother. There are few references to farm life on the prairie.

ANDERSON, BARBARA (HUNTER). See ANDERSON, GEORGE W.

ANDERSON, GEORGE W. and ROBERT N. ANDERSON, eds. Two White Oxen: A Perspective of Early Saskatoon 1874-1905, From the Memoirs of Barbara (Hunter) Anderson. Saskatoon, Sask.: G.W. Anderson, 1974.
Barbara Hunter Anderson participated in pioneer farm life near Saskatoon, Saskatchewan, first with her parents and, later, with her husband. Much of this book is an account of her farming experiences between 1883 and 1905. Among other topics Barbara Anderson describes her family's journey from Ontario to Saskatchewan, the hazards of prairie weather and prairie fires, family chores on the farm, encounters with local Indians, social activities of the surrounding community, and local reactions to the Rebellion of 1885.

BACKSTROM, ELVIRA. "Pioneer Parents." Alberta Historical Review 9 (Autumn 1964): 14-21.
Turn-of-the-century pioneer life in the largely Swedish community of Wetaskiwin, Alberta, is the subject of this article. The author combines her own recollections of growing up on a homestead with recollections from other Wetaskiwin residents to depict the pioneer experiences of her parents, family, and the Wetaskiwin community. This article includes topics concerning women's activities.

BAILEY, MRS. A.W. "Recollections and Reminiscences: The Year We Moved." Saskatchewan History 20 (Winter 1967): 19-31.
The mixed grass prairie south of Regina is the setting for this reminiscence of the drought-stricken 1930's. Mrs. Bailey vividly describes the destruction caused by the drought and duststorms. Unable to remain on their farm the Baileys move to a parkland region two hundred miles north of Regina. Mrs. Bailey recalls her feelings about the decision to move, particularly her reluctance to leave family, friends, and the rolling prairie landscape. She also recalls her first impressions of their new home, especially her negative response to an unfamiliar environment.

BAILEY, MARY C. "Reminiscences of a Pioneer." Alberta Historical Review 15 (Autumn 1967): 17-25.
This reminiscence is both the story of the early history of Leslieville, Alberta, between 1904 and 1911, and an account of the author's pioneer experiences in that region. Mrs. Bailey recalls community efforts to build Leslieville, especially the construction of a church and a school. She notes the active participation of women in community affairs and she remembers their ability to adapt to the hardships of pioneer life.

BANNERT, SYLVIA. Rut Hog or Die. n.p.: The Orris Press, 1974.
Sylvia Bannert tells the story of her life, including her experiences as a child and young adult near Truax, Saskatchewan, during the first half of the twentieth century. As a young girl the author worked as a home-help on local farms. Following their marriage, the author and her husband operated a grain farm near Truax. This autobiography reflects the hardships of pioneer life in modern times.

BINNIE-CLARK, GEORGINA. "Are Educated Women Wanted in Canada." Imperial Colonist, 8 (Feb/April 1910): 22-55.
This three-part article discusses various types of employment

opportunities for British women in Canada. She includes a brief description of daily chores for home-helps on western Canadian farms. It also mentions field chores for women on western Canadian farms. Other parts of the article describe employment opportunities for women as stenographers, nurses, shop-keepers, dressmakers, milliners and school teachers.

_______. "Land and the Woman in Canada." United Empire (1913): 497-508.
Georgina Binnie-Clark presented this paper before the Royal Colonial Institute on April 8, 1913. Her paper argues for equal property rights for women farmers, explains how women can achieve economic independence through farming, and offers advice to potential women farmers. The conclusion of this paper includes a summary of responses to the paper, by male members of the Institute.

_______. A Summer on the Canadian Prairie. London: Edward Arnold, 1910.
Sent by her father to the Qu'Appelle Valley, Saskatchewan, to report on the progress of her brother's homestead, Georgina Binnie-Clark records her first impressions of the prairie, the immigrant experience, and life on a homestead. Among other topics, she notes attributes necessary for successful adaptation to life on the prairie, and the work, attitudes, and responsibilities of women on prairie homesteads.

_______. Wheat and Woman. London: William Heinemann, 1914 and Toronto: Bell & Cockburn. 1914; reprint ed., Toronto: University of Toronto Press, 1979.
Wheat and Woman is Georgina Binnie-Clark's account of her first three years operating a wheat farm in the Qu'Appelle Valley, Saskatchewan, 1905 to 1908. In an effort to assist potential women farmers, the author explains the lessons she learned during her first years farming, and she argues for equal property rights for women.

_______. "Women's Chances in the West." Imperial Colonist 7 (March 1909): 39-40.
The object of this brief article is to describe employment opportunities for British women in western Canada. The author explains personal qualities important to successful adaptation to work in the West. One brief paragraph deals specifically with women's work on the land.

CALLIHOO, VICTORIA. "Early Life in Lac Ste. Anne and St.

Albert in the Eighteen Seventies." Alberta Historical Review 1 (Autumn 1952): 21-26.
The author, of Métis extraction, describes life in the parkland region near St. Albert, Alberta, during the 1870s. Among other topics the author describes the construction of her family's home, family chores, agricultural practices, and community events.

CANADIAN PACIFIC RAILWAY. What Women Say of the Canadian Northwest. n.p., 1886.
This pamphlet is a collection of responses from pioneer women in western Canada to a questionnaire concerning life in western Canada. The publication presents feminine responses to questions about western Canadian climate, prices, schools, and servants, as well as their responses to questions about whether women are personally satisfied with their lives in western Canada. The respondents also offer advice to newcomers.

CANTLON, MRS. F.M. "Breaking the Prairie Sod." Alberta Historical Review 15 (Summer 1965): 22-24.
Mrs. Cantlon remembers the summer in 1917 when she accompanied her husband to a breaking site on a farm near Chinook, Alberta. Among other topics, she remembers the bleakness of the prairie landscape, the thrill of seeing prairie sod broken for the first time, the difficulties of storing food, and encounters with two single brothers living on the prairie.

CASWELL, MARYANNE. Pioneer Girl. Toronto: McGraw-Hill Co. of Canada Ltd., 1964.
In a series of letters written to her grandmother, fourteen-year-old Maryanne Caswell provides a contemporary account of her family's journey from Ontario to Saskatoon, Saskatchewan, in 1887. She also writes of their initial efforts to establish a homestead in that region. The letters reveal family chores, children's pastimes and family reactions to pioneer life in western Canada.

CHAPUT, DONALD. "The 'Misses Nolin' of Red River." Beaver, Winter 1975, pp. 14-17.
Part of this biographical article discusses the activities of Marguerite and Angelique Nolin, founders of the first girl's school in western Canada. There are no references to farm life on the prairie.

COVEY, ELIZABETH. Comrades Two by Elizabeth Freemantle (pseud.). Toronto: Musson, n.d.

Using a diary format, Elizabeth Covey, an English emigrant to the Qu'Appelle Valley in Saskatchewan, explores her feeling about pioneer life and about her impending marriage. Most of this early twentieth century narrative discusses the author's personal relationships.

CRAN, MARION. A Woman in Canada. Toronto: Musson Book Co., 1910.
At the request of the British government, Marion Cran toured Canada during the early 1900s to investigate opportunities for British women. Three chapters report exclusively on opportunities for employment and living conditions on the Canadian prairies. The book includes discussions about farm life and childbirth practices in remote areas of western Canada.

DAVIS, MRS. MAY. "A Pinafore Pioneer." Chatelaine, August 1955, pp. 34-46.
In 1882 nine-year-old May Davis and her family arrived from England to stake a homestead claim near Regina, Saskatchewan. The author recalls numerous topics related to everyday life on the homestead, and she notes the hardships endured by her greenhorn family during their first year homesteading. Unprepared for their first winter, the author's family temporarily sought shelter in Regina in 1883. Her descriptions of this period, combined with later observations of Regina, depict life in an urban prairie setting, and describe growth and change in Regina. Throughout the narrative, the author notes changes in the feelings and the attitudes of her family toward pioneer life on the prairie.

________. "A Pinafored Printer." Saskatchewan History 11 (Spring 1956): 63-69.
Through her work for the pioneer newspaper, Regina Leader, May Davis contributed to the success of her parents' Saskatchewan homestead. In this reminiscence she writes of her experiences working for a paper between 1886 and 1890. She also recalls events occurring in and around Regina during this time.

EBBERS, D.M. Land Across the Border. Sonora, Calif.: The Mother Lode Press, 1978.
This book is a history of the author's family, beginning with her family's decision to homestead near Holbein, Saskatchewan, in the late nineteenth century, and ending with her parent's death in 1937. The author's recollections about her mother's experiences provide general information about homestead life for pioneer women.

ELIOT, ELINOR MARSDEN. My Canada. London: Hodder & Stoughton, 1915.
In search of a job as a working companion on a western Canadian farm, Elinor Marsden Eliot, a financially independent Englishwoman, experiences urban life in Winnipeg, farm life in Elba, Manitoba, and ranch life in southwestern Alberta. Using a diary format she confides her impressions of western Canadian life and work during the early twentieth century; however, much of the diary is devoted to discussions of her personal relationships.

FEILBERG, JULIE. "A Christmas Letter from Nokomis." Jorgen Dahlie, ed. Canadian Ethnic Studies 8 no. 2 (1976): 93-95.
In a brief letter to her sister in Denmark, Julie Feilberg describes her family's efforts to celebrate a traditional Christmas on the prairie. The 1913 letter from Nokomis, Saskatchewan, includes reflections upon the winter beauty of the prairie.

FINLAYSON, ISOBEL. "York Boat Journal." Beaver, September 1951, pp. 32-35; December 1951, pp. 32-37.
In 1840 Isobel Finlayson, an English gentlewoman, traveled by boat from York Factory to the Red River Settlement where she took up residence with her husband, Chief Factor Duncan Finlayson. Extracts from Mrs. Finlayson's diary, published in two parts, describe travel conditions during her journey and her observations of the Red River Settlement.

FITZGIBBON, MARY. Trip to Manitoba. Toronto: Rose-Belford, 1880.
A Trip to Manitoba follows Mary Fitzgibbon's journey to and residence in Winnipeg, Manitoba, during the period of construction of the Canadian Pacific Railway to that city, 1877-1879. While residing in Winnipeg, the author records her impressions of the climate, society, Indians, and Icelandic immigrants; however, much of the book chronicles her journey to and from the prairie province.

GALLOWAY, MARGARET. I Lived in Paradise. Winnipeg: Bulman Bros., 1942.
The location of the author's reminiscences is a prairie town in southern Manitoba, fictitiously named Paradise by the author. Her late nineteenth- and early twentieth-century recollections depict life in a small prairie town and describe highlights of family life.

GOODHAND, HENRIETTA McINTOSH. *Footprints.* Privately printed, 1948.
In this reminiscence the author recalls her life in Ontario and Alberta between 1880 and 1941. Much of this book concerns highlights of her family life. Chapters about her life in western Canada mention Indians, pioneer education, and social and emotional adjustments to the pioneer west.

GRAYSON, ETHEL KIRK. *Unbind the Sheaves: A Prairie Memoir.* Saskatoon, Sask.: Modern Press, 1964.
In this semi-autobiographical account, the author recalls highlights of growing up in a town on the prairie. There are few references to farm life on the prairie.

HALL, MRS. CECIL. *A Lady's Life on a Farm in Manitoba.* London: W.H. Allen, 1884.
The reactions of a British gentlewoman to farm life in Manitoba during the early 1880s are highlights of this book. Mary Hall participated in both farm and household chores during a spring and summer visit to her brother's farm near Winnipeg, Manitoba. The author comments about her chores, living conditions, prairie landscape, and western Canadian customs and manners. She offers advice to potential British emigrants to rural western Canada. Part of this book also chronicles her visit to Colorado.

HARRISON, MARJORIE. *Go West--Go Wise!* New York: Longmans, Green and London: Edward Arnold, 1930.
To assess employment opportunities for British emigrants, and to report on living conditions in western Canada, Marjorie Harrison journeyed across western Canada during the late 1920s. This book is a record of her experiences and observations. Several chapters pertain to life in rural areas, including one chapter about western Canadian farm women.

HICKS, MYRTLE E.J. *The Bridges I Have Crossed.* Brandon, Man.: Myrtle Hicks, n.d.
Southwestern Manitoba is the setting for this autobiography. Born in 1898 the author tells the story of her life to 1966. Her narrative depicts life in both urban and rural settings on the prairie. It also reflects changes occurring in southwestern Manitoba during the twentieth century.

HIEMSTRA, MARY. *Gully Farm.* Toronto: McClelland & Stewart, 1961.
The Barr Colony in Saskatchewan is the setting for Mary

Heimstra's recollections of her immigrant family's frontier homestead. The author recalls the adjustments of family members to their new lives in Canada, and interesting details concerning everyday life on the pioneer prairie. Written in the form of a story, the account depicts female experiences on the prairie frontier.

HOFFER, CLARA and F.H. KAHAN. Land of Hope. Saskatoon: Modern Press, 1960.
Based on the diary of Clara Hoffer, this book portrays the homestead experiences of the Hoffer family in the Jewish community near Estevan, Saskatchewan, during the early decades of the twentieth century. Israel Hoffer, Clara's husband, is the central figure in this readable story.

HOLMES, PEGGY and JOY ROBERTS. It Could Have Been Worse: The Autobiography of a Pioneer. Toronto: Collins, 1980.
The setting for this memoir about modern pioneering is the bush country near St. Lina in northeastern Alberta.

HOPKINS, IDA SCHARF. To the Peace River Country and On. Richmond, B.C.: The Author, 1973.
Parts of this reminiscence describes the author's farming experiences in La Riviere, Manitoba, early in the twentieth century, and in the Peace River Block near Dawson Creek, B.C., during the 1930s and 1940s. The book includes descriptions of pioneer conditions and women's work on Peace River block farms.

HUGHES, LORA WOOD. No Time for Tears. Boston: Houghton Mifflin, 1946.
The prairie grasslands of eastern Kansas and the parkland region of northern Alberta are the backdrops for two chapters of this autobiography. Lora Hughes's family migrated from Missouri to eastern Kansas in 1871. The author recollects details of her family's early sod home and she explains her mother's reactions to pioneer life. The narrative also includes remarks pertaining to the author's appreciation of the prairie landscape and her observations of other prairie settlers.

The author's second grassland experience began in 1915 when she journeyed from Vancouver, British Columbia, to Grande Prairie, Alberta. Among other topics she describes transportation facilities available at that time, and the manners and social customs of pioneers living near Grande Prairie.

HUMPHREYS, RUTH. "Early Days in the Shiny House." Beaver, Summer 1977, pp. 20-28.
Based on letters and written recollections from several family members, the author reconstructs the experiences of the Humphrey family in the English pioneer community of Cannington Manor located in southeast Saskatchewan. The account depicts the setting for educated English immigrants living in this community between 1882 and 1903.

JAQUES, EDNA. Uphill All the Way. Saskatoon, Sask.: Western Producer Prairie Books, 1977.
This book is an autobiography of the life of poet and author Edna Jaques. It contains sketches about pioneer life near Moose Jaw, Saskatchewan, during the first half of the twentieth century. In chapters such as "The First Furrow," "The First Church," "The School," "Washday," and "Threshing Time," the author records her childhood memories of day-to-day life on her family's homestead as well as the people and events in the surrounding frontier community.
In the 1920s the author undertook a second homesteading experience with her husband in the bush country near Tisdale, Saskatchewan. Jaques' unfavorable reaction to this homesteading experience contrasts sharply with her positive account of homesteading as a child.

KILVERT, BARBARA. "The Pioneer Woman." Beaver, Autumn 1957, pp. 16-20.
This biographical sketch is the life story of Mary Jordens, a late nineteenth-century homesteader. As a girl, Mary Jordens migrated with her family from Quebec to the Gotham District in Saskatchewan. At sixteen she married an itinerant school teacher. After several moves, they homesteaded in the Qu'Appelle Valley. The descriptions of Mrs. Jordens' life reveal pioneer conditions of the period, and they illustrate the pioneer woman's role as wife and mother.

KOESTER, MAVIS A. "Childhood Recollections of Lundbreck." Alberta History 26 (Autumn 1978): 23-30.
Early twentieth-century recollections from the author's childhood experiences in the mining community at Lundbreck, Alberta, are the subjects of this article.

LEWTHWAITE, ELIZABETH. "Women's Work in Western Canada." Fortnightly Review, October 1901, pp. 709-719.
Following an extended visit to her brother's farm in Saskatchewan, Elizabeth Lewthwaite enthusiastically writes about her experiences and about employment opportunities and working

conditions for British emigrant women in western Canada. In advice to potential emigrants, she recommends training in domestic skills useful for household work on the frontier and identifies personal qualities important to successful adaptation to life in western Canada.

LOW, FLORENCE. Openings for British Women in Canada. London: William Stevens Ltd., n.d.
The author evaluates employment opportunities for British women in Canada around 1920, and she gives advice related to living conditions in Canada. In chapters concerning opportunities in western agriculture she gives a positive review to women's work on farms in all but the most remote areas, but she discourages single women farmers intent on large-scale farming. Other chapters pertain to employment opportunities in teaching, nursing, clerical positions and small businesses.

LOWES, ELLEN McFADDEN. "Pages from a Pioneer Diary: The Diary of Ellen McFadden Lowes 1881-1886." Part I Manitoba Pageant 22 (Autumn 1976): 21-25; Part II 22 (Winter 1977): 12-17.
Ellen McFadden Lowes participated in two homesteading adventures; first with her parents in Manitoba, and later with her husband in Saskatchewan. In this two-part reminiscence she recalls events pertaining to those 1880's homesteading experiences.

Topics considered in the first part of the reminiscence are train travel from Ontario to Manitoba, establishment of her parents' new home near Brandon, Manitoba, community activities, and homesteading ventures of her future husband.

The second part of the reminiscence briefly describes the author's courtship and eventual marriage to John Lowes. The remainder of the memoir narrates the details of the newlyweds' lengthy journey from Manitoba to their new home near York Colony in Saskatchewan.

McCLUNG, NELLIE. Clearing in the West. 1935 reprint ed., New York: Fleming H. Revell, 1936.
This is the first volume in a two-part autobiography by well-known Canadian author and social activist, Nellie McClung. She recalls childhood memories of the family farm in Grey County, Ontario, the family's decision to homestead in the west, and their journey to the new homestead near Wawanesa, Manitoba. Mrs. McClung describes pioneer life in Manitoba during the 1880s in chapters such as "The First Winter," "Social Activities," and "The Church and School." She also

recalls her experiences as a frontier school teacher in Manitoba. Throughout the narrative the author reflects an awareness of the struggles of pioneer women and their contributions to pioneer life.

_______. The Stream Runs Fast. Toronto: Thomas Allen, 1946.
This is the second volume of Nellie McClung's autobiography. She describes her married life and public career with special attention being given to her work as a social activist. As a member of the W.C.T.U. and the women's suffrage movement, Mrs. McClung was concerned with the social conditions of both rural and urban women during the latter half of the nineteenth century and the first half of the twentieth century. (See also Savage, Candace.)

MACDONALD, AGNES. "By Car and By Cow Catcher." Canada: An Historical Magazine 2 (December 1974): 41-63.
Agnes Macdonald, wife of Sir John A. Macdonald, chronicles her trip across Canada on the Canadian Pacific Railway during the latter part of the nineteenth century. The account describes official stops in the prairie cities of Winnipeg, Regina, and Calgary. There are few details concerning everyday life in the west.

McDOUGALD, MRS. JAMES. "Cypress Hills Reminiscences." Saskatchewan History 23 (Winter 1970): 27-30.
This brief history chronicles the growth and development of the Maple Creek area in southwestern Saskatchewan.

McLEOD, EVELYN SLATER. "Our Sod House." Beaver 308 no. 2 (1977): 12-15.
The author provides a detailed account of the design and construction of her family's sod home near Consort, Alberta. Reasons for the design of the home are linked to the advantages and disadvantages of the use of sod homes. She illustrates her account with a floor plan and architectural drawings.

_______. "Restless Pioneers." Beaver 307 no. 1 (1976): 34-41.
The grassland region near Consort, Alberta, is the setting for Evelyn Slater McLeod's childhood memories of living in a sod house with her family on their Alberta homestead. Her account spans a twelve-year period between 1909 and 1921. It includes descriptions of their wagon train trip from

Stettler, Alberta, to Consort, the construction of their sod house, and the gradual growth of the community of Consort. Includes discussions about children's pastimes, work roles, and the prairie environment. Mrs. McLeod's account is sympathetic to women.

MANN, JESSIE. "Pioneering in Southern Manitoba." *Manitoba Pageant* 15 (Autumn 1971): 16-21.
Southwest Manitoba is the setting for Jessie Mann's recollections of her family's late nineteenth century, bush country homestead. Most of her recollections revolve around her father, especially his work and the homes he built.

MAY, MRS. ERNEST G. "A British Bride-to-be Comes to Calgary." *Alberta History* 6 (Winter 1958): 19-24.
Mrs. Ernest G. May describes her experiences travelling from England to Calgary, Alberta, in 1888. She recalls her "tenderfoot" impressions of the prairie and of frontier Calgary. She also describes events following her marriage when she and her husband established a mixed farm and cattle ranch west of Calgary. There are few details concerning everyday life on the farm.

MAYNARD, FREDELLE BRUSER. *Raisins and Almonds.* Toronto: Doubleday Canada Ltd. and Garden City, N.Y.: Doubleday, 1972.
This book is a collection of sketches about the author's experiences as a Jewish girl growing up in prairie towns during the late 1920s and early 1930s. Birch Hills, Saskatchewan, and Winnipeg, Manitoba, are two locations for the sketches. It includes topics concerning prairie town life, and the author's family, education, and prairie neighbors. An important theme of the sketches is the effect of the land and people of the prairie on the author's experiences.

MIDDLETON, CLARA and J.E. MIDDLETON. *Green Fields Afar.* Toronto: The Ryerson Press, 1947.
After an unsuccessful attempt to homestead in North Dakota, Clara Middleton and her family moved, in 1904, to a homestead near Carstairs, Alberta. In this autobiography she recalls her impressions of the prairie and pioneer life. It includes observations about childbirth practices, women's organizations, and the social and emotional adjustment of women to pioneer life.

MITCHELL, ELIZABETH. *In Western Canada Before the War.* London: John Murray, 1915; reprint ed. (Spectra

Edition) Saskatoon, Sask.: Western Producer Prairie Books, 1981.
Based on her travels in western Canada, Elizabeth Mitchell presents observations about life in western Canada during the early twentieth century. In a chapter entitled "The Women of the West" the author examines women's roles on the rural and urban prairie frontier. Other chapters present useful information about living conditions on the prairies.

MOLYNEAUX, MARIANNE. "Early Days in Alberta." Alberta Historical Review 8 (Spring 1960): 6-14.
In this reminiscence Marianne Molyneaux traces her family's history in western Canada, describes community-building efforts in Calgary and Wetaskiwin, Alberta, and recalls her homestead and business experiences in Leduc. Mrs. Molyneaux's recollections touch upon numerous aspects of late nineteenth- and early twentieth-century pioneer life. Her narrative notes the contributions of women.

MORRIS, ELIZABETH KEITH. An Englishwoman in the Canadian West. Bristol: J.W. Arrowsmith Ltd., and London: Simpkin Marshall, 1913.
The author evaluates employment opportunities for British women in Canada, including work in the rural west as homemakers, domestics, home-helps and homesteaders. She also includes general advice about life in western Canada.

MURPHY, EMILY. Janey Canuck in the West. London and Toronto: J.M. Dent & Sons, 1917; reprint ed. (Heritage Books) McClelland & Stewart, 1975.
One of three books about Emily Murphy's travels in the Canadian west, part of this book consists of her observations about life on the prairies. Of special interest are her observations about Doukhobor women. Other books about her travels are Open Trails, London: Cassell & Co., Ltd., 1912, and Seeds of Pine, London and New York: Hodder & Stoughton, 1914.

NEVILLE, HARRIET JOHNSON. "Pioneering in the Northwest Territories." Harriet Purdy and David Gagan, eds. Canada: An Historical Magazine 2 (June 1975): 1-64.
This memoir is an account of the pioneer experiences of Harriet Johnson Neville and her family between 1882 and 1905. The Nevilles' homestead was located near Regina, Saskatchewan. Mrs. Neville recollects many interesting details concerning their move from Ontario to Saskatchewan, pioneer life on the homestead, and people and events in the

surrounding community. The narration reflects Mrs. Neville's active participation in pioneer life and her ingenuity and resourcefulness when confronted with the hardships of the frontier. The article includes an introduction by the editors, map and photographs.

PARSLOE, MURIEL JARDINE. A Parson's Daughter. London: Faber & Faber, 1935.
One chapter of this autobiography pertains to the author's experiences on a homestead near Swan Lake, Manitoba during the first half of the twentieth century. Mrs. Parsloe's account notes her active participation in farm and household chores and her positive response to the demands of farm life.

PARSONS, NELL WILSON. Upon a Sagebrush Harp. Saskatoon, Sask.: Western Producer Prairie Books, 1969.
Nell Wilson Parsons was nine years old when her parents left Iowa in 1907 to homestead near Lang, Saskatchewan. In this reminiscence the author recalls her childhood impressions of the prairie environment and pioneer life on the homestead. Some of the topics considered are the isolation of pioneer life, the vastness and beauty of the prairie landscape, types of social gatherings, farm and household chores, and children's education. In retrospect the author considers the physical and emotional adjustments of each of her parents to their pioneer life.

PETERKIN, AUDREY and MARGARET SHAW, eds. Mrs. Doctor: Reminiscences of Manitoba Doctors' Wives. Winnipeg: Prairie Publication Co., 1976.
The reminiscences describe the personal and family experiences of doctors' wives on the Manitoba prairie during the first half of the twentieth century. The reminiscences reflect the nature of health care during this period.

PETERSON, FLORA CULP. Life and She. Boston: Christopher Publishing House, 1960.
For approximately seven years, beginning in 1910 the author and her husband owned and operated a farm homestead near Patricia, Alberta, along the Red Deer River. Two brief chapters in this autobiography describe their experiences on the homestead. The book includes descriptions of living conditions, family chores and the prairie landscape.

PINIUTA, HARRY. Land of Pain; Land of Promise. Saskatoon, Sask.: Western Producer Prairie Books, 1978.

This collection of reminiscences about the experiences of Ukrainian pioneers contains translations of reminiscences by four Ukrainian pioneer women. The accounts entitled "Beginnings in Canada," "Encounters with Indians," and "Homestead Girlhood," depict many facts of Ukrainian pioneer women's lives. An introductory essay sketches the social, political and economic history of Ukrainian immigrants. The book includes a bibliography of sources about Ukrainians in Canada.

PINKHAM, MRS. W.C. "Selections from the Unpublished Recollections of Mrs. W.C. Pinkham, an Early Manitoban." Manitoba Pageant. (Part I) 19 (1), 1974: 21-23; (Part II) 19 (2): 19-22; (Part III) 20, 1975: 11-17.
This article is a three-part autobiography of the author's life in the Red River Settlement between 1849 and 1887. In parts I and II of her autobiography, the author recollects family activities, and events occurring in and around Red River during her childhood and adolescent years. Brief sections describe domestic and social activities of women in her family. In part III Mrs. Pinkham describes her marriage and the effects of the Riel Rebellion on her family and the community of Red River.

RABER, JESSIE BROWNE. Pioneering in Alberta. New York: Exposition Press, 1951.
The Browne family left England to homestead in Alberta in 1895. This reminiscence recalls Jessie Browne Raber's childhood impressions of her family's journey to Alberta, and their experiences operating a mixed farm and cattle ranch near Lacombe, Alberta. One of ten children, the author's narrative depicts her role as a daughter on a homestead. Some of the topics considered are household and farm chores, childhood amusements, Christmas celebrations, and local Indians. The narrative reflects the yearly progress and development of their homestead and the surrounding community.

RENDELL, ALICE. "Letters from a Barr Colonist." Alberta Historical Review 11 (Winter 1963): 12-27.
In a series of ten letters written to friends in England, Barr Colonist Alice Rendell chronicles the immigrant experiences of her family during the early twentieth century. In 1902 the Rendell family journeyed from Devonshire, England, to a homestead near Lloydminster, Saskatchewan. The author describes the difficulties they encountered during their journey, various modes of travel required for the trip, and early experiences on their homestead. She includes descriptions

of their new home, cultivation of crops, prairie fires, and the development of the Lloydminster community. In addition to these topics Mrs. Rendell remarks upon her feelings regarding the ownership of land, the prairie landscape, and isolation from family and friends.

REID, IDA MAY. "Good Hope Days." Alberta Historical Review 9 (Spring 1961): 22-24.
Ida May Reid reminisces about early twentieth-century days in the homestead community near Fort Saskatchewan, Alberta. She describes her work as a country school teacher and she highlights various activities of her neighbors and special events occurring in the community.

ROBERTS, SARAH ELLEN. Alberta Homestead: Chronicle of a Pioneer Family. Lathrope E. Roberts, ed. Austin: University of Texas Press, 1971.
Sarah Roberts was fifty-four years old when she and her family began homesteading on a farm east of Stettler, Alberta. In this book, based on her diary, Sarah Roberts chronicles their experiences on the farm between 1906 and 1912. Her account discusses farm life on the prairies from a female perspective, including emotional and social adjustments to life on the prairie, pioneer living conditions and farm chores. Us and the Oxen is the title of an earlier edition of this book published by Modern Press, Saskatoon, Saskatchewan, in 1968.

ROSE, HILDA. The Stump Farm: A Chronicle of Pioneering. Boston: Little, Brown, 1928.
The second part of this book chronicles the experiences of Hilda Rose and her family on a homestead near Fort Vermillion, Alberta, between July 1926 and October 1927. Based on letters written by the author, the account depicts the author's determination to make a home in an isolated frontier area during modern times.

ROWELL, GLADYS. "Memories of an English Settler." Alberta History 29 (Spring 1980): 12-19.
Despite their well-to-do origins Gladys Rowell's family emigrated to Calgary, Alberta in 1902, to make better lives for themselves. Ten years old at the time, the author recalls details of their trip to Canada including descriptions of passenger accommodations and fellow travellers. She describes the appearance of frontier Calgary, and she explains the various jobs obtained by her parents in the Calgary area. In retrospect the author briefly ponders her mother's feelings

about pioneer life, and she remembers her own difficulties adjusting to foreign customs. The reminiscence ends with the location of the family homestead in 1904.

RUTHIG, ELIZABETH. "Homestead Days in the McCord District." Saskatchewan History 7 (Winter 1954): 22-27.
Family homestead experiences are the subject of this reminiscence. In 1909 Elizabeth Ruthig and her family emigrated from Ontario to McCord, Saskatchewan. Mrs. Ruthig describes their wagon journey to McCord, construction of their sod homes and local social activities. Although she notes the pleasant side of their experiences, she also touches upon the physical and emotional strains of pioneer life.

ST. JOHN, SEWARD T. "Diary of Mrs. S.T. St. John." Saskatchewan History (Part I) 2 (May 1949): 25-28; (Part II) 2 (Autumn 1949): 25-30.
In 1902 Mrs. St. John left Omaha, Nebraska, to join her husband at their homestead near present-day Wilcox, Saskatchewan. For two years between March 1902 and March 1904, Mrs. St. John kept a diary of day-to-day occurrences on their homestead. The entries, contained in this article, indicate Mrs. St. John's active participation in farm and household chores, and the progress and development of their farm and the surrounding community.

SALVERSON, LAURA. Confessions of an Immigrant's Daughter. London: Faber & Faber, 1939; reprint ed., Toronto: University of Toronto Press, 1981.
Observations from a female perspective about the prairie, pioneer life, and the immigrant experience are parts of this autobiography. The author recalls events between 1890 and 1923 including her experiences as the daughter of Icelandic emigrants and as a child growing up in Winnipeg, Manitoba. She also recollects two unsuccessful attempts to homestead, once as a child near Selkirk, Manitoba, and, later, as an adult near Prince Albert, Saskatchewan.

SAVAGE, CANDACE. Our Nell: A Scrapbook Biography of Nellie McClung. Saskatoon, Sask.: Western Producer Prairie Books, 1979.
Nellie McClung, a well-known Canadian author and social activist, lived much of her life on the Canadian prairies. The author uses excerpts from Nellie McClung's writings, notes from contemporary observers, and her own analysis to tell the story of Nellie McClung's life.

SAXBY, JESSIE. West-Nor'-West. London: James Nisbit and Co., 1910.
The author offers her impressions and observations of Canada, following a cross-country trip in 1888. She argues for the emigration of British gentlewomen as a means of alleviating the oversupply of unemployed women in the British Isles and as a means of insuring the Imperial character of western Canada. The book presents arguments in favor of the adaptability of British women to life on a pioneer farm.

STEWART, MRS. EDITH C. "Pioneer Days in the Graytown District." Saskatchewan History 10 (Spring 1957): 71-76.
Childhood memories of early twentieth-century pioneer days near Windthorst, Saskatchewan, are the subjects of this recollection. Among the topics recalled by the author are the role of the school in the community social life, types of winter and summer entertainment, and men's and women's farm chores. The author also remembers the isolation of prairie life and its effect on women.

STRANGE, KATHLEEN. With the West in Her Eyes. New York: Dodge, 1937.
A wheat farm in the remote rural community of Fenn, Alberta, during the 1920s is the setting for this autobiography. Kathleen Strange's story covers the ten-year period during which she and her husband developed a successful farm, raised their family, and participated in the development of their local community. She describes her experiences as those of a modern pioneer.

SUMARLIDASON, LILLIAN T. "My Mother, Hallfridur." The Icelandic Canadian 38 (Winter 1979): 28-30.
This biographical sketch focuses on the activities of Mrs. Thorarinn Gudmundson, a late 19th-century Icelandic immigrant to western Canada. Of special interest in this sketch is the author's recollection of her mother's treatment of an itinerant Indian woman.

SYKES, ELLA C. A Home-Help in Canada. London: G. Bell and Sons, Ltd., 1912.
In an effort to investigate employment opportunities for immigrant women in Canada, the author worked briefly as a home-help in five western Canadian homes. In this book she recounts her first-hand experiences as a home-help, and she evaluates the overall employment opportunities and living conditions for immigrant women in western Canada. She notes qualities and training necessary for British gentlewomen to

successfully adapt to life and work in western Canada. The author's experiences took place in 1911. Her comments relate to women's experiences on farms in western Canada.

TEGELBERG, LAURIE. "Catherine Sutherland of Point Douglas--Woman of Head and Heart." Manitoba Pageant 21 no. 1 (1975): 19-24.
This biographical sketch describes the courage and stamina of one of the Selkirk Settlement's earliest female inhabitants, Catherine McPherson Sutherland. To recreate the setting for Catherine's life in Red River the author provides descriptions of women's work roles and entertainment in Red River.

WATSON, MRS. EDWARD. "Reminiscences of Mrs. Edward Watson." Saskatchewan History 5 (Spring 1952): 66-67.
In this brief reminiscence Mrs. Watson recalls her family's initial efforts to establish a homestead near Craik, Saskatchewan, in 1905. It presents details concerning Mrs. Watson's role in building the homestead.

WATT, GERTRUDE BALMER. A Woman in the West. Edmonton, Alberta: News Publishing Co., 1907.
This book is a collection of sketches from the author's newspaper column in the Edmonton Saturday News. The sketches pertain to life in Edmonton, Alberta, and western Canada in general. The sketches do not specifically describe conditions for women in the rural west.

WILKEN, LULU BEATRICE. "Homesteading in Saskatchewan." Canada West Magazine 7 (Spring 1977): 26-34.
Lulu Beatrice Wilken recalls her family's experiences on their turn-of-the-century homestead near Moose Jaw, Saskatchewan. Her childhood recollections include descriptions of pioneer chores, prairie fires and children's amusements. Wilken's recollection is sympathetic to the role of the pioneer mother.

WOYWITKA, ANNE B. "Homesteader's Woman." Alberta History 24 (Spring 1976): 20-24.
The experiences of women as wives and daughters of immigrant homesteaders is the central focus of this biographical sketch of Dominka Rosko. Dominka Rosko and her family emigrated from the Ukraine to Canada in 1900. They homesteaded in the Red River Basin. Dominka's mother actively participated in homestead life helping with field work and providing a cash income, in addition to caring for her family. Dominka followed her mother's hard-working example both at

home and, later, when she and her husband established a homestead in the Peace River region in 1917.

_______. "A Roumanian Pioneer." Alberta History 21 (Autumn 1973): 20-27.
When she was four years old Veronica Kokotailo's family emigrated from Roumania. They settled in the parkland region north of Willingdon, Alberta, in 1898. This short biography of Veronica's life explains the hard work required of Veronica and her mother while their family established a homestead. In 1913 Veronica married and once again helped to establish a new homestead. The narrative reflects the dominance of male authority, despite the active role of these women in pioneer life.

WRIGHT, MYRTLE HAYES. "Mothering the Prairies." Maclean's: Canada's National Magazine, April 1, 1926, pp. 22 and 83.
This two-page biography describes highlights in the life of Mrs. Violet McNaughton, particularly her involvement in the Grain Grower's Association. The author briefly notes Mrs. McNaughton's early life on a farm homestead in Saskatchewan.

United States

The memoirs, letters, diaries, and biographies that follow are representative of female experiences on successive prairie frontiers. The "women worthies" have been excluded and attention focused on the experiences of those females whose stories have been known by only a few--family, friends, and interested readers. The places represented in the works are identified on the map on page four.

ARMSTRONG, ELSIE STRAWN. See ARMSTRONG, JAMES ELDER.

ARMSTRONG, JAMES ELDER. Life of a Woman Pioneer: As Illustrated in the Life of Elsie Strawn Armstrong 1789-1871. Chicago: J.F. Higgins, 1931.
Elsie Armstrong's grandson, using Elsie's autobiographical poems and the memories of other family members, reconstructed the life of a woman who moved from Pennsylvania to Ohio to the prairies of LaSalle County in Illinois. The last move was made after Elsie separated from her husband and had complete responsibility for eight sons under the age of twenty-one. Elsie chooses the homestead site, experiences upheavals resulting from Indian-U.S. military clashes and eventually establishes a farm which is later sold in order to invest in rental property.

BERN, ENID, ed. "They Had a Wonderful Time: The Homesteading Letters of Anna and Ethel Erickson." North Dakota History 45 no. 4 (1978): 4-31.
While visiting friends in Cannon Ball Township, Hettinger County, North Dakota, Anna Erickson (from Iowa) found a desirable claim, filed on it and, with her sister Ethel who joined her and became the first school teacher at Bentley, "proved up" during a fourteen-month period. Their letters, dated from September 1909 to July 30, 1911, describe the activities and perspectives of two young women who find homesteading exhilerating, although they eventually decide that much as they like Dakota and the people, they miss the trees, flowers, fruits, and family back in Iowa.

BLEGEN, THEODORE C., ed. "Immigrant Women and the American Frontier: Three Early 'American Letters.'"

In Norwegian American Studies and Records, vol. V Northfield, Mn.: Norwegian American Historical Association, 1930.

Blegen's introduction to the letters provides background information on the women and the treatment of frontier women in American history. Janiche Saehle, a young woman who emigrated from Norway in 1847 as a maid for an emigrant family, described her Wisconsin experiences at Koshkonong Prairie and in Madison. Henrietta Jensen emigrated in 1849 and tells about her husband's long illness as well as offering advice to other Norwegians considering emigration. Guri Endresen, four years after the 1862 Sioux Massacre, recounts the deaths of family members and neighbors, glosses over her own heroic role, acknowledges her grief and hardships, but also insists on the advantages of emigration.

BONEBRIGHT, SARAH BREWER. The Reminicences of Newcastle, Iowa, 1848: A History of Webster City, Iowa. Narrated by Sarah Brewer-Bonebright; written by Harriet Bonebright-Closz. Des Moines: Historical Department of Iowa, 1921.

This account of the 1848 trip to Iowa and subsequent settlement of what is now Webster City includes chapters on "Cabin Building-Beds," "Illumination--Cabin Conditions," "Women's Work," "Home Manufacture," "Platting of Newcastle, Improvements, Amusements," "Accidents, Births, Weddings, Deaths."

BRADFORD, MARY DAVISON. "Pioneers! O Pioneers!" Evansville, Wisc.: Antes Press, 1940. Originally published in Wisconsin Magazine of History 14 (1930-1931): 3-47, 133-181, 283-313, 354-402; 15 (1931-1932): 47-68, 182-218, 297-349, 446-494; 16 (1932-1933): 47-84.

The memoirs begin with the story of Bradford's grandparents who came to "raw prairie" near Kenosha in 1843. This portion provides useful information about the kinds of arrangements some men made before bringing wives and/or families to the new territory. A chapter on "Home Duties of a Pioneer Mother and Children" focuses on women's work and roles; "Work and Play" describes Bradford's own childhood in the 1860s. Several chapters provide detailed accounts of schools and the education system.

BREMER, FREDRIKA. The Homes of the New World: Impressions of America. Trans. Mary Howitt, 1853; reprint ed. New York: Negro Universities Press, 1968.

Bremer's travel letters include a visit to a Norwegian pastor's house in Koshkonong on "a vast billowy prairie" called Liberty Prairie, about twenty miles from Madison. Here she describes the nineteen-year-old wife of the pastor and her feelings about the prairie to which she has recently emigrated, and the kinds of adjustments she has had to make in a wilderness among "rude peasants." Bremer herself finds the Wisconsin prairie and the prairie near Galena, Illinois, a place where the soul expands and grows but, she admits, she doesn't have to live there.

BRINTON, ADA MAE BROWN. See RILEY, GLENDA.

BURLEND, REBECCA and EDWARD. A True Picture of Emigration: or Fourteen Years in the Interior of North America; Being a Full and Impartial Account of the Various Difficulties and Ultimate Success of an English Family Who Emigrated from Barwick-in-Elmet, Near Leeds, in the Year 1831. 1848; reprint ed. New York: Citadel Press, 1968.
According to the introduction, Burlend represented a peasantry-class woman who had known hard work in Yorkshire and was willing to work hard to make the new world venture successful. The purpose of her account was to inform others in England about the land, climate, problems and advantages on the American prairie. In addition, she provides a long description of the journey. She settled in Pike County, Illinois. Her son, Edward Burlend, edited the work.

CARPENTER, JULIA GAGE. "Prairie Croquet." In To All Inquiring Friends, pp. 154-170. See Hampsten entry.
Julia Gage, after attending Syracuse University, married Frank Carpenter in 1882 and homesteaded in LaMoure County, Dakota Territory. These excerpts from her diary represent approximately the first third of the entire work. Selections have also been published in the Fargo Forum (15 June 1975) under the title "Julia's Diary, Bride on a Prairie Claim."

COLT, MIRIAM, A Heroine of the Frontier: Miriam Davis Colt in Kansas, 1856. Extracts from Mrs. Colt's Diaries. Ed. with Intro. by J. Christian Bay. Cedar Rapids, Ia.: Private printing for friends of the Torch Press, 1941.
The Colts were part of the Vegetarian Settlement Company which planned to homestead near Fort Scott on the Neosha River. Colt's account describes the typical contents of a homesteader's wagon and the good spirits of a woman moving west. In Kansas they discovered the directors had not fulfilled their obligations. There was neither mill nor housing.

Many became ill; the sick had to be moved when Indians reclaimed the cabin. Although help eventually arrived to assist their return East, Mr. Colt and a son died. Mrs. Colt wrote her memoirs to supplement her income from raising chickens and sewing after she and her daughter returned to New York State.

ERICKSON, ANNA and ETHEL. See BERN, ENID.

FAIRCHILD, GRACE. See WYMAN, WALKER O.

FARNHAM, ELIZA W. Life in Prairie Land, 1846. Reprint New York: Arno Press, 1972.
Farnham lived in central Illinois (ten miles south of the village of Washington) between 1836 and 1838. During that period she travelled extensively into prairies both north and south and recorded her observations of the land and of the many kinds of people living in the area. She also collected and retold anecdotes and stories related to the earliest years of settlement.

GILLESPIE, EMILY HAWLEY. See LENSINK, ET AL.

HAMPSTEN, ELIZABETH. To All Inquiring Friends: Letters, Diaries and Essays in North Dakota. Grand Forks, N.D.: Department of English. University of North Dakota, 1979.
Letters between family members and friends, diaries, a doctor's case book, and essays submitted for a pioneer reminiscences contest provide insight into life in North Dakota in the last decades of the nineteenth century and early twentieth century. The doctor's casebook details not only the physical nature of the illnesses but also the sources of women's physical and emotional problems that most pioneer women eliminated from their letters and diaries.

HANSON, EFFIE. See WOLD, FRANCES M.

KINZIE, JULIETTE AUGUSTA. Wau-bun, the "Early Day" in the North-west. New York: Derby & Jackson, 1856.
Juliette Magill, who had attended Emma Willard School at Troy, married John Kinzie, a Yale graduate who had been appointed Indian agent at Fort Winnebago, Wisconsin; she lived there from 1830-1833. Included in her memoirs is a trip through prairie to Chicago (in which she commented on settlers and landscape) and a description of the 1812 massacre based in part on the first-hand accounts of her in-laws.

Of special interest is the description of Chicago in its first years.

KOREN, ELISABETH. See NELSON, DAVID T.

LENSINK, JUDY NOLTE, CHRISTINE M. KIRKHAM, and KAREN PAUBA WITZKE. "'My Only Confidant'--The Life and Diary of Emily Hawley Gillespie." Annals of Iowa 45 (Spring 1980): 288-312.
The article provides background on and interpretation of the diary with lengthy quotations from the diary itself covering the years 1858 to 1888. Emily began the diary at the age of nineteen. In 1862 she married and settled on the Gillespie homestead near Manchester, Iowa. She is unusually candid about family relationships (especially her feelings about her husband), her bouts with depression, her belief in woman's suffrage, her aspirations for herself and her two children.

LEVORSEN, BARBARA. "Early Years in Dakota." Norwegian-American Studies vol. 21, pp. 158-197. Northfield, MN: Norwegian American Historical Association, 1962.
Levorsen describes her experiences as a Norwegian-American child in Wells County, North Dakota. Her mother died at her birth and her grief-stricken father moved, leaving her with foster parents. She provides thoughtful descriptions of her foster mother's activities, manners, and values. She includes refreshing and unusual details that a little girl would notice and remember about prairie farm life and social events. Another chapter is published in Norwegian-American Studies vol. 22 (1965), "Our Bread and Meat," pp. 178-197. Here the emphasis is on foods, preparation, cooking, and supplies.

LEWIS, FAYE CASHATT. Nothing to Make a Shadow. Ames: Iowa State University Press, 1971.
Lewis serves as an interpreter of the homesteading experience on the basis of her early years in Tripp County, South Dakota, where her father established a claim in 1909. Her account serves as a reminder that some settlers were relatively affluent--the children were paid five cents a quart for the gooseberries they picked! She provides portraits of a variety of settlers, their origins, peculiarities, family, and social rituals. She makes the point that there was no "status quo" in a new settlement where everything was possible and class lines still unmarked. The material in the chapter

"Preacher Ladies" provides a rare glimpse of two women from "somewhere in the East" who travelled the prairies, one doing the preaching and one leading the singing.

LONG, FRANCIS A. A Prairie Doctor of the Eighties: Some Personal Recollections and Some Early Medical and Social History of a Prairie State with Two Chapters on "The Prairie Doctor's Wife" by Maggie E. Long. Norfolk, Nebr.: Nebraska Home Publishing Co., 1937.
Maggie Long described the responsibilities of a doctor's wife as "office girl and entertainer" in Madison, Nebraska, in the 1880's. She was also a business manager, bookkeeper, laundress, cleaning woman, receptionist, assistant at surgery on the kitchen table, and cook at all hours. In a small town the doctor's wife was held in "high esteem" and "much was expected of her."

LOOMIS, EMMA MORSE. See NACKMAN, MARK E.

MOORE, MELISSA GENETT. The Story of a Kansas Pioneer, Being the Autobiography of Melissa Genett Anderson. Intro. by Melvin Gillison Rigg. Mt. Vernon, Ohio: Manufacturing Printers Co., 1924.
The Moore family left Kansas in 1857 and settled on "broad prairie" five miles from LeRoy. Moore's account includes typical homesteading situations: two families (fifteen members living in one room; running out of provisions during a blizzard; the mother making children's and her own shoes from men's old boots). When the father decided their homestead was not a good one, they moved to Allen County. She married young (probably at age fifteen) and she and her husband occupied a claim that was "jumpable." Of particular interest is her account of 200 Osage Indians who lived on their farm for two years, providing the family protection. In 1869 she got a sewing machine and shared it with neighbors.

NACKMAN, MARK E. and DARRYL K. PATON, eds. "Recollections of an Illinois Woman." Western Illinois Regional Studies 1 no. 1 (1978): 27-44.
At the age of 89, Emma Morse Loomis recorded her memories, beginning with her childhood in Maine, tracing her father's new start in Jacksonville, Illinois, in 1866, and outlining major family events in Jacksonville and, later, in Pekin. The editors point out in the introduction that Emma's "picture of middle-class society in post-Civil War America .. is not a pretty one." The Western Illinois Regional

Studies editors abridged the memoirs "to concentrate on matters dealing with the region." The Morse and Loomis families were town dwellers.

NELSON, DAVID T., ed. and trans. The Diary of Elisabeth Koren 1853-1855. Northfield, MN: Norwegian-American Historical Association, 1955.
The diary provides an unusually detailed account of the Atlantic crossing in 1853 and the overland trip to Iowa. Elisabeth Koren describes her first year as a young minister's wife in Iowa, six miles southeast of what is now Decorah in Washington Prairie where her husband had responded to a call for a Norwegian Lutheran minister. As the editor notes, the diary reveals "the intelligence, interest, fortitude and clear vision with which Mrs. Koren met the problems of the frontier and made the transition from her assured station in the old country." The diary is supplemented by her letters to family in Norway. Professor Blegen, in the Preface, expresses regret that there are not more details about Rev. Koren. Feminist historians, however, will appreciate the descriptions of a woman adjusting to a new place, adapting to the homes and habits of other church members until her own house has been built, and coping with the frequent absences of her husband.

OLSSON, ANNA. A Child of the Prairie. Trans. Martha Winblad. Ed. Elizabeth Jaderborg. Lindsborg, Kansas: privately printed, 1978. (En Prärieunges Funderinger, 1917.)
Olsson's story for children covers the years 1869 to 1873 in Lindsborg, Kansas, and provides a child's perception of Swedish immigrant customs and American ways.

ORPEN, MRS. Memories of the Old Emigrant Days in Kansas, 1862-1865. Edinburgh & London: William Blackwood & Sons, 1926.
Doaty Orpen recalls the three years when she pioneered in Kansas. Unconventional female roles for both girls and women in the new territory are compared with ways "back East." Doaty thrived during this period in her life when she could live as a boy. Orpen describes the variety of people settling in Kansas, bouts with ague, attitudes toward slavery, and the adjustments that had to be made while her father was away fighting in the Civil War.

OSBORN, JENNIE STOUGHTON. Memories. Medicine Lodge, Kansas: Barber County Index, 1935.

Jennie Osborn, age eighty-seven and just learning to use a typewriter, recorded her memories, demonstrating the varieties of experiences of some young women on the prairie frontier: she taught, tried the millinery business, hauled young fruit trees to Texas. Osborn recorded life in Missouri, Kansas, Texas in the 1870's; then, after her marriage in 1879 her memories provide insights into the life of a young couple trying to establish themselves first with sheep-raising, then with wheat-farming, followed by a three-year period in town where she found life much easier.

PAUL, MATILDA PEITZKE. See RILEY, GLENDA.

PAULLIN, ELLEN PAYNE, ed. "Etta's Journal, January 2, 1874-July 25, 1875." Kansas History 3 (Autumn 1980): 201-219; (Winter 1980): 255-278.

Etta Parkerson's diary reveals the religious, moral and social values of a young woman who supports herself as her uncle's housekeeper over a two-year period preceding her marriage in Manhattan, Kansas. Her religious commitment, concern with family and social relationships, aspirations to teach, concern about her husband-to-be's spiritual state and tendency to use tobacco and alcohol, form the substance of the diary.

PETERSON, SUSAN. "From Paradise to Prairie: The Presentation Sisters in Dakota, 1880-1896." South Dakota History 10 (Summer 1980): 210-222.

The Sisters arrived in Dakota Territory in 1880 from Ireland. Their story provides insights into the similarities and differences between the adjustments made by these women and the typical pioneer woman. They too were affected by the 1880-81 blizzards and the spring floods that followed. Their work required that they move frequently during their first years until in 1886 they settled in Aberdeen and opened a school. In the early 1890s they were plagued by drought and depression, but by 1896 they were firmly established and thriving.

RAAEN, AAGOT. Grass of the Earth: Immigrant Life in the Dakota Country. Northfield, MN: Norwegian-American Historical Association, 1950.

Theodore Blegen's "Foreword" notes that the Raaen family was not "wholly typical of the Norwegian immigrants who turned the prairie sod and made garden of wilderness." Hence the value of the book lies in its analysis of experiences not always found in other memoirs. It is about a family that values intellect and creativity more than materialistic comforts and security, for one thing. While the author says in her "Introduction" that she has omitted "the most tragic scenes," she still gives readers insight into the life of a family coping with a disillusioned male (Far) who turns to alcohol, and into a female's response (Mor) who becomes a militant (and on one occasion saloon-smashing) prohibitionist on the Dakota prairies in the 1870s and 1880s.

REYNOLDS, ETTA PARKERSON. See PAULLIN, ELLEN PAYNE.

RICHARDS, MARILEE, ed. and intro. "Life Anew for Czech Immigrants: The Letters of Marie and Vavrin Strítecký, 1913-1934." South Dakota History 11 (Fall-Winter 1981): 253-304.
Beginning in 1913, the letters from South Dakota (near Colombe) cover two decades, demonstrating changing attitudes and perspectives of immigrants adapting to a new land and a different culture. They comment on American customs and political issues. They kept their correspondents informed about their crops, livestock, and prices. At first they consider returning to Czechoslovakia, but gradually their letters indicate that they consider America a better place to live.

RILEY, GLENDA, ed. "Eighty Six Years in Iowa: The Memoir of Ada Mae Brown Brinton." Annals of Iowa 45 (Winter 1981): 551-567.
Brinton's memoir describes farm and town life in the late 1890's and the first part of the twentieth century in Adair County, Iowa. Her father's and husband's farms were located on savannah, not on prairie.

________. "The Memoirs of Matilda Peitzke Paul." Palimpsest 57 no. 2 (1976): 54-62.
The memoirs, written in 1935, go back to Matilda's girlhood on a Riceville (Howard County, Iowa) homestead in 1865 when, at the age of four, she moved with her family to the farm which eventually she and her husband took over. Of special significance are her descriptions of children's and women's work.

________. "The Morse Family Letters: A New Home in Iowa, 1856-1862." Annals of Iowa 45 (Winter 1980): 212-227.
Included are five letters by Sarah Morse written between August 1858 and September 1862 in which she describes her

disillusionment with pioneer life near Genoa Bluffs, Iowa County. There are no references to the prairie, but she does provide interesting comments on adjusting to a different way of life and conditions.

ROBBINS, VESTA O. _No Coward Soul_. Ames: Iowa State University Press, 1974.
In the preface the author notes that "the names, dates, places and events connected with Susan and her family are recorded as she told them to me." Susan Wyatt was the author's grandmother. After following her husband from Virginia in 1838 to various points in Ohio, Illinois, Missouri and, finally, Iowa, Susan was deserted after she found her husband with a neighbor widow. Susan and her five children then proceeded "to make their homestead pay," thus demonstrating the independence and capabilities of a woman pioneer in the last half of the nineteenth century.

SANFORD, MOLLIE DORSEY. _Mollie: The Journal of Mollie Dorsey Sanford in Nebraska and Colorado Territories 1857-1866_. Intro. by Donald F. Danker. Lincoln: University of Nebraska Press, 1959.
This is one of the best-known journals by a prairie woman. Mollie moved with her family to Nebraska Territory in 1857, three years after it opened for settlement. Mollie's analysis of women's roles and female friendships on the frontier provides important insights into female lives at that time. Mollie helped her mother raise the younger children, served as a seamstress to a townswoman when her father needed financial assistance, taught school, and published some poetry. Her love of adventure and the prairies pervades the journal. After marriage, she and her husband travelled "the 700 miles over the great American desert" to prospect in Colorado.

SNYDER, GRACE McCANCE. See THE WESTERN WRITERS OF AMERICA.

STRITECKY, MARIE. See RICHARDS, MARILEE.

SVENDSEN, GRO. _Frontier Mother: The Letters of Gro Svendsen_. Northfield, Minn.: Norwegian-American Historical Association, 1950.
These are the letters of Gro Svendsen to her parents in Norway from Emmett County, Iowa (near Estherville), where Gro emigrated with her husband in 1862. The daughter of rural aristocracy, Gro's letters reflect the values of an

intelligent, well-informed, and conscientious daughter, wife, and mother. She discusses her concern about her children's education in a pioneer settlement as well as their health and religious training. She understood all aspects of farming and shared decisions regarding crops and machinery. She sheared sheep, wrote letters in Norwegian for her neighbors, taught school part-time, contributed to *Emigranten og Faedrelandet* (the Norwegian-language newspaper) and bore ten children between 1863 and 1878. She died at age 37 in 1878.

TILLSON, MRS. CHRISTIANA. *A Woman's Story of Pioneer Illinois.* Ed. Milo Milton Quaife. Chicago: R.R. Donnelley, 1919.
Christiana Tillson (1796-1872) married in 1822 and set out with her husband for land in Illinois forty miles north of Edwardsville. Tillson's account describes life from the perspective of an educated, affluent easterner confronted with pioneer conditions and people (including many southerners) with whom she has very little in common. Of particular interest are the roles she played as household manager in a home where there were always visitors and a variety of servants. She frequently handled the bookwork and shipments--her husband was "the post office" and ran a store. In 1824-5 they built the first brick house in Montgomery County and moved into town.

VAN CLEVE, CHARLOTTE OUISCONSIN. *"Three Score Years and Ten": Life-Long Memories of Fort Snelling, Minnesota, and Other Parts of the West.* Minneapolis: Harrison & Smith, 1888.
Van Cleve was born in Wisconsin as her parents and a military company were en route to Fort Snelling in 1819. Her childhood was spent at the Fort; these years are described in detail. After her marriage she lived in Cincinnati, on a plantation near La Grange, Missouri, and in Ann Arbor, Michigan. Because of health problems the Van Cleves joined a settlement company establishing a town (Long Prairie) in western Minnesota in 1856 where they lived for five years until her husband was commissioned as a colonel and they moved to Fort Snelling. Van Cleve noted that Juliette Kinzie's book, *Wau-bun,* was a "very pleasant and reliable account" of Fort Winnebago in its early years. (See Kinzie annotation.)

WESTERN WRITERS OF AMERICA. *The Women Who Made the West.* Garden City, NY: Doubleday, 1980.
"Three Wishes" (pp. 43-61) by Nellie Snyder Yost tells the

story of Grace McCance Snyder, a famous quilt artist who grew up on the Nebraska prairie.

WOLD, FRANCES M. "The Letters of Effie Hanson, 1917-1923: Farm Life in Troubled Times." North Dakota History 48 (Winter 1981): 20-43.
A homesteader in Wing Township, Burleigh County, North Dakota wrote letters to her friend Ethel Buck; many of the letters were saved. As the editor notes, Effie Hanson's "accounts of herself, her family, and the everyday events on a small North Dakota farm ... offer a fascinating and sobering view of that life as seen from a woman's perspective."

WYMAN, WALKER D. Frontier Woman: The Life of a Woman Homesteader on the Dakota Frontier. River Falls: University of Wisconsin-River Falls Press, 1972.
Grace Wayne Fairchild accepted a teaching position in South Dakota and left Wisconsin in 1898. There she met and married a widower, Shiloh Fairchild, and emigrated to prairie approximately ninety miles west of Pierre. Her story is typical in her early years of marriage as she worked with her husband and raised a family. However, Shy was not a responsible farmer and Grace gradually took over the homestead, eventually separating from him. By 1940 she "had put together 1440 acres of land and had enough sheep and cattle to keep [her] out of the poor house, and then some." Wyman retold the story from Grace's notes and letters.

WOMEN'S FICTION

Canada

BARCLAY, BYRNA. Summer of the Hungry Pup. Edmonton: NeWest Press, 1982.
A ninety-six-year-old Cree, Medicine Woman, decides to tell her story to Annika, the granddaughter of her Swedish immigrant friend Johanna. Thus every other chapter moves into the past, covering major events in the life of Medicine Woman and her people between 1885 and 1896, providing insight into the experiences of Indian women in Saskatchewan and Montana following the Riel Rebellion. Medicine Woman shows what it is like to be First Woman to Horse-dance-maker with responsibility for his other women, and to be endowed with healing powers and thus responsible to the group in a special way. Childbirth, starvation, deaths, homelessness, friendships, religious experiences and rituals, epidemics, politics, and cultural conflicts are presented from her informed perspective. Over the winter months, while caring for Medicine Woman ("Other-grandmother"), Annika gradually accepts the death of Johanna and eventually experiences "miyopayiwin, the unity of all things under sky" just as Johanna experienced it twenty years before with the guidance of Medicine Woman.

BEYNON, FRANCIS MARION. Aleta Dey. London: C.W. Daniel, 1919.
Aleta Dey, a young Winnipeg newspaper woman, dies from being struck by an object while speaking as a pacifist during World War I. Her story goes back to early years on a prairie farm near the Souris River; the first person narration by Aleta analyzes family relationships and experiences involving religion and education which explain both her radical politics and her love for a conservative Scotsman named McNair. The novel provides insights into the life of a young female radical fighting for women's rights and freedom of speech in the second decade of the twentieth century.

BLONDAL, PATRICIA. A Candle to Light the Sun. 1960; reprint ed. New Canadian Library, Toronto: McClelland & Stewart, 1976.
The action involves David Newman--his growing years, his family situation, his relationship with the people of the Manitoba town, his college education in Winnipeg, and his search for self during the war years. The values and beliefs of Newman are compared with his family's and his townspeoples'; thus Blondal presents a typical prairie town between 1936 and the late 1940s.

CHAPMAN, ETHEL. The Homesteaders. Toronto: Ryerson Press, [1936].
Mary Moran, like many other Canadians, went West because "its growing cities and waiting farm lands needed young men and women." However, in the few years she has been in southern Saskatchewan, drought has transformed the landscape and those who have the financial resources move to other places. When a young farmer she has met briefly goes to the "North country" to make a second start, she agrees to marry him. The remainder of the novel focuses on family and community life in the bush country, noting differences--and some similarities--from the prairie setting of the earlier part of the novel.

CORMACK, BARBARA VILLY. The House. Toronto: Ryerson, 1955.
Mary and Joe Culver watch people come and go from the neighboring farm--"the house"--during the years 1923 to 1950 near an Alberta town named Greentree. The different individuals, couples, and families represent a variety of responses to the land, farming, prairie province politics, and international affairs. However, the story does not reflect a way of life more typical of the prairie than of any other small Canadian farming town during this period.

________. Local Rag. Toronto: Ryerson Press, 1951.
The newspaper files of a "little western town--not so old, not so new--" provide a basis for surveying peoples' lives from 1906-1945 in Alberta. Special emphasis is placed on the narrator, the newspaper owner's daughter, who takes over in 1938 when her father dies. Book Two details the development of the United Farmers Association, the Provincial Wheat Pool, and the Cooperative Creamery. Books One, Three and Four reflect the patriotism of a farming community and the effects of the World Wars. There is no reference to the prairie *per se*.

HAAS, MAARA. The Street Where I Live. Toronto: McGraw-Hill Ryerson, 1976.
A precocious eleven-year-old narrator describes a year's events in Winnipeg's North End in the late 1930s: ritualistic feuds between neighbors; her druggest father boiling Japanese beetles; tenant-landlord conflicts; performances at the Shevchenko Hall against Horbaty the Hunchback's burlap paintings of the Carpathian Mountains; Christmas services in the isolated Ukrainian church on the prairie; a baseball game between the Virgin Mary Maple Leafs and the Star of David

Ukrainian-Canadians; the blizzard and the flood; the gypsy's reading of the Tarot cards; the political candidate's wife canvasing the prairie by bicycle. Against this background of Ukrainian, Jewish, Irish, and British culture (combined with American popular culture--Popeye, True Confessions, Baby Ruth candybars and "Rag Mop"), Maara Lazpoesky begins her writing career and, at the conclusion of her narration, decides she has outgrown Saturday matinees.

HAYES, CATHERINE E. [SIMPSON] (pseud. Mary Markwell). Prairie Pot-Pourri. Winnipeg: Stovel Co., Printers, 1895.
"The La-de-dah from London" takes place in Saskatchewan in the late 1870s. Richard Workman, a hard-working, knowledgeable Canadian farmer is contrasted with D.G. Periwinkle-Brown (the La-de-dah), an English painter sent over by his aunt to see "the raw soide of loife." The La-de-dah experiences several set-backs, but through the positive influences of Workman and Mollie (a "prairie nymph" whom the La-de-dah falls in love with) turns into a respectable farmer. A second story, "The Light of Other Days: A Story of Rebellion and After," brings together (in the latter half of the story) a variety of Ontario people whose fates are worked out on the prairie during the Rebellion. A third story, "How the End Came," describes the ten years of work and want endured by a Métis woman married to a white man who drinks and beats her.

KNOX, OLIVE. Red River Shadows. Toronto: Macmillan, 1948.
This is one of the few prairie novels by a woman with a male hero. The four main female characters receive minimal attention and are important only as objects of men's desire and as mothers for orphans. The novel focuses on conflicts between the Hudson's Bay Company and the independent traders, affirming the good relationships that develop between many of the white settlers--French Canadians, Swiss, Scots, Irish--and the Métis, the English halfbreeds, and the Indians. Also important is the French Canadian priest's vision of a growing, prosperous community where church and school become increasingly important to settlers during the years 1818 to 1849.

LAURENCE, MARGARET. A Bird in the House. 1970; reprint ed. Toronto: McClelland & Stewart-Bantam, 1974.
Vanessa McLeod, granddaughter of a prairie pioneer, describes her town, the townspeople, her family, and her

personal experiences and writing aspirations between the ages of ten and twenty as she grows up during the thirties in a Manitoba town north of Winnipeg.

________. The Diviners. 1974; reprint ed., New Canadian Library, Toronto: McClelland & Stewart, 1978.
Morag Gunn, novelist and mother, has to seek the home of her ancestors in Scotland before she realizes that her true home is "the god-damned prairie town" where she was raised by Christy Logan, the garbage collector. Although Morag acknowledges that she belongs to Manawaka, her hometown in Manitoba, she settles in Ontario. Her daughter, whose father is Jules Tonnerre (Morag's Métis friend in Manawaka and, later, her lover in Winnipeg), returns to the Manawaka area where she can explore the land and the people--Scots and Métis--to whom she belongs.

________. The Fire-Dwellers. 1969; reprint ed. New Canadian Library, Toronto: McClelland & Stewart, 1973.
Stacey Cameron MacAindra, living in Vancouver, comes to terms with her prairie-town origins and what she considers to be her trivial existence as the wife of a salesman and the mother of four children.

________. A Jest of God. 1966; reprint ed., Toronto: McClelland & Stewart-Bantam, 1974.
Rachel Cameron has two options: submitting to her mother's middle-class Scot-Presbyterian morality and living out her life as a "spinster school teacher" in a prairie town, or becoming "her own mother" by affirming her personal beliefs and seeking liberation. To act on the second option requires leaving her hometown and beginning anew elsewhere, but this is the option she finally chooses.

________. The Stone Angel. 1964; reprint ed. New Canadian Library, Toronto: McClelland & Stewart, 1968.
Hagar Shipley, age ninety, comes to terms with her self and her relationships while piecing together her girlhood in a Manitoba prairie town (Manawaka), her rebellious marriage, and her subsequent escape to the west coast when she can no longer tolerate her crude farmer-husband. From her father (a founder of the pioneer prairie town in the 1870s), she inherits arrogance and pride as well as inhibiting puritanism; the town inherits her father's money. At the end of her life, in an abandoned cannery, she shares communion and confession with a fellow sufferer, thus achieving a degree of reconciliation with all her lost men.

LAUT, A.C. Lords of the North. Toronto: William Briggs, 1900.
Rufus Gillespie, the main character, is on a mission to the northwest to rescue his friend's wife and child who have been captured by an Iroquois and a French adventurer. He becomes a trader enmeshed in the Hudson's Bay North-West Company conflict in 1815. The primary female character, Frances Sutherland, is the daughter of a Red River trapper. A typical romantic heroine, she functions in the novel in three ways--as the object of the hero's love, as a rescuer or messenger when the hero is in a tight spot, and as a vision of loveliness to create conflict or tension among the male characters. She is never observed doing the kinds of tasks one would expect of a trader's daughter, nor is she seen in a community with other women. Laut idealizes many of the white characters--the voyageur, the trader, the priest--and the bois-brules. However, she applies only negative stereotypes to the Indians.

LYSENKO, VERA. Westerly Wild. Toronto: Ryerson Press, 1956.
A young Winnipeg school teacher, Julie Lacoste, takes a position in rural southwestern Saskatchewan during the late 1930s and observes the effects of eight drought years on the children, the women, the farmers, as well as on the mysterious Marcus Haugen, the one man who through determination, single-mindedness, and technology has acquired considerable wealth and acreage despite the bad times.

_______. Yellow Boots. Toronto: Ryerson Press, 1954.
As late as 1929 pioneer conditions existed in a Ukrainian community in southern Manitoba. By telling the story of Lilli Landash, Lysenko reveals the hardships of growing up female in an immigrant family of peasant stock. Her mother's Old World superstitions bar Lilli from family affection. Her father sacrifices her in his fanatic accumulation of land. However, brutal work and deprivations do not damage her spirit; she emerges into womanhood as a singer with a talent for learning and singing the songs not only of her own Ukrainian forebears but of other western Canadian immigrants as well. While others, young and old alike, race toward Canadianization, Lilli values the old traditions and through her songs preserves memories of a way of life which, ultimately, the people yearn to preserve.

McCLUNG, NELLIE L. The Black Creek Stopping-House and Other Stories. Toronto: William Briggs, 1912.

This collection includes eight stories dedicated to "the Pioneer Women of the West." In three of the stories, McClung depicts independent women who function in traditional roles yet manage to be themselves rather than conform to others' expectations of what they should be and do. The novella, "The Black Creek Stopping-House," provides portraits of two types of women settlers: the workingclass woman who runs the stopping-house, and the young neighbor woman from an upperclass Toronto home who runs away to Manitoba with the man of her choice. "The Runaway Grandmother" takes a position as a housemaid for a young farmer rather than live out a useless life in her sons' homes. In "You Never Can Tell," a woman writer demonstrates that a woman can be happy and creative on an isolated ranch in Alberta. A fourth story, "The Way of the West," describes how a democratic-loving group of settlers which includes Americans, Canadians, English, and Irish, modify the behavior of an Orangeman who attempts to split the community into factions.

________. Painted Fires. Toronto: Thomas Allen, 1925. A Finnish girl, Helmi, emigrates to America in search of the garden she once saw on a postcard from her American aunt. Her quest takes her from Winnipeg, where she learns the domestic trade, and then is adopted by a single woman who helps her learn the language and customs of Canadians. However, she becomes involved in a drug scandal--innocently, of course--and goes to the girls' reformatory because she wants to protect a neighbor lady she admires. Eventually she escapes to an Alberta mining town where she meets a fine young man, marries, but is again abandoned when he goes to make a fortune at a mine and fails to return. She seeks work in Edmonton where she is taken in by a kindly boarding house owner, assisted in delivering her baby and eventually returns to rural Alberta to live on a farm inherited from an Englishman who has died in World War I. She is reunited with her husband and lives happily ever after. The evils of town and goodness of country become the dominant theme in the novel.

________. Purple Springs. Toronto: Thomas Allen, 1921. McClung's main interest in this story--the third in what could be called the life and times of Pearlie Watson--is the effect of a young woman of intelligence and moral passion on personal lives, social issues and provincial politics. Like Sewing Seeds in Danny and The Second Chance, the novel takes place in southern Manitoba. McClung's famous Mock Parliament, during which women posed as premier and legislators and patiently explained why men should not be given the vote, forms the basis for the chapter called "The Play."

_______. The Second Chance. New York: Doubleday, Page, 1910.
The Second Chance continues the saga of Pearlie Watson and her family--characters introduced in Sowing Seeds in Danny. In this novel the Watson family has a second chance to move from town and start over on a run-down homestead. A variety of minor characters also experience second chances as McClung describes the typical lives, social and religious activities of both farmers and townspeople in southern Manitoba. Temperance emerges as an important issue.

_______. Sowing Seeds in Danny. Toronto: Wm. Briggs, [1908].
Set in a small Manitoba town in the early twentieth century, the novel is more concerned with class differences than with a sense of place, although the prairie is occasionally mentioned. The main character, a youngster named Pearlie Watson, represents the honesty, faith, optimism, and commitment to family and community that makes progress inevitable in a prairie town. Her parents had emigrated from the British Isles thirteen years before and still haven't established themselves. Two characters are representative of two types of people emigrating from England: a young girl who hoped to work as a domestic in order to earn money to save her mother from the workhouse; a young man who is the fifth son of a Kent County rector.

McDOUGALL, E. JEAN. See ROLYAT, JANE.

MACMILLAN, ANN. Levko. Toronto: Longmans, Green, 1956.
In the mid-1940s Ivan, grandson of a Ukrainian immigrant, is confused about his identity because his grandfather tells him he's a Canadian, yet everyone calls the grandfather himself a Galician. The plot evolves around his development and his relationship to Levko, a boy sent from a displaced persons camp to be cared for by Ivan's family in south central Saskatchewan.

OSTENSO, MARTHA. See Fiction: U.S. (next section).
As Desmond Pacey points out in his essay on Canadian fiction 1920-1940, "Ostenso was born in Norway, grew up in Minnesota and North Dakota, and lived in Manitoba only from

1915 to 1921, when she left for permanent residence in the United States." Therefore he classifies her as American although her first novel, Wild Geese, was set in Manitoba. See Literary History of Canada, 2nd ed., Vol. 2. Ed. Carl F. Klinck (Toronto: University of Toronto Press, 1976), p. 188.

PARSONS, NELL W. The Curlew Cried: A Love Story of the Canadian Prairie. Seattle: Frank McCaffrey, 1947.
At the opening of the novel the heroine marries a dark, handsome stranger in Winnipeg rather than the fiancé from Liverpool whom she had left home to marry. This fact would suggest that Victoria Jarvis has the strength and independence essential in pioneer women. However, during her first years on the prairie she vacillates between love and responsibility for the land according to the melodramatic twists in her relationship with her husband. Nevertheless, the novel does record a woman's initiation into pioneer living between 1908 and 1911 on the Saskatchewan prairie south of Regina. The first half records the loneliness of the first pioneers; the second half records the rapid settlement and growth of the town after 1910.

________. Upon a Sagebrush Harp. Saskatoon, Sask.: Western Producer Prairie Books, 1969.
In this autobiographical novel, the narrator Nell opens the story with a description of the last lap of their journey from Iowa (where her English parents had first settled) to a homestead near Lang, Saskatchewan. She acknowledges her parents' continual struggle with finances and bad crops as well as commenting on a variety of subjects--work, fashions, social life, family evenings reading and singing, family treasures, neighbors, and prairie. Nell has to become a teacher rather than the musician or painter that she longs to be. At the end of the account, her parents are forced to move, renting land further north; her father's dream of a prosperous homestead will never be realized.

RIIS, SHARON. The True Story of Ida Johnson, 1976. Toronto: Women's Educational Press, 1977.
The narrator-waitress describes growing up during the 1950s in Longview, Alberta, and then experiencing marriage, motherhood, and disaster--the deaths of husband and children--followed by a period of wandering from job to job through western Canada. By the end of the story, we see a survivor, a woman of strength, although we still do not know which parts of her story are fact and which fiction.

ROLYAT, JANE, pseud. (E. Jean McDougall) The Lily of Fort Garry, 1930. Rpt. London & Toronto: J.M. Dent & Sons Ltd., 1933.

Farm and town life in the Red River settlement at mid-century are described. Margaret, the heroine, has been trained and educated to marry into one of the "first families" of the settlement, but she falls in love with Koominah Koush, an educated half-breed who is admired and respected by both Indians and Anglos. Margaret's father, an Irish immigrant, is a trapper and adventurer incapable of settling down; he has left his wife to manage house and fields, but at the time of the story the eldest son Don, a progressive young farmer, has taken over the farm. Indian life receives sympathetic attention; Indian-government relationships are discussed in detail.

ROY, GABRIELLE. Children of My Heart. Trans. Alan Brown. Toronto: McClelland & Stewart, 1979. (Ces enfants de ma vie, 1977.)

The young narrator, a school teacher who has come to a prairie community, "a village on the threshold of virgin land" in the 1930s, becomes absorbed into the lives of her students and their families. Her account focuses particularly on five boys who are sons of immigrants and a sixth who is half Indian. She tells about her visit to "Little Russie" where there are more Poles and Ukrainians than Russians; her visit to Andre's mother who is confined to bed before childbirth to avoid a miscarriage; and her responses to the songs of Nils' Ukrainian mother. She also describes the prairie landscape from a variety of perspectives and moods.

________. Garden in the Wind. Trans. Alan Brown. Toronto: McClelland & Stewart, 1977. (Un jardin au bout du monde, 1975.)

Two of the stories, "Hoodoo Valley" and "Garden in the Wind" provide detailed descriptions of two immigrant groups--the Doukhobors and the Ukrainians--and their reactions to the Canadian prairies. "Hoodoo Valley" deals almost entirely with the landscape and the immigrants' search for a place like the old country. "Garden in the Wind" focuses on an old woman, Marta, who had urged her husband (in their youth) to leave Poland and find a place on the prairies. The story covers Marta's last summer before her death and shows how a woman survived isolation on a farm, alienation from Ukrainian traditions, and loss of children to Canadian cities; she survived because she loved the prairie winds and, especially, the flowers in her garden.

_______. The Road Past Altamont. Trans. Joyce Marshall. Toronto: McClelland & Stewart, 1976. (La Route d'Altamont, 1966.)
Christine, the narrator of the earlier work Street of Riches (1955), again provides a perspective on women's lives on the prairie. In the first story of the collection, Christine visits her old grandmother on the prairie homestead, and absorbs her grandmother's ambivalent attitudes toward emigration and the prairie landscape. In the final story, "The Road Past Altamont," Christine and her mother try to interpret the reasons for the grandmother's alienation from land and family while at the same time revealing their own feelings about Manitoba and the excitement of new beginnings.

_______. Street of Riches. Trans. Harry Binsse. Toronto: McClelland & Stewart, 1967. (Rue Deschambault, 1955.)
This is a portrait of girlhood in St. Boniface, on the edge of Winnipeg, during the early twentieth century. Four of the stories emphasize various aspects of prairie life: in "The Gadabout" Christine and her mother return to Quebec, thus providing contrasts in landscapes and attitudes; "The Well of Dunrea" provides an outsider's view of Ruthenians and their search for the promised land as Christine's father relates his efforts to help them find suitable land; "My Aunt Theresina Veilleux" describes a woman's search for health and home; "To Earn My Living" is about Christine's first teaching position in Cardinal, Manitoba, about fifty miles from Winnipeg.

SALVERSON, LAURA G. The Dark Weaver. Toronto: Ryerson Press, 1937.
This is one of the few prairie novels that provides extensive background on the characters' personalities and lives before emigrating to Canada. Salverson focuses on four groups which represent Danish aristocracy, Danish middleclass, Russian peasant, and German professional backgrounds. These people settle near Winnipeg and are instrumental in developing all aspects of the new town. The last part of the novel emphasizes the influence of place and time on the second generation.

_______. The Viking Heart. 1947; reprint ed. New Canadian Library, Toronto: McClelland & Stewart, 1975.
Writing about the years 1876-1918, Salverson focuses first on the Icelandic community of pioneer farmers in the Gimli, Manitoba, area, then on city life in Winnipeg. Through her

portrayal of the experiences of the pioneer generation and the Canadianization process that is completed with the second generation, Salverson presents an optimistic view of emigration while at the same time describing the ordeals of the farmer and the advantages and disadvantages of life in a relatively young prairie city. Attention is given to the conflict in values that emerge between the two generations as well as to the preservation of cultural traditions and values.

SEITZ, MARY ANN. Shelterbelt. Saskatoon, Sask.: Western Producer Prairie Books, 1979.
The novel takes place in the southern part of Saskatchewan from 1938 to the late 1940s, tracing the growth of Francie Polanski, daughter of a Ukrainian immigrant and his first generation Polish wife. The events emphasize the attempt on the part of the adults to preserve their Ukrainian culture and their religious customs. Of equal importance is the analysis of a young girl's sense of increasing alienation within a farm family with eight sons and of the mother's determination to help Francie to a better life through education.

SLUMAN, NORMA. Poundmaker. Scarborough, Ont.: McGraw-Hill Ryerson, 1967.
In the process of telling the story of Poundmaker and his role in Indian-white affairs during the 1880s, Sluman provides insights into the lives of Indian and Métis women during that period.

TRUSS, JAN. Bird at the Window. Toronto: Macmillan, 1974.
This is a contemporary work about an Alberta prairie farm girl who becomes pregnant and fears that her aspirations as an intellectual and writer will never be realized. She escapes to her grandparents in England and undergoes a series of ordeals ending in a premature delivery and death of the baby. When word comes that her father is being operated on for cancer, she returns to her home near the foothills of the Rockies and comes to terms with her feelings about both parents. She is determined to stay on her father's farm and learn the art of writing.

VAN DER MARK, CHRISTINE. Honey in the Rock. Toronto: McClelland & Stewart, 1966.
Dan Root comes to teach in a remote prairie community in Alberta in 1936. There he observes the lives of a group of people devoted to the Brethren in Christ church. Two families dominate the religious and educational sectors of the

community, and the plot centers around the women of these families. The mothers were "newspaper wives" who came to Ulna hoping for a new start in life--one with an unborn child comes from northern Alberta; the other comes from Russia with her four daughters. Van Der Mark emphasizes the limited options for females growing up in remote prairie areas; moreover, she is critical of the narrow-mindedness and suspicious natures of zealously religious individuals.

_______. In Due Season. 1947; reprint ed. Vancouver: New Star Books, Ltd., 1979.
The novel focuses on a woman homesteader in the Peace River Country who has been forced to leave the southern Alberta prairie because of droughts. Lina is a frontier type who believes that hard work and good land will eventually bring prosperity. Van Der Mark provides insights into several immigrant groups--Ukrainians, Poles, and Swedes--and the Métis. Following the epigram, Van Der Mark writes that it is a story of a woman, alone, forced to work like a man; that it is about a pioneer community which grows while the spirit of the woman degenerates.

VAN HERK, ARITHA. Judith. 1978; reprint ed. Toronto: McClelland & Stewart-Bantam, 1979.
Judith Pierce, after six years as a secretary in Edmonton, buys a farm and begins raising pigs. The events cover fall to early spring of her first year on her own farm as she tries to recreate her father's way of life. The novel traces her development from an alienated, disjointed city woman to a woman who, at twenty-three, is emotionally and sexually comfortable with herself, and gradually able to integrate into the life of the community and the natural cycles of her pigs. In addition, the author emphasizes that female friendships like those that sustained so many pioneer women continue to be essential in the lives of women on the contemporary farm.

WISEMAN, ADELE. Crackpot. 1974; reprint ed. New Canadian Library, Toronto: McClelland & Stewart, 1978.
Hoda, one of the "crackpots," is the daughter of immigrant Jews from Russia living in North Winnipeg in the early twentieth century. Her father is blind; her mother is a hunchback; Hoda is obese. All three are outsiders, cut off from the Jewish community because of their physical handicaps, their poverty, their inability to understand the new ways, and their innocence. Nevertheless, Hoda good-humoredly and optimistically perseveres, easing into prostitution as a way of surviving. She eventually comes to terms with her

own particular version of the human predicament as an immigrant in a prairie city.

_______. The Sacrifice. 1956; reprint ed. Laurentian Library 8, Toronto: Macmillan of Canada, 1977.
While the novel can be read as a religious allegory, it also gives insight into the life of an immigrant Jew who settles in Winnipeg with his family, but refuses to give up Old World beliefs and customs. Consumed with what he considers to be his mission, Abraham becomes insane; his son Isaac dies in a synagogue fire. Perhaps the grandson, however, will be able to reconcile the best of Old World values with those of the new land.

ALDRICH, BESS STREETER. A Lantern in Her Hand. New York: D. Appleton, 1928.
The character Abbie Deal, based on Aldrich's mother, is eleven years old at the opening of the story in 1857. In 1865 she marries Will Deal; in 1869 the young couple heads for a homestead thirty-five miles from Nebraska City despite Abbie's reluctance to leave family and civilization. As years pass Abbie realizes that her own aspirations to paint or to write will have to be realized in her children, and the years are taken up with motherhood and the struggle against nature. In the 1880s and 1890s life becomes somewhat easier, the children become successful in numerous fields, and Abbie realizes she indeed belongs to the prairie. In fact, after her husband's accidental death, she takes complete responsibility for the farm and lives there (long after her children leave) until her death at the age of eighty. A granddaughter, Laura, becomes her spiritual heir.

________. The Rim of the Prairie. 1925; reprint ed. Lincoln: University of Nebraska Press, 1966.
The main story concerns a young woman, Nancy Moore, who returns to visit her beloved Nebraska prairie after four years as a sophisticate in Chicago. Through Nancy the cynical Warner Field comes to see and to write about the natural beauty of the prairie and to acknowledge the vision and courage of the old pioneers like Nancy's Aunt Biny ("delicate and gentle and refined") and Uncle Jud ("courageous and energetic and strong"). Aldrich weaves details from the pioneer past into the contemporary story, thus demonstrating continuities in place and character as well as marked differences.

________. Song of Years. New York: D. Appleton-Century, 1939.
A New England youth, Wayne Lockwood, establishes a claim in the unsettled Cedar River Valley in 1854. The story follows his activities over the next ten years and those of his nearest neighbor, Jeremiah Martin, his wife, two sons, and seven daughters. Based on the life of Aldrich's grandfather, the character Jeremiah takes active interest in political developments in the new country and eventually represents Black Hawk County at the State Legislature. The female characters are lively and interesting but traditional in their roles and aspirations.

________. Spring Came on Forever. New York: D. Appleton-Century, 1935.
The lives of two individuals are traced from 1866 to the 1930s: Matthias Meier and Amalia Stoltz meet, fall in love, and part immediately when Amalia is forced to emigrate from Iowa to Nebraska and to marry a man of her father's choice in the new Lutheran settlement in the new town, Nebraska City. The remainder of the novel alternates between the two families--Amalia's family on a farm and Matthias' family in the town--thus providing an account of prototypical developments on the prairie.

AYDELOTTE, DORA. Across the Prairie. New York: D. Appleton-Century, 1941.
The story takes place in a small town near the Kansas-Oklahoma border during the early 1880s. The main character, Tenny Weber, raises a son and twin daughters after her husband died of pneumonia following a Boomer excursion into Oklahoma. Tenny symbolizes the pioneer woman who finally puts down roots and resists the efforts of the men and young girls around her to pull up stakes and start anew in Oklahoma territory. Her son Buff represents the next generation of pioneers--he finds silver in Nevada--and the novel ends with his departure to Nevada with an adventure-loving bride. Another major figure in the novel is the charismatic David Payne who repeatedly led the Boomers into Oklahoma.

________. Full Harvest. New York: D. Appleton-Century, 1939.
The story takes place in Illinois at the turn of the century and explores farm and town life. However, there is very little relationship between characters and the prairie.

________. Trumpets Calling. New York: D. Appleton-Century, 1938.
Aydelotte's main male character, David Prawl, is the prototypical adventure-loving American male; he expends most of his energy on public causes while adroitly avoiding daily drudgery whether on the farm or in the town. In creating the character of the wife, Martha Prawl, Aydelotte insists that the intelligence, managerial talents, hard work and commitment to family of the woman are what make it possible for certain families to survive in pioneer situations. Martha has spent her life watching men--first her father and then her husband--uproot their families and head for new territories. After settling a homestead on the outskirts of a new Oklahoma town at the time of the 1894 landrush Martha refuses to go any

further. While Dave fights the powerful railroad's decision to locate a station on a railroad townsite, Martha establishes the homestead and a reputation as prairie angel caring for the needy.

BEERS, LORNA DOONE. Prairie Fires. New York: E.P. Dutton, 1925.
The town-country conflict, with emphasis on the parasitic nature of townspeople--especially bankers, merchants, lawyers, and grain dealers--receives careful attention as Beers traces the exploitation of the farmers and their rebellion, set-backs, and eventual success in organizing politically. Against this background we are told the story of Christine Erickson, the daughter of a successful, intelligent, ethical, far-sighted Dane who arrived in South Dakota during the last years of the nineteenth century. Christine, remembering none of the difficult pioneer years, dreams romantic encounters in exotic places where men will adore her and provide her with status and material comforts. Against her parents' wishes she marries a banker, and the final chapters detail her disillusionment and acceptance of her role as wife and mother in the midst of prairie town mediocrity.

BRENEMAN, MARY WORTHY, pseud. (MARY WORTHY THURSTON and MURIEL BRENEMAN.) The Land They Possessed. New York: Macmillan, 1956.
The responses of a mother and daughter to the prairie in Dakota territory are explored and compared during the period 1885-1894. This is one of the most honest portrayals in the tradition of prairie literature of growing up female; both puberty and pregnancy are dealt with. Even an outhouse is described in some detail. The father is an adventurer-type, always looking for a new business proposition. The Dakota years represent another stage in a series of moves West, and the novel ends with his uprooting of the family for yet another move. Another dominant theme relates to class consciousness and prejudices against the increasing population of German-Russian immigrants in the new prairie town. This theme is resolved symbolically by the marriage of the New England girl to a "Rooshan" farmer.

CANNON, CORNELIA JAMES. Red Rust. Boston: Little, Brown, 1928.
At the beginning of the novel a young Swedish immigrant who is an uneducated but curious student of nature reads about "variation and selection" in a farm journal. He recognizes the possibilities for making Minnesota a great wheat-producing

country if he can develop an early-maturing grain with thick stalks and heavy heads that is also rust resistant. He develops such a grain, but only because his wife Lena commits her life to making his dream become a reality through her sacrifices, hard physical labor, and quiet manipulation of finances and household affairs; nothing must interfere with Matt Swenson's experiments. The plot also accommodates portrayals of Matt's sister and stepdaughter--their lives on farms and gradual Americanization as hired girls.

CATHER, WILLA. Lucy Gayheart. 1935; reprint ed. Vintage Books, New York: Random House, 1976.
Lucy Gayheart leaves her Nebraska town on the Platte and goes to Chicago to study music. The novel establishes sets of contrasts: the "purchased" elegance of the successful prairie town businessman is compared to the "personal" elegance of the Chicago-born, internationally-known singer, Sebastian Clement. The lack of privacy in the flimsy prairie town house is compared to the lonely but comforting anonymity of Chicago crowds. Nevertheless, Lucy has what Sebastian Clement does not: "a relation with the earth itself, with a countryside and a people," and it is the first of these, the earth, that helps Lucy regain emotional stability after Clement's death. In the end, however, nature--the river--takes Lucy's life as a result of her inattentiveness to her surroundings.

________. My Ántonia. Boston: Houghton Mifflin, 1917.
This is the story of Antonia, the daughter of a Bohemian immigrant to the Nebraska prairie as perceived by her childhood friend, Jim Burden, who has become a lawyer for one of the railroads. Through Jim's memories of Ántonia and others, Cather portrays the ordeals of immigrant prairie girls in Nebraska, their roles on the farm and in the town, their options, and their responses to American life in the late nineteenth century. The character Ántonia is based on Annie, a Bohemian girl Cather knew in Red Cloud.

________. O Pioneers! Boston: Houghton Mifflin, 1913.
A Swedish woman, Alexandra Bergson, takes over the management of the family farm after her father's death. She demonstrates that a woman can love the Nebraska prairie at the same time she turns it into a successful economic venture by using modern agricultural techniques.

________. "A Wagner Matinee," 1905. In Willa Cather's Collected Short Fiction 1892-1912. Introduction by Mildred R. Bennett. Lincoln: University of Nebraska Press, 1965.

A Nebraska woman who returns to her New England home for a visit is overcome, at the end of a concert, with a sense of the cultural deprivation she has endured as a hard-working farm wife.

CATHERWOOD, MARY HARTWELL. "The Bride of Arne Sandstrom," in The Queen of the Swamp and Other Plain Americans. 1899; reprint ed. New York: Garrett Press, 1969.
Elsa descends from a train in a typical prairie town expecting to find her betrothed, Arne Sandstrom, who left Sweden to make a home in America. After a series of misunderstandings are corrected, Elsa and Arne are reunited, married, and reassured that the American dream will be fulfilled.

_______. "The Career of a Prairie Farmer." Lippincott's Magazine 25 (June 1880): 706-713.
The story insists that even the affluent farmer is affected by the hard work and the monotonous years required to achieve success on the prairie. His wife and sister, who found the prairie "novel" at first, gradually become like the other women as their silks are replaced with calico and the faces are altered by the constant winds. Catherwood provides an early interpretation of social life, women's work, and growth of a prairie settlement. Brief portraits are provided of a young female school teacher, a prosperous Dutch farmer, and "Old Mary," a domestic who manages to marry well.

_______. "A Little God." Weekly Dispatch (Kokomo, Indiana), 19 December 1878; 26 December 1878; 2 January 1879; 9 January 1879.
Early pioneer town life is described by "the little god," a promising young New Englander who goes West to prove himself as a journalist in what he feels is a new empire. Within six months' time his "rugged and unconquerable New England spirit came out"; he exhibited tremendous power over the prairie people by his presence and by his writing. He has, indeed, become "a kind of human deity" who, disciplined and renewed, can return East to marry a charming Easterner. Ultimately he belongs to the East, not to the prairie that made him a man.

_______. "The Monument of the First Mrs. Smith. A True Story of Today by 'Lewtrahl.'" Weekly Dispatch (Kokomo, Indiana) 7 November 1878, n.p.
This "true story" is a blunt comment on the prairie pioneer farmer who literally works his wife to death. The first

Mrs. Smith foregoes all personal comforts and satisfactions to raise her children and help her husband establish a prosperous farm. The husband, completely blind to her hardships and sacrifices, attributes her death to a sickly nature. The story ends with an admonition to readers: "MORAL--girls, if you must marry Mr. Smith, don't take him on the first ballot--i.e.: wait till the monument [the nice house that the first Mrs. Smith gave her life for] is built, and then enter as the second Mrs. Smith."

_______. "The Spirit of an Illinois Town." Atlantic Monthly, 78 (August-October 1896): 168-174; 338-347; 480-491. Seth Adams, disillusioned and penniless, accepts a friend's offer to establish a newspaper in a pioneer Illinois prairie town. At first Adams is cynical about the townspeople's belief that they have arrived in the promised land where everyone will succeed. As he gradually becomes a part of the town, his respect for the ambition and energy of the settlers increases and he undergoes a kind of resurrection. He falls in love with a young woman, Kate Keene, who aspires to "a life of high breeding" and intently pursues her goal of becoming an actress. However, nature intervenes and Kate is killed in a cyclone. Nevertheless, Adams feels that Kate's spirit lives on in the townspeople: they stand for "pluck and genius and humility, boundless energy and vision, and a personal power...."

DONOVAN, JOSEPHINE. Black Soil. Boston: Stratford, 1930.
A young Boston woman, Nell Connors, marries an adventurous Irishman and emigrates to Iowa in the mid-to-late 1860s. The plot accommodates an exploration of one woman's feelings about the land, the European immigrant neighbors, the Indians, the difficulties of raising children in a new land, and the role of the pioneer woman. Many years of hardship precede the arrival of the railroad, the growth of a town, and a civilized way of life.

ERDMAN, LOULA GRACE. The Edge of Time. New York: Dodd, Mead, 1950.
A young Missouri woman, Bethany, proposes to Wade Cameron and convinces him to take her with him to establish a prairie homestead in the midst of Texas panhandle cattle country. The story covers the years 1885 to 1887, a transitional period preceding the arrival of the train and settlers. Wade and Bethany Cameron are portrayed as ideal frontier types; a variety of cowboys and "nesters" provide contrasts.

Bethany's three neighbor women represent alternative responses to the land and the frontier experience: one is passive, one moves on to unexplored territories, the third returns to eastern Texas.

FAIRBANK, JANET AYER. Rich Man Poor Man. Boston: Houghton Mifflin, 1936.
The novel focuses on the relationship between a woman with a Kansas farm background and a rich Chicagoan from a banking and steel family. The setting and situations of the novel are rooted in the city with occasional sentimental references to prairie farm life.

FARALLA, DANA. A Circle of Trees. Philadelphia: J.B. Lippincott, 1955.
The story covers one year on the Minnesota prairie as experienced by two children in the 1880s. The mother died shortly after their arrival from Denmark; the father, formerly a seaman, is disillusioned by life in "Beulah Land." Trees--their presence or absence on the prairie--provide thematic unity for the story. Indian values and beliefs are affirmed as well as certain Danish customs.

FERBER, EDNA. So Big. Garden City, N.Y.: Doubleday, Page, 1924.
A city girl and daughter of a gambler, Salina accepts a teaching post in a Dutch farming community in High Prairie, Illinois. There she marries a farmer, becomes a truck farmer, and eventually sends her son, Dirk (So Big) to college in Chicago. The values of the city--success, money, fame--are contrasted with the values of Salina--life and beauty.

FERNALD, HELEN CLARK. Plow the Dew Under. New York: Longmans, Green, 1952.
In 1874 a group of Mennonites arrive from the Crimea, bringing with them the wheat grains that will make Kansas famous. The main character, Ilya, is intent on becoming Americanized and becomes part of the mercantile world as soon as he can conscionably leave his father's farm. His mother, Sophie, represents the type of immigrant woman who is anxious to adapt to American ways. The villains are those who exploit or discriminate against foreigners.

FORD, ELISABETH. Amy Ferraby's Daughter. New York: Coward-McCann, 1944.
Caroline Ferraby, a New York aristocrat, is an unwilling

emigrant to Prairie Grove, Iowa, when she marries after the Civil War. She remains a recluse in the midwestern town and raises her daughter to feel superior to others. As a result, both women live lonely, meaningless lives.

________. No Hour of History. New York: I. Washburn, 1940.
Victoria Ash, born in a young Iowa town just before the Civil War, lived through major changes in family and society, the nation and the world. After a full life (she died in 1927) with ample opportunities to travel and meet a wide variety of people, she still admired her town and affirms its way of life.

FRENCH, ALICE (pseud. OCTAVE THANET). "Mrs. Finlay's Elizabethan Chair." In Knitters in the Sun. 1887; reprint ed. New York: Garrett Press, 1969. Pp. 97-132.
Two armchairs--an Elizabethan one and a Jacksonian one--symbolize the allegiance of Mrs. Finlay to what is European and aristocratic and the allegiance of the citizens of a small prairie town to what is American and democratic.

GATES, ELEANOR. The Biography of a Prairie Girl. New York: Century, 1902.
The narration includes many convincing details about growing up female on the prairie in the late nineteenth century ten miles west of Sioux Falls, South Dakota, but the underlying sentimentality of character and plot undercut the realistic portions. Edenic scenes are juxtaposed with incidents of violence by men and nature, and the author's final statement is that the prairie offers women drudgery, limited options, and minimal cultural opportunities. So the "little girl," after a year of school teaching, obeys her mother's dying wish and with the financial backing of "biggest brother" leaves the prairie to participate in the educational and cultural advantages of an eastern city.

________. The Plow-Woman. New York: Grosset & Dunlap, 1906.
Conflict over a land claim, an Indian's ordeal in regaining his honor, the attempt of imprisoned Sioux to join their tribe and attack the military fort, trials of love, and parent-child conflicts provide the plot lines for a novel whose main point is that women like twenty-year-old Dallas Lancaster also settled the frontier. In 1875 Dallas, her crippled father, and younger sister began developing a section of rich prairie

on the Missouri River in Southern Dakota Territory. Dallas makes the decisions, plows the land, and fights a lonely, complicated battle to maintain her place on the piece of land she loves. Gates demonstrates that a woman who chooses a non-traditional role is an outcast among ladies but the object of admiration among men; Dallas is rewarded with clear rights to her claim and a fine, frontier-type husband.

HEACOCK, NAN. Crinoline to Calico. Ames: Iowa State University Press, 1977.
The main characters, Castle and Jonathan (patterned after Heacock's grandparents), come from a prosperous Pittsburgh family and the Welsh cottager class respectively. They are among the first settlers near Anita, Iowa, where Castle is put through the typical frontier ordeals and succeeds not because she is committed and heroic but because pride drives her to surpass the neighboring women in cooking, needlework, gardening, and doctoring.

HUDSON, LOIS PHILLIPS. The Bones of Plenty. Boston: Atlantic-Little, Brown, 1962.
Shifting perspectives reveal different responses to farm life in the drought-and depression-ridden thirties in North Dakota. Will and Rose Shepherd began farming when a good living could be made. Their daughter, while a young schoolteacher, marries George Custer and settles on the next farm. When the story opens Lucy Custer is eight years old and portions narrated from her point of view provide yet a third response to prairie life.

________. Reapers of the Dust: A Prairie Chronicle. Boston: Little, Brown, 1957.
Hudson's note to readers indicates that she relies heavily on real people and actual events in constructing what she contends is a "true statement about a particular time that should not be forgotten." She records the experiences of a girl born in the third year of drought (1927) and traces her feelings and observations about nature, about being female during the drought and depression of the 1930s. The concluding chapter pieces together what she remembers or has heard about her two grandmothers who pioneered on the North Dakota prairie.

KIRKLAND, CAROLYN. Western Border Life; or, What Fanny Hunter Saw and Heard in Kanzas and Missouri. New York: Wiley & Putnam, 1856.
Kirkland's intent, as the preface notes, is to "sketch a picture of the social and moral life which the border counties

of Missouri are endeavoring to force upon the new territory." She proceeds to describe what Fanny Hunter, a genteel New England school teacher, saw and heard in Kanzas and Missouri: abuse of slaves by southern mistresses; limited educational and economic opportunities for the poor; immorality; excessive religious zeal; blatant disregard for the law. The heroine has accepted the teaching post in order to be independent; she also finds ample opportunity to demonstrate an ability to adapt to primitive living conditions, to act daringly and ingeniously in saving endangered lives, and to make specific gains against superstition, immorality, class and racial prejudice, and religious slackness. The novel concludes with Fanny's return east with her bridegroom, a St. Louis lawyer who is entering divinity school because he can do far more good as a minister than as a lawyer. They take with them the daughter of Fanny's host family who is an equally zealous do-gooder and committed to being trained for missionary work in the West.

LANE, ROSE WILDER. Free Land. New York: Longmans, Green, 1938.
This novel analyzes the homesteading experience in greater depth than Lane's earlier work, Let the Hurricane Roar. Beginning in 1879 and ending in 1884, the plot enables the author to explore the complex relationship between Mary and David who leave their comfortable family homes and relocate west of Tracy, Minnesota, on a homestead site. The pride of a man in succeeding as an independent farmer, the growth of community spirit, the constant battle of human beings with nature, the varied types, goals and responses of settlers in the new land are some of the subjects that receive in-depth analysis. As the novel unfolds, the reader becomes aware that the title, Free Land, is ironic on several levels.

________. Let the Hurricane Roar. New York: Longmans, Green, 1933. (Also published as Young Pioneers, 1976.)
The setting of the novel is familiar to readers of Laura Ingalls Wilder's On the Banks of Plum Creek. The archetypal plot shows the growth of a young couple from naïve idealism as they head west to experienced realism after two years of working a homestead. The last third of the novel describes the pride, stamina and ingenuity of the young pioneer wife isolated with her infant son on the homestead from October to February when her husband is unable to return from his summer job in Iowa.

LeSEUR, MERIDEL. "Corn Village." Scribner's Magazine,

August 1931, pp. 133-140. Also in Salute to Spring. New York: International Publishers, 1940; Corn Village. Sauk City, Wisc.: Stanton & Lee, 1970.
The narrator describes the "blackness, weight, and terror of childhood in mid-America" where there is no community; people are brought together only through violence--a love-murder and suicide or a frantic revival meeting. Some (like the narrator) stay on the Kansas prairie, trying to love the land, trying to bring it to life.

_______. "O Prairie Girl Be Lonely." In Cross Section 1947, pp. 40-71. Ed. Edwin Seaver. New York: Simon & Schuster, 1947.
To a farm girl who sought work and love in the city, the Iowa prairie is a sacred place where she can bury her lover who dies from a bullet wound received during a bank robbery. This story, slightly revised, was integrated into LeSueur's novel The Girl which is set in St. Paul during the depression. (Cambridge, Mass.: West End Press, 1978.)

_______. "Salute to Spring," In Salute to Spring, pp. 144-158. New York: International, 1977.
A farm woman, after experiencing several years of drought, joins her husband at a farmer's alliance meeting and finds hope for the future through community action.

LOVELACE, MAUD HART. Early Candlelight. New York: John Day, 1929.
Lovelace records life in and around Fort Snelling and the growth of St. Paul from a small settlement called Pigs Eye. The story centers on Deedee Du Gay, twelve years old at the opening of the story, whose father is a settler from Quebec. Contrasts are presented between the easterners at the Fort, the squatters, and the Indians.

_______ and DELOS. Gentlemen from England. New York: Macmillan, 1937.
Clergymen's sons, second and third sons of nobility and gentry, and retired military men are duped into coming to southern Minnesota to make their fortunes raising beans. Their wealth, sense of superiority, and adherence to English customs keep them alienated from the Americans. Most of them fail as gentlemen farmers. The one admirable Englishman, Richard Chalmers, works hard, loves the prairie, and remains committed to the land--all characteristics which are desirable by American standards and win him respect among the native settlers. The English women are unsuited to the

prairie--one has a title and a serving maid, another, though the mother of numerous children, knows nothing about running a household in a land where hired help is scarce; but she and her daughters make an attempt to learn and, predictably, Richard falls in love with one of these strong, attractive girls. The only American girl in the story dies in childbirth, unwed, because her English lover was too weak to demand that his family recognize the relationship.

LYNN, MARGARET. A Stepdaughter of the Prairie. New York: Macmillan, 1916.
The sketches move from the narrator's sense of self as "stepdaughter" of the prairie in the first chapter to "daughter" in the last chapter, thus indicating her acceptance of and identity with the land that she at first rejected. Some of the sketches focus on the early years of settlement--"the movers" passing through, "the stoppers" needing a place to spend the night, and "the visitors" spending time with the narrator's family. Children's activities and routines are described as well as a trip to the city and her last year in the one-room school house before being sent East to complete her education.

McCARTER, MARGARET HILL. The Price of the Prairie: A Story of Kansas. Chicago: A.C. McClurg, 1910.
The narrator of the novel, a prominent Kansas lawyer of New England descent, looks back forty years and recalls his youth in Kansas between 1853 and 1868. He focuses on his role in the Free Soil movement, the Civil War, and the removal of Indians to reservations. The heroes of the novel are those who vow to give their lives to protect women and "the hearthstones of the West." Before joining General Custer's troops, the hero sees himself, like Coronado years before, "... going now to put the indelible mark of conquest by a civilized Government, on a crafty and dangerous foe [the Indian], to plough a fire-guard of safety about the frontier homes."

McDONALD, JULIE. Amalie's Story. New York: Simon & Schuster, 1970.
The first two-thirds of the novel takes place in Denmark; the last third recounts the successful business venture of Amalie's husband in late nineteenth-century Iowa, his rise to a leadership position in the community, and Amalie's gradual adaptation to a new country and new ways.

NORTH, JESSICA NELSON, Morning in the Land. New York: Greystone Press, 1941.

The family of Thomas Wentworthy from Derbyshire, England, settles in an English community called Hampstead Prairie located in Rock County, Wisconsin, south of Lake Koshkonong. Beginning in 1840, the story traces the growth of farms and town, presenting cameo portraits of several women while focusing on the main character, Richard, younger son of Thomas Wentworthy. The author emphasizes the sacrifices demanded by wife and sons of a man determined to succeed materially in the new land. Richard rebels by rescuing and marrying a French girl who had been captured and raised by the Winnebagos. The treatment of this female character is sympathetic and unsentimental; however, the couple is eventually separated and Richard is free to marry the daughter of a prominent Madison family. The novel concludes with Richard riding off to the Civil War.

OSTENSO, MARTHA. O River, Remember! New York: Dodd, Mead, 1943.
Two stories are told: the main story is about the Shaleens and the Vinges (changed to Wing) in the 1870s in the Red River Valley near Fargo and Moorhead; the second story briefly touches on the lives of two of their descendents in Minneapolis in the early 1940s. The pioneer generation is represented by three types of settlers: Magdali Wing, but not her husband, is materialistic and speculates in land to make money (and eventually becomes a "town father"); her husband Ivar, on the other hand, loves the land for itself and for its potential for bearing fine crops if scientifically cultivated; Kate Shaleen is the artistic, cultured, school teacher whose life weaves in and out of the Wings' to provide tension as well as contrast.

________. Wild Geese. 1925; reprint ed. New American Library, Toronto: McClelland & Stewart, 1961.
Set on a prairie homestead in the lake district of Northern Manitoba, the novel describes the attempt of Caleb Gare to hold his family in bondage to the land. Only his daughter Judith rebels from what she sees as a dehumanizing situation for her mother and brother and sister. Much as she loves the land itself, she needs to escape even after her father's death. An outsider's perspective is provided by Lind Archer, the school teacher who lives with the Gare family. [Research by Peter E. Rider indicates that the novel was written with Douglas Durkin; however, to be eligible for the Dodd, Mead prize, Wild Geese had to be submitted by an unpublished novelist. Thus Ostenso received credit for the novel. (See Rider's introduction to Douglas Durkin's The Magpie. Toronto: University of Toronto Press, 1974.)]

PEATTIE, LOUISE REDFIELD. American Acres. New York: Triangle Books, 1936.
The first chapters describe homesteading on the prairie, but the majority of the novel deals with the expatriot son and granddaughter. However, the novel concludes with the return of the granddaughter to the homestead where she and a second cousin marry and the farm is once again under plow. The novel provides only fleeting glances of prairie life.

SCARBOROUGH, DOROTHY. The Wind. 1925; reprint ed. Austin: University of Texas Press, 1979.
An eastern woman becomes the victim of nature in the West Texas setting before the prairie has been transformed from ranch country to farm land.

SOULE, MRS. CAROLINE A. The Pet of the Settlement: A Story of Prairie-Land. Boston: A. Tompkins, 1860.
The central figures are the upperclass Belden family from New England. Belden's business failed and he moved with his son and daughter to start over on the prairie near the Des Moines River. During the next fifteen years he becomes founding father of the town and witnesses people living in peace and plenty on the prairie who formerly were struggling, homeless, debt-ridden, and hungry in the crowded cities of the East. The daughter, Margaret, rejoices over the opportunity to educate and convert to Christianity two young Indians who happily forsake their tribes and accept the Anglo way of life. She marries her old lover from the East who has become purified as a hunter-priest on the prairie. The huntsman Billy and the prairie angel Grandma Symes represent idealized types from the lower classes who initiate newcomers into the ways of the wilderness. The prairie is represented as a new heaven on earth, but with the recognition that the serpent exists; however, the warring Sioux, the black bear, the unscrupulous white adventurer, the blizzards of winter never fully succeed in harming the occupants of the prairie garden. In fact, the "pet of the settlement"--abandoned on the prairie as an infant, discovered, nursed, and raised to young womanhood--represents the possibility for perfection in the new prairie environment.

STOCKWELL, NANCY. Out Somewhere and Back Again (The Kansas Stories). Washington, D.C.: Women in Distribution, 1978.
The first and last stories in the collection demonstrate the effects of people and place on an individual. Although the narrator has to escape the conservative values of the small

Kansas town that threaten her creativity and her lifestyle, she acknowledges her debt to her pioneer forebears, to Kansas heroes like John Brown and the pioneer women, and to the land which has been a source of renewal and insight.

SUCKOW, RUTH. Country People. New York: Alfred A. Knopf, 1924.
After a brief survey of several immigrant German families in Turkey Creek, Iowa, the novel focuses on the family history of August Kaetterhenry. Unlike many novels tracing the lives of a family, emphasis is placed on the latter part of August's life--middle age and retirement--with special attention to his wife, Emma--her trip to Rochester, Minnesota, for an operation after having been overworked for years, her leisure-time activities after they retire and build a house in town, her new-found freedom and independence after August's death. One of the strengths of the novel is its portrayal of women's changing roles beginning with August's mother in the 1850s to the granddaughter Marguerite in the 1920s.

_______. The Odyssey of a Nice Girl. New York: A. Knopf, 1925.
Suckow develops several themes typical of midwestern literature: the town-country conflict, the education of a young woman in the East, the inability of some to adapt to a small town with its limited opportunities. The story traces the life of Marjorie Schoessel from her Iowa girlhood to her marriage to a mechanic in Colorado.

THANET, OCTAVE. See FRENCH, ALICE.

THURSTON, MARY WORTHY. See BRENEMAN, MARY WORTHY.

WILDER, LAURA INGALLS. By the Shores of Silver Lake. 1939; reprint ed. Harper Trophy Book, New York: Harper & Row, 1953.
Pa finds the Minnesota homestead unsatisfactory. He moves the family to Dakota territory, sixty miles west of Brookings, when he has an opportunity to work in a railroad camp while looking for the perfect homestead site. Laura, now fourteen years old, has to adjust to greater responsibilities and behave properly in the shanty town. Ma, who had been reluctant to move from Minnesota, vows to settle in the Dakotas and raise her daughters as properly as possible. The story ends with their move from town to the claim.

_______. Little House on the Prairie. 1935; reprint ed. Harper Trophy Book, New York: Harper & Row, 1953.
When some Washington politicians announce that Kansas is going to open for settlement, the Ingalls head for Kansas and settle forty miles west of Independence. Laura observes her father's enthusiasm and her mother's caution as they try to create a home in the new territory. She realizes there are a wide range of attitudes toward Indians among the adults, and that lives are occasionally threatened not only by hostile Indians but by wolves, prairie fires, and fever 'n' ague. At the end of the story the Ingalls have to leave Kansas because they are living three miles into Indian territory and the government is moving the settlers out.

_______. Little Town on the Prairie. 1941; reprint ed. Harper Trophy Book, New York: Harper & Row, 1953.
The story opens in the spring of 1881. Although Laura, age fifteen, prefers living on the farm, she enjoys observing town life and people while she works at the dry goods store sewing so there will be cash to send her blind sister to college. The narration includes descriptions of social life in a new pioneer town and the types of social issues that arise.

_______. The Long Winter. 1940; reprint ed. Harper Trophy Book, New York: Harper & Row, 1940.
An old Indian, after the four-day blizzard in October, predicts seven months of blizzards. Pa trusts the Indian's wisdom and moves the family from the farm into town. Blizzards, their characteristics and consequences, provide the main focus as people in the new town of DeSmet in Dakota Territory adjust their way of living to snow and wind in the winter of 1880-1881.

_______. On the Banks of Plum Creek. 1937; reprint ed. Harper Trophy Book, New York: Harper & Row, 1953.
This is the third story in Wilder's autobiographical experiences and recounts life in Minnesota. The pioneer's stamina is tested by a fire, a grasshopper plague, and a blizzard.

WILSON, MARGARET. The Able McLaughlins. New York: Grosset & Dunlap, 1923.
The events of the story take place between 1864 and 1866 in a Scots settlement twenty-five miles west of Davenport. The eldest son of the McLaughlin clan returns from the Civil War, marries, and establishes his farm on land adjoining his father's which had been purchased in 1854 upon their emigration

from Ayrshire. The characters provide a variety of male and female responses to the prairie, to farming, to America, and to Scottish values and customs.

LITERARY BACKGROUNDS

ADAMSON, ARTHUR. "Identity Through Metaphor: An Approach to the Question of Regionalism in Canadian Literature." Studies in Canadian Literature 5 (Spring 1980): 83-99.
"Identity comes through metaphor and so culture is essentially regionalist in its creative forms. Metaphor is derived from immediate experience, and is linked ... to regionalism." See related article in Essays on Canadian Writing: Prairie Poetry Issue.

________. See also Essays on Canadian Writing.

ALDRICH, BESS STREETER. "The Story Behind A Lantern in Her Hand." Nebraska History 56 no. 2 (1975): 237-241.
According to Paul Riley's introduction to the essay, this is one of the last articles written by Aldrich and published in Christian Herald in March 1952. She traces the pioneer experiences of her grandparents and mother which form the basis of A Lantern in Her Hand. She was consciously attempting to alter the stereotype of pioneer women as "gaunt, browbeaten creatures, despairing women whom life seemed to defeat." These images, says Aldrich, do not represent her mother.

ANDREWS, CLARENCE. A Literary History of Iowa. Iowa City: University of Iowa Press, 1972.
This survey traces Iowa literature from the first publication of poems in 1836 to the 1970's. Four of the fourteen chapters are devoted to individual authors: Alice French, Hamlin Garland, Herbert Quick, and Ruth Suckow. Andrews also discusses the works of Bess Streeter Aldrich, Susan Glaspell, and Josephine Herbst.

APONIAK, NATALIA. "The Problem of Identity: The Depiction of Ukrainians in Canadian Literature." Canadian Ethnic Studies/Etudes Ethniques au Canada 14 no. 1 (1982).
Vera Lysenko's Yellow Boots is one of the novels examined for its depiction and interpretation of the Ukrainian experience in

Canada. Lilli, the protagonist of Yellow Boots, succeeds because she acquires the characteristics essential to assimilation; at the same time, however, she is able to retain customs and values of her Ukrainian background.

ARMITAGE, SUSAN H. See LEE, L. L. and MERRILL LEWIS, eds.

ARNASON, DAVID. "The Development of Prairie Realism: Robert J. C. Stead, Douglas Durkin, Martha Ostenso and Frederick Philip Grove." Ph.D. dissertation, The University of New Brunswick, 1980.
Arnason traces the development from sentimentality to realism in the works of four prairie novelists whose works reflect the political and intellectual climate of the times. "Their belief in human progress was one rooted in their acceptance of evolution. They tried to create accurate psychological portraits against a complex social environment." DAI 41 no. 5 (November 1980.)

ATKINS, ANNETTE. "Women on the Farming Frontier: The View from Fiction." The Midwest Review, 2nd series, 3 (Spring 1981): 1-10.
"Historians have portrayed pioneer women as stereotypes, almost all in virtual imitation of Beret Hansa," the female protagonist in Rölvaag's Giants in the Earth. This stereotype is refuted by reference to Beret's characterization in the remainder of Rolvaag's trilogy and in the Nebraska novels of three women writers: Aldrich's A Lantern in Her Hand and Spring Came on Forever; Cather's O Pioneers! and My Antonia; and Sandoz's short-grass prairie novels, Old Jules and Slogum House. These works "suggest a ... complex and subtle view not only of frontier women but of frontier men as well."

BAKER, BRUCE, II. "Nebraska Regionalism in Selected Works of Willa Cather." Western American Literature 3 (Spring 1968): 19-35.
Baker traces Cather's response to the Nebraska environment. Her work reflects "an attitude at first vindictive but soon ambivalent." While portraying the harsh realities of the region, Cather also admires the people who endure and accomplish their goals.

BECKER, MAY LAMBERTON, ed. Golden Tales of the Prairie States. New York: Dodd, Mead, 1932.
The collection includes stories by Dora Aydelotte, Ruth Suckow, Mary Katharine Reely, Caroline Dale Snedeker, Alica French, Bess Streeter Aldrich. The remaining thirteen stories are by men. The stated purpose of the anthology is to preserve "an

America that has ceased to be." The stories emphasize characters, situations and values frequently associated with the midwest. Short biographies of each writer are included.

BENNETT, MILDRED R. "Willa Cather and the Prairie." Nebraska History Magazine 56 no. 2 (1975): 230-235.
Willa Cather responded passionately and positively to the prairie, according to comments quoted by Bennett from the Omaha Daily Bee. After a fruitless search for books about the beauty of the prairie, the strength and heroism of the people, Cather decided to write O Pioneers! Cather's love of the prairie brought her back to Nebraska innumerable times throughout her life, and she would have approved of the site selected for the Willa Cather Memorial Prairie located near Red Cloud, Nebraska.

BLODGETT, E.D. "Gardens at the World's End or Gone West in French." Essays on Canadian Writing no. 17 (Spring 1980): 113-126.
Works by Gabrielle Roy, Maurice Constantin-Weyer, and Georges Bugnet form the basis for this analysis of the Canadian West since 1885 as presented in fiction by French writers. Roy, "by transforming space into a metaphysics of time" is able to "play constantly on life as it may have been within a perspective of how one would like it to be." Blodgett uses The Road Past Altamont to demonstrate how, in Roy's work, the closure of the Old West affected the French population in the Prairie Provinces.

CARP, ROGER E. See LEE, L.L. and MERRILL LEWIS, eds.

CARPENTER, DAVID C. "Alberta in Fiction: The Emergence of a Provincial Consciousness." Journal of Canadian Studies 10 no. 4 (1975): 12-23.
The Alberta writer interprets his region for the reading public, creates his region and, at the same time, is created by his region. Alberta is distinguished by its antipathy to Ottawa and by its associations with the images of the "promised land." In literature characters seek the promised land--Neil in McCourt's Music at the Close, Lina In Due Season by van der Mark; the promise remains unfulfilled in Bugnet's La Forêt, O'Hagen's Tay John, and Kroetsch's But We Are Exiles. Carpenter concludes that "Alberta voices still speak of romantic nonrealities and great expectations haunted by the conflict between natural and civilized values...."

________. "Patrified Mummies and Mummified Daddies: A Study of Matriarchs and Patriarchs in Canadian Prairie Fiction," in The Settlement of the West, pp. 153-173. Ed. Howard Palmer. Calgary: University of Calgary, 1977.

Settlement fiction endures when it transcends "merely regional considerations," becoming not only a source for sociological data but also art. The study focuses on four works representing the *roman du terroir*: Stead's *Grain*, Ostenso's *Wild Geese*, Grove's *Fruits of the Earth*, and Bugnet's *La Forêt*. Stead and Grove fail in their characterizations of women and men. Ostenso takes essentially the same story as Grove and, by providing rich characterization, goes beyond documentary naturalism. Of the four novels, however, Bugnet's is the most successful.

CHADBOURNE, RICHARD and HALLVARD DAHLIE, eds. *The New Land: Studies in a Literary Theme*. Waterloo, Ont.: Wilfrid Laurier University, 1978.
Chadbourne's essay, "Two Visions of the Prairies: Willa Cather and Gabrielle Roy," pp. 93-120, analyzes the biographical similarities between the two authors and then discusses their prairie works--Cather's short stories, *O Pioneers!* and *My Antonia*, and Roy's *Street of Riches*, *The Road Past Altamont* and *The Garden in the Wind*. The Prairie West nourishes the imaginations of both. They were pioneers as artists, introducing a new landscape and new subject matter into literature. At the same time, neither is a regional writer in the sense of being "merely a local coloris." In Clara Thomas's "Women Writers and the New Land," pp. 45-59, McClung, Salverson, Laurence and Wiseman all have a common identity as prairie fiction writers. McClung's and Laurence's preference, however, is for the agrarian way of life; Salverson's characters prefer the security of the city. Many of the male characters in the works of these writers are dreamers and losers; frequently the women are adventurers and heroes exploring new territories.

CHAMBERS, ROBERT D. "Notes on Regionalism in Modern Canadian Fiction." *Journal of Canadian Studies/Revue d'etudes canadiennes* 11 (May 1976): 27-34.
Chamber's purpose is "to work towards a concept of regionalism in literature." He points out that any such theory must consider 1) the writer's awareness of identity in relation to roots; and 2) the reader's sense of "common ground" when reading a particular work. He concludes the essay with excerpts from Laurence's *The Stone Angel*, a work that represents a writer's intense response to a specific region while also helping the reader to know and to feel "the historical development of Canada as a whole."

COMMAGER, HENRY S. "The Literature of the Pioneer West." *Minnesota History* 8 (December 1927): 319-328.

Realism has won out over romance in Rölvaag's Giants in the Earth, marking a significant point in American literature: "the westward movement ceases to be the victim of romances and becomes a great physical and spiritual adventure." The psychological and spiritual aspects of the frontier--not the economic alone--represent an important trend in realistic works of the Middle Border. Rölvaag's major contribution in Giants in his refusal to "draw the veil of silence over the 'tragic futility' of the women's suffering.... Indeed, it might be said that his volume is primarily concerned with the 'futility of their suffering'...."

DAVIDSON, CATHY N. "Geography as Psychology in the Writings of Margaret Laurence." Kate Chopin Newsletter 2 (Fall 1976): 5-10.
In Margaret Laurence's Canadian novels, characters who come to terms with their physical, psychological and social landscapes are able to survive.

DONDORE, DOROTHY ANNE. The Prairie and the Making of Middle America: Four Centuries of Description. Cedar Rapids, Iowa: The Torch Press, 1926.
Chapters four through eight review literature about the prairie; early accounts of the prairie by eastern and European travellers, popular songs, poetry and romantic fiction by both Americans and Europeans, the development of realism in midwestern fiction. Women writers discussed include Alice Cary, Mary Hartwell Catherwood, Willa Cather, Mary Borden, Susan Glaspell, Zona Gale, Carolyn A. Soule, Caroline Mathilda Kirkland, Margaret Lynn, and Katherine Keith.

DYRUD, DAVID L. "Varieties of Marginality: The Treatment of the European Immigrant in the Middlewestern Frontier Novel." Ph.D. dissertation, Purdue University, 1979.
Seventy-seven novels published between 1880 and 1970 form the basis for an analysis of the European immigrant experience in the middle west. Dyrud identifies four major themes discussed in chapters II through V: "Familial Tensions: Connubial, Generational and Communal," "Cultural Deprivation in a New Land," "Yankee Resentment," "Nature: Minor Impediment or Major Obstacle." He concludes with a survey of the "melting pot" proponents and opponents. Willa Cather, Bess Streeter Aldrich, Mary Worthy Breneman (pseud. for Mary Worthy Thurston and Muriel Breneman), Helen C. Fernald, Maud Lovelace, Dana Faralla, Borghild Dahl, Karen Peyton, Julie McDonald are among the women novelists discussed.

EGGLESTON, WILFRID. *The Frontier and Canadian Letters.* Toronto: Ryerson Press, 1957.
Eggleston analyzes the reasons why Canadian western literature of quality was slow to emerge. He concludes that educational, social, and cultural conditions have become conducive to writing but the works available are appreciated by only a select few among the population.

ENGEL, MARY FRANCES. "Bankrupt Dreams: The Isolated and the Insulated in Selected Works of Canadian and American Prairie Literature." Ph.D. dissertation, Kent State University, 1978.
Canadian and American agricultural settlement patterns and conditions are compared. The study focuses on the use of a dream motif for structure, thematic development and characterization. "The dream is pursued by a male protagonist who invariably fails to consider his wife (or intended wife) as an individual with dreams of her own...." Much of the literature indicates that family and the woman's happiness were sacrificed in the process of settling the prairie.

ERISMAN, FRED. "Western Regional Writers and the Uses of Place." *Journal of the West* 19 (January 1980): 36-44.
The works of Cather, Guthrie, Steinbeck, Horgan, and Graves demonstrate that the writers shared "a conscious concern with Western materials and Western themes." As regionalists, their works are, not only "nominally located in the region ... but derive actual substance from that location." They explore the effects of landscape and climate on specific individuals and explore themes of loneliness, ambition, social change, and attitudes toward the city.

Essays on Canadian Writing: Prairie Poetry Issue. Nos. 18-19 (Summer/Fall 1980).
This issue includes interviews and articles about prairie women poets Lorna Uher, Elizabeth Brewster, and Ann Szumigalski. Checklists of recent prairie poetry in English and in French provide a useful guide to the women poets and their works. An article by Arthur Adamson argues that good art is regional because its language and metaphors are rooted in a particular time and place; "international" art is inferior and provincial because it lacks identification with place--"Notes from a Dark Cellar: Ruminations on the Nature of Regionalism and Metaphor in Mid-Western Canadian Poetry," pp. 223-241.

FAIRBANKS, CAROL. "Lives of Girls and Women on the

Canadian and American Prairies." International Journal of Women's Studies 2 (September/October 1979): 452-472.
Two autobiographies and seven novels which provide detailed accounts of female experiences on the prairies serve as the basis for an analysis of the vision of the prairie settlers, the effect of that vision upon the daughters, and the reactions to the prairie of the girls growing up there. Canadian works include novels by Ostenso, Wild Geese; Grove, The Fruits of the Earth; Laurence, The Diviners, and a memoir by Maynard, Raisins and Almonds. American novels include Cooper's The Prairie, Rölvaag's Giants in the Earth; Muilenberg's Prairie, Donovan's Black Soil, and Cather's My Ántonia. Also included are Stockwell's short fiction Out Somewhere and Back Again: The Kansas Stories and Garland's autobiography Son of the Middle Border.

FAULKNER, VIRGINIA and FREDERICK C. LUEBKE, eds. Vision and Refuge: Essays on the Literature of the Great Plains. Lincoln & London: University of Nebraska Press for the Center for Great Plains Studies, 1982.
In an essay entitled "Agrarian versus Frontiersman in Midwestern Fiction," pp. 44-63, Barbara Howard Meldrum states that 'Defeat and disullusionment haunt the characters of western fiction when the better life they seek so often eludes them or proves to be a hollow achievement." This can be better understood by examining the interrelationships of agrarian and frontiersman traits and values. Rölvaag's Giants in the Earth, Keith Winther's Grimsen trilogy, and Manfred's This Is the Year provide the basis for the analysis. John R. Milton, in "Materialism and Mysticism in Great Plains Literature," analyzes the materialistic relationship of man with the land in twentieth century literature of the plains, focusing almost entirely on works by male writers (pp. 31-43). Skårdal's "Life on the Great Plains in Scandinavian-American Literature," pp. 71-92, comments on a variety of issues: responses to the land, ordeals with nature, housing, farming techniques, attitudes toward work and women's roles. The presence of Indians and their rights to the land are rarely acknowledged in the novels. Church is a major subject; politics is not. Alcoholism and materialism are considered the downfall of many immigrants. Bernice Slote's essay, "Willa Cather and Plains Culture," pp. 93-105, summarizes Cather's response to the physical landscape in her personal life and her fiction.

FREDERICK, JOHN T. "Town and City in Iowa Fiction." Palimpsest 35 (February 1954): 49-96.

The survey covers writers before World War I through the 1950's. Short analyses are provided of works by Bess Streeter Aldrich, Margaret Wilson, and Elisabeth Ford. The works of Alice French (Octave Thanet) and Ruth Suckow receive more detailed critical attention.

FRIESEN, VICTOR CARL. "The Rural Novel and the Great Depression." *Prairie Forum* 2 no. 1 (1977): 83-96.
Canadian prairie novels dealing with the Depression were written after the 1930's, unlike the American novels that were written during the Depression as weapons of protest. Lysenko's *Westerly Wild*, Laurence's *The Stone Angel*, and Blondal's *A Candle to Light the Sun* are discussed, as well as works by Ross, Kroetsch, McCourt, and Mitchell. The works of these writers document the economic and political situation; however, they are even more important for their insights into the search for emotional security in an adverse environment.

GARLAND, HAMLIN. "The West in Literature." *Arena* 36 (November 1892): 669-676.
Garland issues a charge to writers: "Write of those things of which you know most, and for which you care most. By so doing you will be true to yourself, true to your locality, and true to your time." He predicts the rise of a new group of Western novelists "(Will they be women?)" who will repudiate their conservative training and explore new forms. "They must be born of the soil. They must be products of the environment. They must stand among the people, not above them, and then they can be true, and being true they will certainly succeed."

GOM, LEONA. "Margaret Laurence: The Importance of Place." *West Coast Review* 10 no. 2 (1975): 26-30.
Gom enumerates the positive attitudes toward nature (country) of the female characters in the five Manawaka novels and their negative responses to small town and city. Yet each character eventually accepts her prairie town origins as part of her past and personality.

GRIDER, SYLVIA. See LEE, L.L. and MERRILL LEWIS, eds.

HARRISON, DICK. "Across the Medicine Line: Problems in Comparing Canadian and American Western Fiction." In *The Westering Experience in American Literature: Bicentennial Essays*, pp. 48-56. Bellingham, Wash.: Bureau for Faculty Research, Western Washington University, 1977.

Readers comparing midwest fiction with Canadian prairie fiction will be struck more by the differences than similarities. Writers like Cather, Garland, and Morris have more in common with rural Ontario writers than with Grove, Ross and Wiebe. However, there are exceptions: Ross can be compared with Lewis; Grove can be compared with Rölvaag. In American western fiction, the relationship between man and nature is more stable; in Canadian fiction man is in greater harmony with society than with nature.

_______, ed. Crossing Frontiers: Papers in American and Canadian Western Literature. Edmonton: University of Alberta Press, 1979.

Perspectives on regional literature and comparisons of Canadian and American western literature are provided in the following essays: Howard R. Lamar's "The Unsettling of the American West: The Mobility of Defeat," pp. 35-54; "Prairie Settlement: Western Responses in History and Fiction, Social Structures in a Canadian Hinterland," pp. 59-72, by Lewis G. Thomas; Eli Mandel's "The Border League: American 'West' and Canadian 'Region,'" pp. 105-121, which is followed by W.H. New's "Response," pp. 122-130. Don D. Walker explores the relationship between history and fiction in "On the Supposed Frontier Between History and Fiction," pp. 11-29. Kroetsch's essay "The Fear of Women in Prairie Fiction," pp. 73-83 (with a response by Sandra Djwa, pp. 84-88) is annotated under Kroetsch, Robert.

_______. "Rölvaag, Grove and Pioneering on the American and Canadian Plains." Great Plains Quarterly 1 (Fall 1981): 252-262.

Several similarities between the two authors are noted: both are immigrants describing representative immigrant experiences; both present factual information about the homesteading process. Their novels, Giants in the Earth and Fruits of the Earth represent pioneer efforts in fiction in that they realistically present the physical, mental, emotional, and spiritual aspects of pioneering. Both works are about giants--natural leaders with bonds with the land while at the same time demonstrating pride, stubbornness and ambition that eventually lead to their failures in family relationships. They differ in that Grove's homestead experience was not in a wilderness, as was Rölvaag's.

_______. Unnamed Country: The Struggle for a Canadian Prairie Fiction. Edmonton: University of Alberta Press, 1977.

A survey of the ways early writers saw and described the prairies provides a basis for the analysis of the various traditions included in prairie fiction--romance, realism, adventure romance, and sentimental comedy. Works by Kate Simpson Hays, Agnes Laut, Nellie McClung, and Vera Lysenko are discussed briefly. Margaret Laurence's and Martha Ostenso's fiction are treated more fully as are works by Ralph Connor, Grove, Kroetsch, McCourt, Mitchell, Ross, Stead, and Wiebe. Recurring themes and images are identified and an analysis reveals the degree to which they reflect the cultural baggage of the writers. The final chapter acknowledges the ability of writers like Laurence, Wiebe and Kroetsch to re-name the landscape and the prairie experience according to their imaginative insights.

HAZARD, LUCY LOCKWOOD. The Frontier in American Literature, 1927; reprint ed. New York: Frederick Ungar, 1961.

Chapter VII, "The Frontier and the Nester," identifies similarities and differences between the frontier farm experiences portrayed by Crèvecoeur, Garland, and Norris. The chapter ends with a discussion of Willa Cather's works. Hazard notes that "no American writer since Crèvecoeur has made so vivid the love of land as a ruling passion" as Willa Cather.

KAROLIDES, NICHOLAS J. The Pioneer in the American Novel 1900-1950. Norman: University of Oklahoma Press, 1964.

The study includes novels published between 1900 and 1950 which describe the frontiersman on the overland trail, the forest, the mountain, the range, and on the farming and mining frontiers. The dominant themes considered are the wilderness ideal vs. progress, East vs. West, good vs. evil, class attitudes, responses to Indians, law and justice. Special attention is paid to the evolving images of heroes and heroines. Romantic treatments dominate the majority of works during the first two decades (Cather's works are the exception), and increasingly realistic treatments of men and women, their relationships and their roles, emerge from 1930 to 1950. A few prairie women writers are discussed briefly: Aldrich, Cather, Erdman, Ferber, Hargreaves, and Wilson.

KAYE, FRANCIS W. "The 49th Parallel and the 98th Meridian: Some Lines for Thought." Mosaic 14 no. 2 (1981): 165-175.

Kaye emphasizes the differences in literature of the American

West and the Canadian Prairie each side of the 98th meridian. On the east side, both men and women agreed, for the most part, on the importance of law and order. West of the meridian, American males rebelled while Canadian males acknowledged and respected the pre-established laws and acted responsibly toward women and family. Included in the analysis are works by Cather, Laurence, Kroetsch, Ross, Stegner, and Twain.

_______. "Hamlin Garland and Frederick Philip Grove: Self-Conscious Chroniclers of the Pioneers." *Canadian Review of American Studies* 10 (Spring 1979): 32-39.
Garland and Grove, in searching for their own identities, became chroniclers of the prairie frontier era. Both writers "believed their lives served as texts for their nations." Indeed, Garland's *A Son of the Middle Border* and Grove's *A Search for America* were used as school texts; each believed "that he was in his own life an exemplar of the last and most characteristic frontier."

KRIESEL, HENRY. "The Prairie: A State of Mind." In *Contexts of Canadian Criticism*, pp. 254-266. Ed. Eli Mandel. Chicago: University of Chicago Press, 1971.
Although many characters in Canadian fiction (like Sinclair Ross's Mrs. Bentley) demonstrate that the prairie is "a state of mind," all discussions of literature must begin with the actual landscape. In order to tame the land, settlers had to first "curb their passions and contain them within a tight neo-Calvinist framework"; hence two themes develop: 1) puritanism and the inevitability of violent disruptions; 2) the imprisoned spirit of the individual. Another portion of the discussion focuses on sea imagery in describing the prairie.

KROETSCH, ROBERT. "A Conversation with Margaret Laurence," in *Creation*, pp. 53-63. Toronto: New Press, 1970.
Kroetsch and Laurence agree that the writer must go away and learn about the rest of the world before s/he can return physically or spiritually to their homelands and understand their origins. When Laurence notes that Kroetsch's writing is "a strange kind of humour" because of its irony and at the same time "profoundly sad," Kroetsch replies that "maybe that's in the nature of the prairie experience. Or in the nature of comedy itself." The conversation concludes with Laurence pointing out that "Fiction relates to life in a very real way." This conversation includes Kroetsch's often-quoted

statement, "In a sense, we haven't got an identity until somebody tells our story. The fiction makes us real."

_______. "Fear of Women in Prairie Fiction: Erotics of Space." Canadian Forum, October-November 1978, pp. 22-27; also in Crossing Frontiers, see Harrison, Dick, ed.
Kroetsch raises the question, "How do you make love in a new country," especially where distance is the dominant characteristic. After establishing that external space is male and internal space female, he discusses Sinclair Ross's As for Me and My House and Willa Cather's My Ántonia. He suggests that male fear of space limits possibilities for satisfactory sexual relationships between couples. Male characters are unable to move freely and surely in either internal or external space; they are unable to define themselves.

LAMAR, HOWARD R. See HARRISON, DICK, ed. Crossing Frontiers.

LAURENCE, MARGARET. Heart of a Stranger. Toronto: McClelland & Stewart, 1976.
This collection includes two essays that analyze the importance of place in one's identity and view of the world. In "A Place to Stand On" (published as "Sources" in Mosaic, 1970), Laurence notes that two aspects--the geography and the people--have influenced her writing. She points out similarities between her hometown, Neepawa, and her fictional town, Manawaka (both in Manitoba). In "Where the World Began" (1971), Laurence compares her perceptions of the prairie landscape with those of others, insisting that the prairie is "never merely flat or uninteresting. Never dull." Although the prairie town may have stifled the mind, it never stifled the imagination. Both essays stress the influence of her pioneer grandparents and their generation in her life and work.

LEE, L.L. and MERRILL LEWIS, eds. Women, Women Writers, and the West. Troy, NY: Whitson, 1979.
This collection includes the following essays on the female experience and the prairie: Susan H. Armitage, "Women's Literature and the American Frontier: A New Perspective on the Frontier Myth," pp. 5-13; Jeannie McKnight, "American Dream, Nightmare Underside: Diaries, Letters and Fiction of Women on the American Frontier," pp. 25-44; Roger E. Carp, "Hamlin Garland and the Cult of True Womanhood," pp. 83-99; Sylvia Grider, "Madness and Personification in Giants in the Earth, pp. 111-117; Bernice Slote, "Willa Cather and the Sense of History," pp. 161-171.

LENNOX, JOHN WATT. "Manawaka and Deptford: Place and Voice." Journal of Canadian Studies/Revue d'etudes canadiennes 13 (Automne 1978/Fall): 23-29.
Through an extended comparison with Robertson Davies' Deptford trilogy, Lennox analyzes the use of place and voice in Margaret Laurence's Manawaka cycle. He finds that Laurence "illuminates the mystery and experience and knowledge of the familiar and the commonplace." Her Manitoba town is distinctly Canadian in its population (Scots, Irish, Ukrainian, and Métis), in its economic and religious values (mercantile and Calvinistic), and in its character ("practical, aggressive, and proud"). Hence her characters, though "ordinary" Manawaka citizens, speak with an authority that is frequently qualified by experience.

McCOURT, EDWARD A. The Canadian West in Fiction. Toronto: Ryerson Press, 1949.
McCourt first traces the images imposed on the prairie by early travellers whose cultural baggage prevented them from really seeing the landscape as it was. Major male writers considered are Ralph Connor, Frederick Niven, Frederick Philip Grove and R.J.C. Stead. Of the women writers McCourt says that Nellie McClung was "a robust optimist" but not necessarily a sentimentalist; Salverson (who made the first serious attempt to describe a mass migration movement) was "a romantic optimist"; Christine Van der Mark was the first realistic novelist of the new frontier of Peace River country. McCourt does not feel that at the time of his writing the western novelists had adequately told the story of the prairie region.

________. "Prairie Literature and Its Critics." In A Region of the Mind: Interpreting the Western Canadian Plains, pp. 153-162. Ed. Richard Allen. Regina: University of Saskatchewan, 1971.
A very brief survey of major prairie publications is followed by a discussion of the function of the prairie literary critic.

MacEWAN, GRANT. ...And Mighty Women Too: Stories of Notable Western Women. Saskatoon, Sask.: Western Producer Prairie Books, 1975.
Kate Simpson Hayes and Nellie McClung--as well as prairie poet Edna Jaques--are represented in this collection of influential women. MacEwan describes Hayes' arrival in Reginia in 1885 with her two young children (she was separated from her husband) and then traces her varied career up to 1895 when Prairie Pot-Pourri was published. In his essay

on McClung, MacEwan focuses on the publication of her first novel in 1911, her move to Winnipeg where she became active in the suffrage movement and starred in the famous "Mock Parliament," and concludes with her move to Edmonton and subsequent election to the Alberta legislature.

McKENNA, ISOBEL. "As They Really Were: Women in the Novels of Grove." English Studies in Canada 2 (1976): 109-116.
Frederick Philip Grove, in his work In Search of Myself, points out that in his sympathies he was always on the side of the pioneer woman, not with the man. McKenna traces Groves' sympathetic treatment of female characters in the prairie novels Settlers of the Marsh, Our Daily Bread, Yoke of Life, Fruits of the Earth, Master of the Mill, and in the Ontario novel, Two Generations. "The women in the prairie novels had been condemned to lives completely lacking in any other purpose than running the home, and for this Grove pitied them." In the Ontario novel, the land has been tamed and people, especially women, are free to develop in other ways.

McKNIGHT, JEANNIE. See LEE, L.L. and MERRILL LEWIS, eds.

MacLEOD, GORDON DUNCAN. "A Descriptive Bibliography of the Canadian Prairie Novel 1871-1970." Ph.D. dissertation, University of Manitoba, 1974.
Prairie fiction over a one-hundred year period is discussed, item by item, in terms of story-line, setting, dates; pertinent biographical information about the author; literary merit.

MAINIERO, LINA, ed. American Women Writers: A Critical Reference Guide from Colonial Times to the Present, vols. 1-4. New York: Frederick Ungar, 1979, 1980, 1981.
Several prairie writers are included: Aldrich, Barnes, Cather, Catherwood, Fairbank, Ferber, Glaspell, Lane, Laut, LeSueur, Suckow and Wilder. Each entry provides biographical information, a brief synopsis for major works, titles of books with date of publication, abbreviated bibliographical citations for biographical and critical works on the author.

MANDEL, ELI. "Images of Prairie Man." In A Region of the Mind: Interpreting the Western Plains, pp. 201-209. Ed. Richard Allen. Regina: University of Saskatchewan Press, 1971.

Three approaches lead to the images we have of prairie man: the pluralistic approach (a listing of the numerous images), the sociopolitical approach, and the mythic approach. In fact, Mandel argues, prairie is "a mental construct, a region of the human mind, a myth." Attempts to find "a certain coherence of unity or identity" among prairie works have failed because "accuracy of fact and of tone is essentially superficial.... If there is a distinctive regional prairie literature, it would have to be ... mythic."

_______. "Romance and Realism in Western Canadian Fiction." In Prairie Perspectives 2, pp. 197-211. Eds. A.W. Rasporich and H.C. Klassen. Toronto: Holt, Rinehart & Winston, 1973.

Beginning with Robert Kroetsch's statement that "fiction makes us real," Mandel asks: "In what sense could we say a fiction, particularly of America or Greece or Judea, makes us real, defines our identity?" Using Watson's The Double Hook and Kroetsch's The Studhorse Man to demonstrate his points, Mandel argues that the literature of Western Canada can be identified not by place, society, or history, but by its "own developing forms."

_______. See also HARRISON, DICK, ed. Crossing Frontiers.

MARSLAND, ELIZABETH. "La chaine tenue." Canadian Literature no. 77 (Summer 1978): 64-72.

Marsland draws attention to the symbolism of the railroad in prairie fiction. In French literature, there is no "garrison mentality"; characters are in harmony with nature and have a sense of the railroad and roads both going and returning; thus characters accept their environment and feel connected to distant places. In English prairie fiction railroad tracks don't go any place. There's either no escape or journeys into oblivion; hence characters feel isolated and vulnerable.

MELDRUM, BARBARA. "Images of Women in Western American Literature." Midwest Quarterly 17 (April 1976): 252-267.

Three approaches to the subject of women in western American literature are suggested: 1) a thematic approach--woman as civilizing force; 2) an archetypal approach--masculine vs. feminine ideals as a source for dramatic tension; 3) an historical approach--images of pioneer women. Meldrum relies more on the works of male writers than on those by females; only Cather, Sandoz, and Foote are included.

________. See also FAULKNER, VIRGINIA and FREDERICK C. LUEBKE, eds.

MEYER, ROY W. *The Middle Western Farm Novel in the Twentieth Century*. Lincoln: University of Nebraska Press, 1965.
The genre consists of works that deal with farm life, using accurate details; also, a large part of the action takes place on a farm and main characters are farm people. Works must use the vernacular and also reflect typical attitudes and beliefs such as conservatism, individualism, anti-intellectualism, hostility to the town, and a type of primitivism. Works by the following prairie women writers receive some attention: Beers, Cather, Hudson, Lane, and Suckow.

MILLER, JAMES E., JR. "*My Ántonia* and the American Dream." *Prairie Schooner* 48 (Summer 1974): 112-123.
Cather's *My Antonia* has been given a place in the American fiction canon because it "clings tenaciously in the mind" and comments on "the American experience, the American dream, and the American reality." Jim Burden is trying to understand and find an answer to what went wrong with the American dream. Comparisons are made with the failure of the American dream in Fitzgerald's *The Great Gatsby* and in Williams' *Paterson*. Jim Burden's "longing for something missed in the past is a national longing."

MILTON, JOHN R. See FAULKNER, VIRGINIA and FREDERICK C. LUEBKE, eds.

MITCHAM, ALLISON. "Roy's West." *Canadian Literature* no. 88 (Spring 1981): 161-163.
The harsh landscape of the West has a strong impact on the individual and on the artist. In Roy's fiction, the harsh environment is a testing ground and those who survive achieve greater health, vigour, and understanding of self. Roy, unlike Ross and Grove (and other prairie writers with the exception of W.O. Mitchell), exudes tenderness, gentleness, and humor in her delineation of character. *Un jardin au bout du monde* is the best example of this: Martha survives without bitterness, finding meaning in defending her flowers from wind and drought year after year. The essay concludes with a discussion of Roy's concern with accuracy in descriptions and portrayal of characters.

O'CONNOR, JOHN JOSEPH WILLIAM. "The Last Three

Steppes: The Canadian West as 'Frontier' in Prairie Literature." Ph.D. dissertation, University of Toronto, 1977.
The degree to which the view of the Canadian west as "frontier" influences characters and themes in both French and English prairie literature is examined in detail. In the fiction, most dreams were unfulfilled. Solitude and monotony are presented as conditions affecting women in particular.

________. "Saskatchewan Sirens: The Prairie as Sea in Western Canadian Literature." Journal of Canadian Fiction nos. 28-29 (1980): 157-171.
Early writers see the prairie as some form of sea, regardless of the season. Behind the clichés "lay a genuine heritage and ancestral memory." In recent fiction Grove and Ross have probed the deeper implications of the prairie-sea imagery. O'Connor concludes that "the metaphor is both appropriate and illuminating" in representing the physical and psychological impact of the landscape.

OSTER, JOHN. "The Ukrainian Canadian in Prairie Fiction." Alberta English 15 (Winter 1975/1976): 5-9.
Changing social attitudes toward Ukrainians are reflected in the fiction of non-Ukrainian novelists--Connor's The Foreigner, MacMillan's Levko, Storey's Prairie Harvest; Grove's The Fruit of the Earth; Marlyn's Under the Ribs of Death; Laurence's A Jest of God; Mitchell's Who Has Seen the Wind. Works by Ukrainians stress "the rigours of pioneer life and the transference and transformation of customs from the old world to the new": Lysenko's Yellow Boots; Kiriak's Sons of the Soil; Bhataia's The Latchkey Kid.

PAUSTIAN, SHIRLEY I. "Saskatchewan in Fiction." Saskatchewan History 1 (October 1948): 23-26.
This review article devotes a paragraph each to Grove's Our Daily Bread (recommended as "a good attempt to represent the Saskatchewan farmer in fiction"), Ross's As for Me and My House (excellent picture of small town life), Mitchell's Who Has Seen the Wind (excellent details), Stringer's trilogy (lacks accuracy), and Grayson's Willow Smoke (unconvincing heroine).

PETERMAN, MICHAEL. "'The Good Game': The Charm of Willa Cather's My Ántonia and W.O. Mitchell's Who Has Seen the Wind." Mosaic 14 no. 2 (1981): 93-106.
The two novels are similar in that they appeal to readers, provide contrasts between open prairie and sheltering town,

present two male youths who are fascinated by the land. In addition, both are "conscientious as artists, as western humanists ... and, above all, romantics. They strive to create a vision of possibility and hope for mankind, based on the ministering power of the open prairie and the development in childhood of the fullest capacities of imagination and individuality."

PORTER, ELIZABETH. "*Sarah Binks*: Another Look at Saskatchewan's Sweet Songstress." *World Literature Written in English* 21 (Spring 1982): 95-108.
The satire in Paul Hiebert's *Sarah Binks* preserves much of "the detail and flavour of life in a bygone era and, with lighthearted nostalgia, brings into comic perspective the trials of rural living in the early days on the Canadian prairie."

PRICE, ROBERT. "Mrs. Catherwood's Early Experiments with Critical Realism." *American Literature* 17 (1945): 140-151.
The years between 1878 and 1882 represent the realistic period in Catherwood's writings about "the old corn belt." She was able to be more realistic in her treatment of materials at this time because she was not having to support herself with her writings. Works discussed include "The Monument to the First Mrs. Smith," "A Little God," "The Career of a Prairie Farmer," and *Craque-o'-Doom*.

QUANTIC, DIANE DUFVA. "The Ambivalence of Rural Life in Prairie Literature." *Kansas Quarterly* 12 (Spring 1980): 109-119.
No prairie writer feels neutral about the prairie or ignores the prairie. The land is at the center of every work. Works by Cather, Rölvaag, Howe, Garland, Morris, Woiwode, White, Wilder, and Sandoz reflect ambivalence about the farm and the prairie town. Characters are attracted to, challenged by, or overwhelmed by the land. The same ambivalence carries over into the town experience; the town may seem unstable, stagnant, or unfulfilling.

RAY, JO ANNE. "Maud Hart Lovelace and Mankato." In *Women of Minnesota: Selected Biographical Essays*, pp. 155-172. St. Paul: Minnesota Historical Press, 1977.
Besides biographical information, this essay provides background on the prairie novel, *Gentlemen from England* (coauthored with her husband) about English immigrants to Martin County.

RICOU, LAURENCE R. "Circumference of Absence: Land

and Space in the Poetry of the Canadian Plains." In Canadian Plains Studies 6: Man and Nature and the Prairies, pp. 66-76. Ed. Richard Allen. Regina: Canadian Plains Research Center, University of Regina, 1976.
The images and abstractions created by plains poets enable people to live with the space. Two women poets are discussed briefly: Dorothy Livesay and Elizabeth Brewster.

_______. "Empty as Nightmare: Man and Landscape in Recent Canadian Prairie Fiction." Mosaic 6 no. 2 (1973): 143-160.
A phrase from Wallace Stegner's Wolf Willow points to the unifying image in Canadian prairie fiction: "empty as nightmare." Man is an intruder; he sticks out. In both rural and urban novels of the 1950s and 1960s, man is exposed, a vertical object on a flat landscape. Only in Margaret Laurence's landscapes is there a "gentler" quality; Laurence's prairie is lonely and isolated but also beautiful, fertile, and open. In Kroetsch's novels the heroes rebel and defy the emptiness of the prairie.

_______. Vertical Man/Horizontal World: Man and Landscape in Canadian Prairie Fiction. Vancouver: University of British Columbia Press, 1973.
"The theme of solitude is the most persistent in Canadian prairie fiction, rooted as it is in cold climate and lacking the psychological comfort of substantial vegetation or significant contours of landscape." Other themes include the benign prairie of Stead, the implacable prairie of Grove, the invisible prairie in minor fiction (including Beynon's Aleta Day, Grayson's Willow Smoke, Parson's The Curlew Cried, and Rolyat's The Lily of Fort Garry); the obsessive prairie in Ostenso's Wild Geese, the prairie internalized in Ross's As for Me and My House, the bewildering prairie in recent fiction (including Laurence's novels).

ROY, GABRIELLE. "Mon heritage du Manitoba." Mosaic 3 (Spring 1970): 69-79.
The responses of three generations of females to the prairie provide insight into Roy's own prairie works. Roy's grandmother was a reluctant immigrant, yet as an old woman she became attached to her prairie home; Roy's mother, who emigrated as a young girl, responded positively to the new landscape. Both women influenced Roy in her perceptions of place. An understanding of what is to be of French Canadian descent living in Manitoba leads, perhaps, to an understanding of what it is to be Canadian.

SALVERSON, LAURA GOODMAN. "An Autobiographical Sketch." Ontario Library Review 14 (February 1930): 69-73.
Salverson comments on the frequent moves she made as a child after her parents emigrated to Canada. She compares farm and town in both Canada and the United States. Sources for her feminism are found in her mother and aunt who provide stability whenever Salverson's father's ventures fail. However, both parents contribute richly to her literary heritage.

SAVAGE, CANDICE. Our Nell: A Scrapbook Biography of Nellie L. McClung. Saskatoon, Sask.: Western Producer Prairie Books, 1979.
This collage of McClung's writings and speeches combined with newspaper articles, letters, comments by family members and Savage's biographical, social, and political backgrounds provides essential information for reading and analyzing McClung's fiction.

SCHLEUNING, NEALA J.Y. "Meridel LeSueur: Toward a New Regionalism." Books at Iowa no. 33 (November 1980): 22-41.
An examination of the facts of LeSueur's life, the relationship between her writings and her politics, and the themes of her work lead to an appreciation of a writer's intense commitment to her people and her land. The discussion of LeSueur's relationship to the land provides a model for new ways of thinking about the portrayal of women and the prairie in literature, history, and criticism.

SKARDAL, DOROTHY BURTON. The Divided Heart: Scandinavian Immigrant Experience Through Literary Sources. Lincoln: University of Nebraska Press, 1974.
Although the work focuses on the Scandinavian immigrant experience, Skårdal's discussions provide insights that can be applied to the study of other immigrant groups on the prairie. She analyzes the reasons Scandinavians emigrated to America and describes their ocean and overland journeys. She identifies the major problems encountered: language barriers, prejudices of natives, Scandinavian distrust of Americans, homesickness, negative reactions to the landscape, pressures to become Americanized, and generational conflicts in values. Also emphasized are the important bonds between those speaking the same language, kinship ties, strong church affiliations, positive self-images, and preference for the new life in America to the hardships of former

days because of opportunities to own land in America, better jobs, and education for a greater number of individuals.

________. See also FAULKNER, VIRGINIA and FREDERICK C. LUEBKE, eds.

SLOTE, BERNICE. See LEE, L.L. and MERRILL LEWIS, eds.; FAULKNER, VIRGINIA and FREDERICK C. LUEBKE, eds.

SORFLEET, JOHN R., ed. "The Work of Margaret Laurence." Journal of Canadian Fiction no. 27 (1980): special issue.
The collection includes two early stories and an essay on form and voice by Margaret Laurence. Four critical essays illuminate place and people in Laurence's Manawaka novels: Joan Caldwell's "Hagar and Meg Merrilies, The Homeless Gypsy," (pp. 92-100) relates Keats' ballad to the character Hagar in The Stone Angel and provides insights into Hagar's Scots ancestry. The Scots-Presbyterian background of all the female protagonists in the Manawaka novels is examined in Melanie Mortlock's "The Religion of Heritage: The Diviners as a Thematic Conclusion to the Manawaka Series" (pp. 132-142). Leslie Monkman's "The Tonnerre Family: Mirrors of Suffering," (pp. 143-150) analyzes the roles of a Métis family. Angelika Maeser, in the process of interpreting the individuation process of the women in Laurence's novels, discusses the city-country, civilization-nature correspondence to the male-female principles in "Finding the Mother: The Individuation of Laurence's Heroines" (pp. 151-166).

THOMAS, CLARA. "Proud Lineage: Willa Cather and Margaret Laurence." Canadian Review of American Studies 2 (Spring 1971): 1-12.
A cycle beginning with the American wilderness in My Ántonia and O Pioneers!, through Laurence's The Stone Angel and A Jest of God, is completed in the urban wilderness of The Fire Dwellers. The "energy and life-affirming spirit" found in Antonia emerge in the character of Stacey (The Fire Dwellers). Only the tone shifts; the sense of possibility and fulfillment of the dream found in Antonia is replaced by an ironic tone in the Canadian works which is Irish, or Scots-Irish, in origin. Images of the cave, the garden, the wilderness, and the matriarch persist in both the Canadian and American novels.

________. See CHADBOURNE, RICHARD and HALLVARD DAHLIE, eds.

THOMAS, G. LEWIS. See HARRISON, DICK, ed. *Crossing Frontiers*.

THOMPSON, ERIC. "Infinite Spaces: Canadian Prairie Writers." *Literary Review* 24 (Fall 1980): 168-175.
A review essay of Ken Mitchell's anthology, *Horizon: Writings of the Canadian Prairie*.

________. "Prairie Mosaic: The Immigrant Novel in the Canadian West." *Studies in Canadian Literature* 5 (Fall 1980): 236-259.
The immigrant novel in prairie writing needs to be examined more fully. To partially offset this neglect, Thompson examines five themes in immigrant literature: "The Anglo-Canadian Preserve," "The Saga of Settlement," "Confrontation and Assimilation," "The Outsider Mentality," and "Tradition and Change." The only "true" prairie woman writer included is Salverson; works by Rasheviciite-Eggleston, Van Der Mark, and Wiseman are also examined along with numerous male novelists.

________. "The Prairie Novel in Canada: A Study in Changing Form and Perception." Ph.D. dissertation, The University of New Brunswick, 1974.
The study is concerned with the "larger cultural matrix" out of which prairie novels emerged. Major and minor writers are examined in relation to the periods in which they wrote, changing conditions, as well as popular and critical tastes. The Quest emerges as the over-riding motif in prairie fiction. In stage one, the late nineteenth century, the prairie stirred the imagination of travellers and settlers to respond in fictional forms. In stage two, the age of settlement, writers glorified the last days of the open ranges and the first days of human conquest of the land. In stage three realism became the dominant form. In stage four the "inner territory" of the individual's experience in the prairie environment is explored.

WAINWRIGHT, J.A. "You Have to Go Home Again: Art and Life in *The Diviners*." *World Literature Written in English* 20 (Autumn 1981): 292-311.
In Laurence's *The Diviners*, Morag Gunn is unable to become a good writer "until she admits that there can be no farewell to what she has inherited from Manawaka," her

prairie hometown. The inheritance waiting to be acknowledged includes 1) the ability to tell a story, a talent she has inherited from her step-father Christie Logan; 2) the ability to use the painful facts of one's life and history. She also learns that she is not only an inheritor but an ancestor in the flow of time.

WALKER, DON D. See CHADBOURNE, RICHARD and HALLVARD DAHLIE, eds.

WASSERSTROM, WILLIAM. "The Lily and the Prairie Flower." American Quarterly 9 (Fall 1957): 398-411.
Midwestern literature shaped a new myth based on a belief in freedom, human perfectibility and human vigor; the "unrestrained freedom" of the West was tempered by the "noble and ancient traditions" of the East. In addition, midwestern literature insisted that denial of sex disrupts life and that passion could be dignified. This balance is represented by the midwestern heroine who, in fact, became the ideal for all Americans: the "vigorous angel" as an image of womanhood won out over the chaste eastern woman and the tempestuous western woman.

WEBB, WALTER PRESCOTT. The Great Plains. Boston: Ginn, 1931.
This classic study of the plains includes a chapter on the literature of the Great Plains with a sub-section called "The Literature of the Farm." Quick, Cather, Lewis, Ferber, Anderson, and Grove are mentioned. Rölvaag's Giants in the Earth is singled out to represent what Webb considers typical male and female responses to the prairie.

WOOD, SUSAN. "God's Doormats: Women in Canadian Prairie Fiction." Journal of Popular Culture 14 no. 2 (1980): 350-359.
Wood analyzes the images of women in popular fiction by Ralph Connor, Nellie L. McClung, and Robert J.C. Stead. The "prairie angel" archetype persists in the works of Connor and the secondary heroines of McClung. However, McClung's primary heroines "do everything"--they have careers, participate in politics, organize the community, and keep their families happy, just as McClung did. While Stead's women characters frequently are portrayed realistically as overburdened by farm work and motherhood, his female heroes--like Connor's and McClung's--are idealized in their consciousness of self and situation and their ability to rebel against existing conditions. Leading "literary works" (in

contrast to "popular works") by Ostenso, Grove, and Ross rejected romantic formulas and stereotypes and failed to attract large audiences of readers.

INDEX

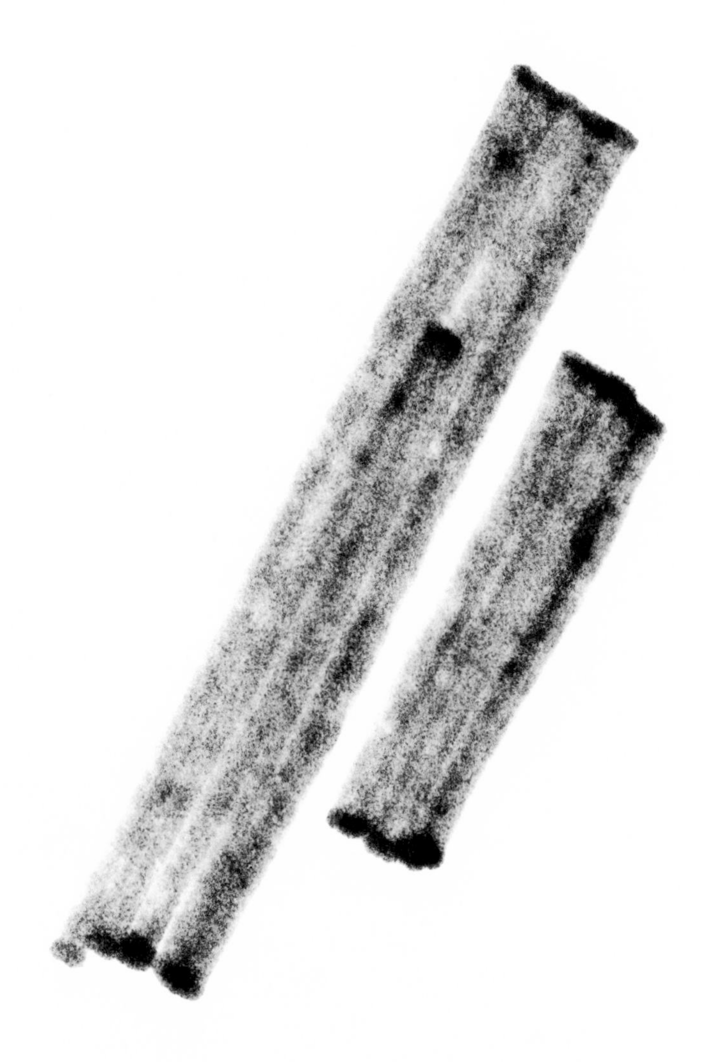